L I E

*f*P

THE FREE PRESS
A Division of Simon & Schuster Inc.
1230 Avenue of the Americas
New York, NY 10020

THE FREE PRESS and colophon are trademarks
of Simon & Schuster Inc.

Manufactured in the United States of America

10   9   8   7   6   5   4   3   2   1

Library of Congress Cataloging-in-Publication Data

Lieberman, Myron, 1919–
     The teacher unions: how the NEA and AFT sabotage reform and hold students,
   parents, teachers, and taxpayers hostage to bureaucracy
   / Myron Lieberman.
         p.   cm.
     Includes bibliographical references and index.
     ISBN 0–684–84282–3
     1. Teachers' unions—United States.   2. National Education
   Association of the United States.   3. American Federation of
   Teachers.   4. Collective bargaining—Teachers—United States.
   I. Title.
   LB2844.53.U6L56   1997
   331.88'113711'0973—DC21   97-2982
                                                                        CIP

THE

TEACHER

UNIONS

How the NEA and AFT Sabotage
Reform and Hold Students, Parents, Teachers,
and Taxpayers Hostage to Bureaucracy

MYRON LIEBERMAN

THE FREE PRESS

New York   London   Toronto   Sydney   Singapore

For her unwavering support and commitment to the cause of better teacher organizations, this book is dedicated to

CHARLENE K. HAAR

CONTENTS

PREFACE

My first book, *Education as a Profession*, was published in 1956. It was widely and favorably reviewed in Canada, England, and Australia as well as the United States. The book was adopted for courses at several universities and launched a professional career that emerged, in almost linear fashion, to this book.

Education as a Profession urged and predicted teacher unionization. For 20 years thereafter, my publications continued to support collective bargaining in education. Beginning in the late 1970s, however, my views on this issue began to change. I had embraced teacher bargaining before having had any school district level experience with it. As my experience with it increased, I realized that my advocacy of it had overlooked several issues pertaining to its desirability as public policy. This fact led me to read more widely on the subject; as a result, my doubts eventually culminated in the early 1980s in opposition to collective bargaining in public education.

The most important reason for my change of position was the realization that collective bargaining in public education is inconsistent with democratic, representative government. Although the details are spelled out in this book, the basis for this conclusion is simple enough: In teacher union bargaining, school board representatives, that is, government officials, negotiate public policies with one special interest group in a process from which other parties are excluded.

Important as it is, this conclusion was not the only factor in my change of position. Thus as I began to question the basic rationale for teacher unions, I also began to take cognizance of other issues that had been ignored when teacher unionization was becoming institutionalized. For instance, to my knowledge, no one raised any hard questions about the costs of the process, but costs are an important criterion for evaluating the efficacy of any method of dispute settlement.

Although my views on teacher unionization have changed a great deal since 1956, much of the analysis that led me to support it remains valid. One point in particular is especially relevant. My initial interest in teacher unions grew out of the fact that teacher associations were weak organizations. Whereas others dismissed teacher organizations in the 1950s because of their weakness, I became interested in the reasons for their weakness and what could be done to strengthen them. My conclusion was that the NEA (National Education Association) and its affiliates were weak organizations because they enrolled school administrators as members. The latter used their power over teachers at work to stifle militant action by organizations in which teachers outnumbered administrators. My conclusion was that teacher organizations would be much more powerful if they excluded administrators; inasmuch as such exclusion is inherent in collective bargaining, my support for the latter was a logical next step in my search for the keys to stronger teacher organizations. It was also my view that as teacher organizations became more influential, they would be scrutinized more intensively than in the past. This book provides some of that scrutiny. I hope that others will add to it.

Although my publications were not responsible for the emergence of teacher unions, they may have played a minor role in their emergence and growth. In any event, I certainly have been in a unique position to observe the emergence, operations, and consequences of teacher unions: Experience as a long-time member of the National Education Association (NEA) and the American Federation of Teachers (AFT); delegate to more than twenty state and national union conventions; candidate for AFT president in 1962; labor negotiator in about 200 school district contracts in seven states; consultant to state and federal legislative bodies on collective bargaining in public education; professor of graduate courses devoted to teacher bargaining at several universities from Long Island to Hawaii; consultant and expert witness on racial discrimination in public education for the NAACP Legal Defense and Education Fund in six states, candidate for state superintendent in California—all of these experiences and others not mentioned have affected the discussion that follows.

Although critical of the teacher unions (as well as of their opposition), I have tried to avoid "bias" in the analysis. Certainly, it is partisan, as is every analysis that supports one course of action over another. If "bias" is merely a synonym for "partisan," the term is not a criticism.

I regard "bias" as a pejorative term, which I hope is not applicable to this book. My goal has been to provide an objective analysis of the teacher unions, but "objective" is not synonymous with "nonpartisan." On the contrary, objective analysis of an issue often results in a partisan position with respect to it.

Of course, it is for readers to decide whether my analysis is objective. Certainly, many who profess the label do not deserve it. Furthermore, objectivity is not to be confused with a subjective state of mind. In countless situations, analysts reflect bias even if they are not aware of it. My plea is that the analysis not be dismissed as "biased" simply because it is partisan. If my analysis overlooks significant evidence, or weighs it on a double standard, or ignores arguments that belong in the discussion, I neither seek nor deserve exemption from criticism as "biased."

Finally, let me explain why personal references are so frequently mentioned in this book. Generally speaking, I prefer not to rely on personal experience to demonstrate a point of broad applicability. If an author's point is indeed broadly applicable, the author should be able to cite nonpersonal data or experience to confirm it.

This book, however, includes several personal experiences. One reason is that readers are in a better position to evaluate my objectivity if they know more about my actual involvement with the individuals, organizations, and issues discussed in this book. Furthermore, if I am writing about an individual or organization with whom I have had extensive face-to-face experience over a long period of time, my experience may be a reliable source of information. In some cases, I was in a unique position to assess the matters discussed in this book. For this reason, failure to refer to my experience would be grounds for legitimate criticism.

ACKNOWLEDGMENTS

I am deeply indebted to the Social Philosophy and Policy Center, Bowling Green State University and to its Deputy and Associate Directors, Ellen and Jeffrey Paul, for the encouragement and editorial assistance that made it possible for me to write this book. I am also indebted to Andrea Millen Rich, Kermit Hummel, and Max Green for their criticisms and suggestions; to Charlene K. Haar for help on all fronts; also to several individuals who are not acknowledged by name. Of course, I am solely responsible for the contents of this book.

1

INTRODUCTION

Why This Book?

The National Education Association (NEA) and the American Federation of Teachers, AFL-CIO (AFT) are the nation's largest teacher unions. These unions are the major components of "the education establishment," and they play an extremely influential role, not just in education but in politics and the economy as well. How do the NEA/AFT decide upon their objectives, what are the sources of their power, and how do they exercise their power to promote their objectives? Neither the public nor the union rank and file know the answers, and I hope that this book provides them.

I begin with a paradox. The U.S. labor movement is in a declining mode and has been since the 1960s. Analysts who differ about the desirability of the decline nevertheless agree that it exists. Private sector union membership has declined from a peak of 17 million in 1970 to 9.7 million in 1995. As a percentage of the nonagricultural private sector labor force, union membership has dropped from 36 percent in 1953 to 10.7 percent in 1995.

Against this backdrop, the teacher unions have experienced phenomenal growth. Since 1961, membership in the NEA has increased from 766,000 to 2.2 million, almost 300 percent. Actually, this increase vastly understates NEA growth. In 1961, teachers could join the NEA without having to join their state or local association. Thus NEA membership in 1961 included many teachers who were not members of either their state or local associations. In 1973, however, the NEA required membership in the local and state associations to be an

1

NEA member. Consequently, a much higher percentage of the 2.2 million are also enrolled in state and local unions. AFT membership, which always required unified dues, increased from 70,821 in 1961 to 947,000 in 1997.

During this same period, NEA/AFT revenues also increased dramatically. The NEA budget just for its national office increased from $7.7 million in 1960–61 to $186 million in 1995–96; as Chapter 9 shows, state and local union revenues have also increased in similar fashion.

Perhaps one other point will drive home the striking contrast between the decline of private sector unions and the tremendous growth of the teacher unions. In 1960, I wrote that: "The foremost fact about teachers' organizations in the United States is their irrelevance in the national scene."[1] True then, but what a different story today. More delegates to the 1996 Democratic national convention (405) were NEA members than from any state in the union, except California. The NEA's state affiliates are among the most powerful interest groups at the state level; often they are the most influential. The AFT, which almost always supports the same candidates and the same objectives, only strengthens the picture.

In some respects, the most striking feature about the explosive growth of the teacher unions is that it has occurred during reported declines in student achievement and huge increases in spending for public education. The NEA argues that there has been no decline in student achievement and even if there were, the union bears no responsibility for it. The AFT concedes the fact of decline but contends that union activities are not a causal factor. I will assess these matters in detail in Chapter 12, but at the very least, even if there has been no decline in student achievement, the large increases in educational expenditures above the rate of inflation reflect significant declines in productivity. Something is clearly wrong.

Public opinion assumes that the NEA/AFT affect only students, teachers, parents, and school officials. Certainly, parents' concern for their children should be a primary reason to read this book. Yet the idea that the teacher unions affect only education is a fallacy with enormous consequences. From the economy to taxes, health care, immigration, or any other major public policy, the NEA/AFT play an important role in its resolution. Unfortunately, union members themselves are frequently uninformed about what their unions, especially state and national, are doing and why. Consider one major example.

The NEA/AFT are the major political opponents of public funding for private schooling (I refer to "private schooling" in order to bypass the issue of whether public funds are used for private schools, or are assistance to parents who spend the funds in private schools). NEA/AFT publications, conferences, and legislative programs assert that public funding for private schools would:

- Lead to the demise of public education
- Help the affluent at the expense of poor children
- Exacerbate racial and economic stratification
- Violate the constitutional separation of church and state
- Foster extremist schools that would teach antidemocratic doctrines

Just about everyone is aware of NEA/AFT opposition to public funding for private schooling, and the reasons they cite for their opposition. Very few, however, are aware of the fact that in 1947, the NEA/AFT and American Federation of Labor (AFL) supported federal aid to education that would have provided substantial federal aid for private schooling.[2]

This fact raises some interesting questions. If federal aid for private schooling was a good thing in 1947, why is it a threat now to our way of life? Conversely, if it is such a threat now, why wasn't it then? My only point here is that the inconsistency is not discussed, either in teacher union publications or in the media generally. The NEA/AFT may have a satisfactory explanation for the shift in position, but what is it? Neither the public nor the union membership is aware of the change, let alone any explanation for it. And if the public as well as the rank and file membership can be as uninformed about a matter of such importance, we should not be surprised that they are uninformed about a host of other matters as well.

The preceding example underscores the importance of the distinction between teachers and their unions. The unions characterize any criticism of unions as a criticism of teachers. This strategy was evident in the NEA/AFT reaction to Bob Dole's acceptance speech at the 1996 Republican national convention; despite Dole's explicit disclaimer that his criticisms of the teacher unions should not be interpreted as a criticism of teachers, the NEA/AFT immediately charged that Dole's speech had attacked teachers. The union charge was false but politically effective. On some matters, the union interests coincide with teacher interests, but on others, there is an actual or potential conflict of interest. For example, the teachers are consumers of representational services. The unions are producers of them. In this capacity, it is in the union's interest to be paid more, in the teacher's interest to pay less. The union's interest lies in persuading members that they are receiving excellent service for their dues; the member interest lies in getting all the facts, not simply those which strengthen the union's position. In short, criticism of the teacher unions cannot be equated with criticism of teachers, much as the NEA/AFT characterize it this way.

An Overview

By the time readers come to the end, this book reaches the following conclusions:

• The most important outcome of teacher unionization is its effect on the way public policy is made. This outcome overshadows the effects of teacher unionization on teacher welfare and student achievement.

• The NEA and the AFT are among the most powerful interest groups in U.S. society; their influence on noneducational issues at the federal and state levels is arguably more important than their influence on educational issues per se.

• Public and academic opinion vastly underestimate NEA/AFT influence partly because private sector unions have been declining since the 1950s. Meanwhile, the public sector unions, especially the NEA and AFT, have experienced huge increases in membership and influence. Failure to distinguish the trends in the two sectors leads to neglect of the explosive growth and consequences of teacher unionization.

• Jointly considered, the NEA/AFT enroll over three million members and their dues revenues exceed one billion dollars annually. In addition, the revenues of NEA/AFT subsidiary organizations, such as their political action committees (PACs) and foundations, probably amounts to $100 million annually, and the revenues over which the teacher unions share control with others are much greater.

• On a full-time equivalent basis, I estimate that the NEA/AFT employ more political operatives than the Republican and Democratic parties combined. My estimate is based upon NEA publications, especially those specifying the duties of UniServ directors. AFT staff perform the same work, but the AFT does not publish manuals on the subject.

• About 3,000 NEA/AFT employees, including the officers elected at various levels, earn more than $100,000 annually in salary and benefits. Teacher union compensation plays a major but widely neglected role in shaping educational policy in the United States.

• Collective bargaining in public education was initially advocated because political action was ineffective in protecting teacher interests. Ironically, collective bargaining has greatly increased the political influence of teacher unions, far beyond the expectations of its early proponents.

• Collective bargaining by public sector unions shares all of the important characteristics of political action and should be subject to the legislation governing political action.

• U.S. Supreme Court decisions which distinguish collective bargaining in public education from political action were legal blunders with far-reaching negative consequences for our political and educational systems.

• The NEA is engaged in questionable accounting practices to understate their financial support for their political operations and to maximize the revenues they can require nonmembers to pay to the unions.

• The NEA and the AFT illustrate the tendency of producer groups to rely on government protection or regulation instead of better service at lower cost to protect and promote their interests.

• School boards and school administrators are largely unaware of the ways that collective bargaining contracts in public education maximize union revenues and political influence.

• Generally speaking, the activities of state and local affiliates of the NEA and the AFT are governed by state, not federal, legislation. The state legislation does not include the safeguards for union members and the public that have been included in federal legislation regulating unions in the private sector. The absence of these safeguards renders it virtually impossible for teachers to monitor union activities or expenditures, especially the total compensation of union officers and staff.

• Like unions generally, the NEA and the AFT are adamantly opposed to competition in their labor markets, and to any policy that would shrink the market for teacher services. Thus the NEA/AFT oppose vouchers, tuition tax credits, contracting out, home schooling, or lowering the compulsory age limit for education. On the theory that the camel must not be allowed to poke its nose into the tent, the NEA/AFT are as adamantly opposed to "trial projects" or "demonstration projects" as they are to large scale programs to allow competition in the education industry.

• The NEA completely dominates the policies and programs of the National Congress of Parents and Teachers, widely referred to as "the PTA." As long as the PTA is unwilling or unable to abolish NEA domination, parents will need either a new parent organization not controlled by the NEA; or school choice plans that enable parents to enroll their children in a wide range of private schools.

• The teacher unions are highly vulnerable in several ways, but their critics have failed to recognize and hence to exploit these vulnerabilities. Union revenues, membership and political influence experienced substantial growth during the twelve years of the Reagan and Bush administrations; the post-November 1994 conservative emphasis on school prayer and abolition of the U.S. Department of Education merely continues conservative ineptitude on education issues.

• The NEA and the AFT overwhelmingly support Democratic candidates for public office. The NEA's claim to be "bipartisan" is based upon its endorsements of a minuscule number of liberal Republican candidates for public office. The basic causes of overwhelming teacher union support for Democratic candidates are not likely to change; however, the NEA may increase its contributions to Republican party organizations to preserve the appearance of bipartisanship when it cannot identify any Republican candidates to endorse.

• There are some important differences between the NEA and the AFT, but they have little or no bearing on educational or political policies. The neoconservative notion that the AFT is a more enlightened union or more hospitable to educational reform or innovation resulted from AFT President Albert Shanker's ability to manipulate media, not to any substantive differences between the unions. The latter overwhelmingly endorse the same candidates for public office, and adopt the same positions on legislative issues. Internal union issues, not differences over educational or political policy, are the main obstacles to an NEA/AFT merger.

• In the private sector, it is taken for granted that basic changes in our system of employment relations are essential to union viability. Labor relations experts often disagree about the changes that should be made, but few, if any, anticipate a union resurgence under prevailing labor law. In education, however, the NEA/AFT are trying to neutralize the factors responsible for the decline of private sector unions. The NEA/AFT are winning some battles but are not likely to win the war.

• Because of competitive factors, private sector unions are beginning to emphasize productivity over redistribution. It is unlikely that teacher unions can do the same.

The Point of View

Because this book is often critical of both teacher unions and their critics, readers should know my basic attitudes toward unions generally and the NEA/AFT in particular.

First, I believe that employee organizations are essential in both the private and public sectors. It is especially not desirable that government be able to treat employees with impunity. Employee organizations should be strong enough to challenge government but not able to cripple it in the pursuit of the special interests of their members.

Private sector unions have been declining in members and political influence, not only in the United States but in most if not all Western industrial nations.[3] Some of the reasons are not applicable to teacher unions; for instance, the latter are not threatened by competition from products made by cheaper labor in other countries. This is why generalizations about organized labor do not necessarily apply to the NEA/AFT.

Indisputably, the NEA/AFT are the main political opponents of privatization. Any study of the NEA/AFT that ignored their antiprivatization activities would be substantially incomplete. Nevertheless, although I support market oriented changes, promoting them is not the purpose of this book. Because the NEA/AFT are so heavily involved in antiprivatization activities, discussion of them is unavoidable in a book about the unions, but my purpose is to raise different and broader issues.

For example, school boards allow payroll deductions to NEA and AFT political action committees (PACs) and transmit the amounts to the union PACs at no cost to the unions. Many citizens who are opposed to market oriented changes in education also believe that school boards should not collect and distribute PAC funds for private organizations. This is the kind of issue that should not be overlooked in the conflict over privatization issues.

Although critical of the NEA and AFT, my analysis often diverges from popular criticisms of them. For instance, the Heritage Foundation, *Forbes* magazine, the *Wall Street Journal*, and a host of other union critics have alleged that public school teachers enroll their children in private schools in higher proportions than the public at large. This allegation is frequently cited to demonstrate that NEA/AFT opposition to privatization is not justified. Aside from the fact that the allegation is false, it has no bearing on the issues to be discussed. As a matter of fact, NEA/AFT critics typically embrace the same babble ("Every child can learn"; "parental involvement"; "world class standards") as their union counterparts, and their policy prescriptions just as frequently serve only symbolic or narrow interest group purposes.

The Plan of This Book

With several detours and add-ons, the plan of this book is as follows:

Chapter 2 is devoted to the emergence of teacher unionization, especially since the early 1960s. Having participated in this emergence as an author, professor, union activist, and true believer who interacted frequently with the key personalities in the situation, my account cites both personal experience as well as historical records.

Labor unions bargain collectively on behalf of the employees they represent; in this process, their objectives are to maximize employee and union benefits. Chapter 3 is an effort to explain the NEA/AFT political and social agendas as well as their so called "bread and butter" objectives. Chapter 4 discusses the way NEA/AFT objectives are implemented through collective bargaining. Without an understanding of this process, it is impossible to understand how the NEA/AFT fund their local, state, and national activities; without an understanding of how union operations are funded, it is impossible to appreciate their sources of power and their vulnerabilities.

Chapter 5, which is devoted to NEA/AFT political operations at the national level, documents the interaction of union political and bargaining objectives; also the way union objectives affect their political preferences. These interactions are also evident in Chapter 6, which takes up NEA/AFT political operations at the state and local levels; as we shall see, it is difficult if not impossible to distinguish collective bargaining from political activity in public education. This point is further expanded in Chapter 7 by an analysis of NEA/AFT opposition to contracting out by school boards. Chapter 8 is devoted to the compensation of union staff, which I regard as the most important neglected fact in American education. Chapter 9 then tracks union revenues; the data show that representing teachers is a billion dollar industry, perhaps much more. The teacher unions control huge member benefit corporations and insurance trusts that have yet to be thoroughly scrutinized. Chapter 9 also explains how the NEA maximizes its revenues by means of dubious accounting practices.

Having considered the NEA/AFT role in collective bargaining and political action, Chapter 10 challenges the distinction between these two processes. Chapter 10 also discusses teacher rights to disassociate from union policies and programs. These issues are especially salient in the light of NEA/AFT political and social agendas.

Chapter 11 explains the unique role of AFT President Albert Shanker. Shanker's prestige in education, the labor movement, and politics is shown to have deflected critical inquiry away from his modus operandi, a topic with significant implications for the future of teacher unions. The discussion of Shanker, who died on February 22, 1997, leads into Chapter 12, which sets forth my assessment of the impact of teacher unions on teacher welfare and pupil achievement. It then takes up some of the unintended consequences of teacher unionization, such as its effects on the PTA. On most issues, my assessment challenges both pro and anti-union critiques, partly because of the limited range of the outcomes they consider.

Even without merger on the horizon, it is unlikely that the NEA/AFT will continue to function as they do now. With due regard for the speculative nature of the issue, Chapter 13 takes up the likelihood of an NEA/AFT merger and affiliation with the AFL-CIO. Chapter 14 concludes by assessing how teachers, parents, and citizens can address the issues raised in the preceding chapters.

Definitions and Dimensions

Legally, a union is an organization that exists in whole or in part to represent employees to their employers on their terms and conditions of employment. In the United States, unions ordinarily fulfill this role through collective bargaining, which is defined in the National Labor Relations Act (NLRA) as: ". . . the performance of the mutual obligation of the employer and the representative of the employees to meet at reasonable times and confer in good faith with respect to wages, hours, and other terms and conditions of employment, or the negotiation of an agreement, or any question arising thereunder, and the execution of a written contract incorporating any agreement reached if requested by either party, but such obligation does not compel either party to agree to a proposal or require the making of a concession."[4] Although this definition includes terms which require further clarification, it is the one adopted or followed since 1935 under federal and most state statutes on the subject.

Throughout this book, I refer to "teacher unions" or "teacher bargaining" or some other phrase that limits the discussion to teacher unions or public education. In many cases my comments would be just as applicable to other unions representing state and local employees; however, repeated discussion of applicability to other unions would have been distracting in a book about the NEA/AFT. For this reason applicability issues are usually left to the reader with no comment from the author.

Technically, we might distinguish unions that bargain collectively from unions that try to promote employee welfare through other means. In about one-third of the states, there are teacher organizations that oppose collective bargaining and would be dismayed at being categorized as "unions" merely because they try to represent teachers on employment issues. At the same time, the NEA/AFT would ridicule the idea that organizations opposed to collective bargaining should be categorized as "unions." Consequently, I refer to teacher organizations opposed to collective bargaining as "nonunion," even though they engage in some union type activities.

2

THE TAKEOFF

One event overshadows all others in the rise of teacher unions: the 1961 election to choose a bargaining agent for New York City's teachers. After 1961, teacher unionization boomed; before it, teacher unions were marginal players, limited geographically to a few large urban centers.[1]

American Federation of Teachers (AFT)

Prior to the merger of the American Federation of Labor (AFL) and the Congress of Industrial Organizations (CIO) in 1956, teacher unions were overwhelmingly AFT locals affiliated with the AFL. Although teacher unions emerged before 1900, the first to affiliate with the AFL was one in San Antonio, Texas, in 1902. In the same year the Chicago Teachers Federation, which had been organized in 1897, affiliated with the Chicago Federation of Labor. Two patterns of affiliation thus appeared at the outset. One was affiliation with a national labor organization, the other, with a local body.

From 1902 to 1916, the teacher union movement had little success in enlisting the nation's teachers. In 1916, however, a small group of teacher union leaders agreed upon the desirability of a national teacher union. At the time, there were three teacher unions in Chicago fighting with the Chicago Board of Education for their very existence. The board had amended its rules in 1915 to prohibit "membership by teachers in labor unions or in organizations of teachers affiliated with a trade union." The Chicago Teachers Federation secured an injunction which restrained the board from enforcing this prohibition. However, at this time teachers in Chicago were hired on a year-to-year basis, and the board refused to rehire many teachers who belonged to unions.

As a result of the board's action, the Chicago teachers took the lead in forming a national union of teachers. An invitation to form such a union was sent to all teacher organizations affiliated with labor or interested in such affiliation. Only four locals sent delegates to the first meeting in Chicago on April 15, 1916, but teacher organizations in Chicago, Gary, Ind., New York City, Oklahoma City, Scranton, Pa., and Washington, D.C., received charters from the new organization, designated the "American Federation of Teachers." An application for affiliation with the American Federation of Labor was granted on May 9, 1916.

From its inception, the AFT has attracted some nationally known scholars. John Dewey, the most prestigious academic personality of his era, received the AFT's first membership card. At one time, Dewey was president of the American Association of University Professors; also of the American Psychological Association. "The father of progressive education," he was also a union supporter.

In its first two years, the AFT had to struggle desperately to survive. The Chicago Teachers Federation withdrew from the AFT in 1917 as the price for the reinstatement of the Chicago teachers who had been fired because they were union members. Many other locals disbanded under heavy pressure from school boards. However, from 1918 to 1919, the number of AFT locals increased from 24, with a membership of less than 2,000 to over 160, with a membership of close to 11,000. For a short time, AFT membership exceeded membership in the NEA, which had been established in 1857; teachers were increasingly dissatisfied with the association's failure to raise teacher salaries in the inflationary period at the close of World War I.[2]

After World War I, school boards and school administrators, encouraged by the anti-union political climate in the early 1920s, launched a major effort to crush the teacher unions. By 1927, less than one-fifth of the AFT locals which had been issued charters were still operating. After 1927, membership increased steadily until 1939, suffered a short setback until 1941, and then slowly turned upward with only minor reverses until the 1960s.

Nevertheless, the increases in AFT membership in the 1950s did not reflect any increase in the proportion of teachers who were AFT members. Before the mid-1960s, the AFT never enrolled five percent of the nations public school teachers. AFT inability to organize a larger proportion of teachers ended dramatically in 1961–62. To understand how and why this happened, we must review briefly developments in the NEA up to that time.

National Education Association (NEA)

The NEA was founded by school superintendents in 1857. For over one hundred years thereafter it was an anti-union organization even when its teacher members greatly outnumbered administrators. In 1906, a congressional charter exempted NEA property in the District of Columbia from taxation. The other organizations that have received such charters are the American Legion, AMVETS, American War Mothers, American National Red Cross, Boy Scouts of America, and Disabled American Veterans. The fact that no other union has been chartered by Congress or received a congressional tax exemption reflects the nonunion character of the NEA in 1906. Ironically, in the 1920s and 1930s, school boards often required teachers to join the NEA and its state and local affiliate; school districts with 100 percent membership were regarded as demonstrating professional leadership. Needless to say, the practical implications of 100 percent membership at the behest of management are very different from 100 percent membership at the behest of unions.[3]

Obviously, school management had no interest in requiring teachers to join organizations that would challenge management over teacher interests. Nevertheless, a strategy for advancing teacher interests was essential to justify the inclusion of teachers in the NEA, an organization dominated by school management. The solution was to promote teacher interests through state legislation. In addition to avoiding conflict at the local level, state legislation often provided benefits for school administrators as well as teachers; for example, improvements in the state retirement system benefited the administrators as well as the teachers.

The emphasis on state legislation was reflected in the NEA's membership structure. Teachers could join the local, state or national association without having to join at all levels, whereas unified membership is normal practice in labor unions. In the preunion era, local association dues were extremely low. State dues were much higher, and the state associations employed the vast majority of full-time association personnel. The officers of the state associations were usually teachers elected for honorific one year terms; sometimes these officers did not even move to the state capitols where the state association headquarters was located. The real power in the state association was exercised by their executive secretaries, who also dominated NEA policies and programs.

The foregoing organizational structure did not represent teacher interests effectively for at least three reasons. First, the power of school administrators on the job site ensured their power in the associations at all levels. The teachers could not conduct effective legislative campaigns over the opposition of their administrator members. For example, some states did not enact tenure laws because administrators in the state association opposed tenure protection for teachers; consequently, their state associations did not support it.[4]

Second, legislation is a highly problematic, protracted way to achieve teacher benefits. Under the legislative approach, teachers could not achieve a benefit until all teachers in the state were entitled to it. Since benefits were often achievable in school districts with potentially strong local associations, the emphasis upon state legislation was not a productive strategy for teachers in such districts. The NEA emphasis on legislation was also flawed by its weakness at the local level. NEA local affiliates lacked the resources to provide effective grassroots support in political campaigns.

Although these weaknesses offered promising opportunities for a rival organization, the AFT was unable to take advantage of them. In 1961, however, the United Federation of Teachers (UFT), the AFT's affiliate in New York City, persuaded the New York City Board of Education to conduct an election on whether the teachers wanted to bargain collectively with the board. When the teachers voted overwhelmingly to bargain collectively, the board conducted another election for teachers to choose the organization to represent them in collective bargaining. After an intensive campaign, the election results, announced on December 16, 1961, were as follows:

United Federation of Teachers (AFT)	20,045
Teachers Bargaining Organization (NEA)	9,770
Teachers Union of the City of New York	2,575
No union	662
Spoiled ballot	67
Total votes cast	33,119

The UFT enjoyed a remarkable advantage in the election; it received information on a daily basis from a spy in the NEA office. Remarkably, the late AFT President Albert Shanker, was instrumental in arranging this espionage. I never discussed this with Shanker, but I did raise the issue in the late 1980s with David Selden, who had directed the UFT campaign. I wanted to know how anyone presumably opposed to labor espionage could utilize it as he and Shanker had done in New York City. Selden's answer was clear, even if his logic was not: Labor espionage is perfectly acceptable if the unions employ the spies![5]

The NEA conducted an extremely inept campaign in New York City, but two aspects of the election had profound consequences for American education. One related to the labor relations issue known as unit determination: Should all teachers collectively decide whether to be represented by a union, and if they did, what union should represent them? Or should groups of teachers, such as elementary, junior high school, and senior high school make these decisions independently of what the other groups decided to do? The UFT was a "wall to wall" union, that is, one that enrolled all teachers, regardless of grade level or subject. The NEA did not have a similar New York City affiliate. Instead, there were several NEA affiliates, each enrolling teachers categorized by grade level or subject. When the election became unavoidable, the NEA argued that elementary, junior high school, and senior high school teachers should be in separate bargaining units. Under this arrangement, teachers in each division would decide what union, if any, would represent them. Inasmuch as the NEA had local affiliates corresponding to these divisions and the AFT did not, the NEA sought to have the election conducted on a divisional basis.

The decision maker on this issue, as on most others pertaining to the election, was Dr. George Taylor, a professor of labor relations at the University of Pennsylvania. Taylor was perhaps the nation's most prestigious expert on labor relations. The New York City board of education had employed him to recommend the rules governing the election to the board. Taylor recommended a "wall to wall" unit, so the voting was on which union, if any, would represent all teachers.

Because of the enormous publicity associated with the election, the prestige of the decision maker, and the strong influence of precedent in labor relations generally, Taylor's decision became the national pattern. If Taylor had accepted the NEA's position, elementary and secondary teachers probably would be negotiating separate contracts in a large number of school districts.

The aftermath of the New York City election was bizarre, to say the least. The NEA had been founded by school superintendents and had always allowed unrestricted administrator membership. In contrast, the AFT had been founded as a union and had excluded top level administrators from membership from the beginning. Since its founding in 1916, the AFT had argued that the NEA enrolled more teachers only because administrators forced teachers to join the NEA. Allegedly, if teachers had an uncoerced choice, they would vote for AFT representation.

The AFT's victory in New York City appeared to be dramatic confirmation of the AFT's position on teacher representation. Although it enrolled only 5,200 members, about half of whom had joined during the past year, the UFT received 20,045 votes in the election. As a result, public education immediately witnessed an unprecedented pattern of union representation elections. Inspired by the UFT victory in New York City, AFT leaders in other large urban school districts began to clamor for such elections. Usually unions do not call for representation elections unless a substantial proportion of the workers involved have expressed support for the union. To do otherwise is to run the risk of defeat or even worse, of entrenching a rival union. After the New York City election, however, AFT locals which often enrolled far fewer members than NEA in the same district began to call for representation elections.

Controlled as it was by school management, the NEA dithered in responding to the challenges. Since it had always opposed teacher unionization, the NEA could not formally embrace "collective bargaining." Nonetheless, it had to come up with a strategy for more effective teacher representation at the local level. The NEA solution was "professional negotiations"; the alleged difference was that "collective bargaining" was limited to terms and conditions of employment, whereas "professional negotiations" supposedly implied a teacher right to negotiate on any matter of teacher concern.

From a labor relations standpoint, the NEA's appeal to an unlimited scope of bargaining was absurd. Autoworkers may be concerned about the price of cars, their color and safety features, the number of dealers, and scores of other matters that are not subject to bargaining. The United Auto Workers bargains on "terms and conditions of employment"; even on the most expansive definition, the phrase falls far short of "any matter of concern." Nonetheless, as soon as the NEA urged an unlimited scope of negotiations, the AFT asserted that teacher unions should bargain about anything that concerned them. Unfortunately, this nonsense was and still is taken seriously by many teachers.

The right to strike was another point of disagreement that vanished in the 1960s. Prior to that time, the AFT had wavered between silence on the issue and renunciation of the teachers' right to strike; in 1964, however, the AFT embraced the teachers' right to strike. Not having the right would allegedly lead to school board failure to bargain in good faith; knowing that teachers would continue to work, school boards would not feel any pressure to give good faith consideration to union proposals. The AFT also argued that since private sector employees had the right to strike, denial of a teacher right to do so was an "inequity." The federation further contended that a teacher right to strike did not endanger public health or safety, an argument often cited to justify prohibitions against strikes by public employees. After all, schools were not open during Christmas, Easter, and Thanksgiving vacations, as well as 2 to 3 months in the summer; shutdowns as a result of collective bargaining were not likely to continue for more than a few days.

Inasmuch as the NEA enrolled school administrators, it could not embrace the right to strike without antagonizing its administrator members. Neither could it avoid the issue of how local associations should deal with unreasonable school boards; to do so would give the AFT a huge advantage in the representation elections. The uneasy compromise was an NEA policy that tried to finesse the strike issues. In brief, the NEA urged "professional sanctions" as the way to deal with unreasonable employers. The idea was that in extreme cases of unfair treatment, the

NEA would send a team to investigate and report on the situation. The report would be widely publicized and the profession would supposedly shun the recalcitrant district. Colleges would not send candidates for teaching positions; teachers would not apply for employment; employment agencies would boycott the district, and so on. In the real world, however, "professional sanctions" were too convoluted to be a practical option for dealing with hard cases.

Essentially, NEA policy was that teacher strikes would not happen if everyone was reasonable. When "everyone" (that is, the school board) was not reasonable, NEA news releases announced that teachers had taken "professional holidays." When the Newark Teachers Union (AFT) went on strike in 1964, the NEA denounced the strike as irresponsible lawlessness; when the Newark Teachers Association, an NEA affiliate, won representation rights, and went on strike in February 1966, the NEA pointed out that NEA did not have a no-strike policy. Finally, in 1969, the NEA embraced the right to strike without equivocation, and has ever since.

The Legislative Front

In the history of unions, their legal status has been the single most important factor in their development. Unless employers are legally obligated to bargain collectively with unions, many will not do so. Education was no different; school boards often asserted lack of authority to recognize and bargain with a union. And even when they did not refuse to bargain for this reason, the absence of a state statutory framework meant that school boards resolved procedural issues. The New York City board of education held a union representation election in 1961 because the mayor and city administration were strong union supporters, but elsewhere, the political environment was not so hospitable to teacher unionization.

When the AFT won the New York City election in 1961, no state statutorily authorized collective bargaining in public education. As AFT locals and other public sector unions began to clamor for bargaining rights, the absence of state legislation on the subject emerged as a legislative problem. How many teachers had to sign a petition for an election? Who would conduct and monitor the election? What was the scope of bargaining? Were strikes allowed or prohibited? What remedies were available if one of the parties did not bargain in good faith? Scores of issues such as these had to be resolved. Naturally, the teacher unions did not want them resolved by school boards; likewise, other public employee unions did not want the issues resolved by the government agencies that employed their members.

Along with other public employee unions, the NEA/AFT launched major campaigns to enact state legislation that resolved these issues. In making this effort, the NEA and AFT differed on which employees should have the right to bargain collectively. Along with other AFL-CIO unions eager to organize public sector workers, the AFT argued for legislation applicable to state and local public employees generally. The NEA, however, supported "professional negotiations" applicable only to teachers. The NEA feared that if the legislation was applicable to state and local employees generally, the state agencies that administered the laws would be more sympathetic to AFT than to NEA positions. In particular, the NEA was concerned that its middle management members would be excluded from bargaining units and be forced to drop their NEA membership. In several states the outcome was decided by the fact that the AFL-CIO shared the AFT position in the state legislatures.[6]

Paradoxically, public sector bargaining laws were not enacted in some states due to the opposition of strong public sector unions. Because of their strength, these unions had negotiated contracts despite the absence of a state bargaining law. They were willing to support enactment of bargaining laws only if the laws did not weaken the rights they already enjoyed, such as a broad scope of bargaining. Whereas weak unions preferred a weak bargaining statute to none, strong unions were opposed to weak statutes that restricted their freedom of action.

The NEA faced a much different problem. School boards outside of large urban areas were not under pressure to recognize and bargain with NEA locals, and the locals seldom took militant action to gain recognition as a union. The locals would request recognition if state law required school boards to grant it, but very few NEA locals were willing to press the issue in the absence of state legislation.

The NEA realized that it is very difficult to oust an incumbent union. Thus, its primary objective was legislation that required school boards to recognize its locals as the bargaining agent. The NEA wanted such legislation enacted before the AFT was able to challenge NEA locals in most school districts. Also, the NEA quickly realized that AFT affiliates received many more votes than their membership in representation elections; in contrast, NEA locals often failed to receive as many votes as they had members. Consequently, the NEA sought legislation that authorized or required school boards to recognize locals on the basis of membership instead of votes in a secret ballot election. To enact such legislation, the NEA's state affiliates were willing to accept highly unfavorable restrictions, such as a narrow scope of bargaining and severe penalties against striking teachers and unions.

The upshot was a split among the public sector unions. The NEA, American Federation of State, County, and Municipal Employees (AFSCME), and the International Association of Firefighters (IAFF) supported legislation that prohibited strikes by public employees; these unions accepted antistrike provisions as essential to the enactment of state bargaining laws. In contrast, the AFT and some other public sector unions refused to support bills of this kind. The positions of both teacher unions reeked of hypocrisy. The NEA was willing to accept virtually any legislation that allowed recognition to be based on membership. Meanwhile the AFT opposed legislation that prohibited strikes that endangered public health or safety. Since teacher strikes did not fall under this category, the AFT would not have been adversely affected by the prohibition, but the AFT's real motivation was to block any collective bargaining legislation that would lock in NEA's membership superiority.

Paradoxically, anti-union sentiment also played an influential role in the enactment of the state bargaining laws. Many public officials were concerned about strikes by public employees, especially recognition strikes. These are strikes by public employees to force public officials to be recognized and bargain with their union. Thus, some public officials viewed bargaining legislation as the way to prevent recognition strikes; also as the way to limit the scope of bargaining, which was thought to be inevitable.

Today, the NEA and AFT contend that teacher bargaining was a spontaneous reaction to low salaries and arbitrary treatment of teachers. Historically, the contention is indefensible. In Wisconsin, the public employee bargaining bill introduced in 1959 did not include teachers. The bill was amended by public employers to include teachers; it was assumed that the amendment would kill the bill. When it did not, Wisconsin teachers had bargaining rights without any effort or even any strong interest on their part.

Similarly, in New York City, teachers did not have to struggle to achieve bargaining rights. New York City's mayor in 1961 was Robert Wagner; his father, Robert Wagner, Sr., was the author of the National Labor Relations Act (NLRA), widely referred to as the Wagner Act. Mayor Wagner's pro-union director of labor relations, Ida Klaus, observed that New York City's public employees achieved bargaining rights because of the mayor's desire to demonstrate his pro-union credentials; according to Klaus, who drafted the executive order that authorized bargaining with the city's municipal unions, employee pressure was not a factor. Interestingly enough, AFT president Albert Shanker agreed with this conclusion; in Shanker's view, collective bargaining by municipal unions in New York City resulted from the city's takeover of New York City's unionized subway system; municipal authorities accepted public sector bargaining as a result of the takeover.

The New York City situation illustrates several critical reasons for the rapid growth of teacher unions. Unlike private sector employers, school boards did not oppose unionization very much, partly because school boards were not under competitive pressures from nonunion employers. Furthermore, school board opposition to unionization often was not politically attractive. Also, male teachers are more supportive of unionization than female teachers; unionization took off at a time when larger than usual proportions of males became teachers to avoid the draft. It is difficult to assess the weight to be accorded these factors, but they undoubtedly contributed to the phenomenal increase in teacher unionization in the 1960s and early 1970s.[7]

The Impact of Collective Bargaining on NEA/AFT Membership

Both the NEA and the AFT tried to enact legislation that reflected their membership policies. For example, the NEA wanted supervisors to be in the same bargaining unit as teachers. Under such legislation, the association would not be forced to exclude principals and assistant principals from membership in the NEA. On most statutory issues that divided the two unions in the 1960s, the NEA shifted to the AFT position after the NEA no longer feared losing any election advantage by doing so.

As AFT affiliates racked up victory after victory in large school district elections, the NEA finally realized it faced a membership free fall unless it changed its position on collective bargaining. Within a short time, the NEA embraced the concept, albeit, not the term itself. The more intense the NEA/AFT union competition, the more NEA resources were devoted to it; from 1961–62 to 1964–65 NEA expenditures for collective bargaining increased from $28,000 to $885,000. Inevitably, the probargaining forces in the NEA expanded their control of the association as their share of the NEA budget increased.

Membership in both the NEA and AFT also increased rapidly under collective bargaining. From 1961–62 to 1964–65, AFT membership increased from 60,715 to 112,000. During the same period, however, NEA membership increased from 765,616 to 943,581. This pattern has continued to the 1990s; while both unions have increased their membership substantially as a result of collective bargaining, NEA gains have exceeded the AFT's by wide margins.

Obviously, both unions could not increase their total membership by recruiting members from the rival union. Increases at the expense of the rival union usually materialize when a union gains bargaining rights in a school district which includes some members of the rival union. For example, New York City affiliates of the NEA enrolled 30,000 members in 1961; today, NEA membership in New York City has virtually disappeared. In other school districts, when NEA affiliates became the bargaining agent, AFT membership usually dwindled or disappeared altogether. Generally speaking, membership growth in both unions resulted from the fact that the unions that win representation elections are much more able to recruit teachers who are not members of any union. This fact explains the intense NEA/AFT interest in enacting bargaining statutes in the states that have not done so.

Theoretically, NEA or AFT affiliates can win representation elections even if they have no members in the school district. All teachers in the bargaining unit, regardless of membership, are entitled to vote on what union, if any, they want to represent them. Consequently, nonmembers often vote to be represented by a union. Furthermore, unions, even with employer support, cannot require employees to become union members. The AFT especially was faced with situations in which it represented teachers in large school districts but did not have an adequate membership base to support its operations. Over time, however, unions that win representation elections are usually able to increase their membership.

A major reason is that the winning union becomes the "exclusive representative" of the employees in the bargaining unit. Under exclusive representation, individual teachers can no longer negotiate their terms and conditions of employment. The union negotiates for all teachers, not just all union members. Suppose, for example, that veteran teachers are concerned about their low maximum salaries. The veterans cannot necessarily rely on support from the younger teachers; the latter may be more interested in negotiating family health insurance than higher maximum salaries for veteran teachers. At some point in the bargaining process, the union negotiators have to set their priorities; the negotiators cannot satisfy everyone's wish list. However, teachers who are nonmembers of the union cannot participate in the process of setting union priorities or ratifying a proposed contract. For tactical reasons, a union may allow nonmembers to participate, but the union interest lies more in excluding than including them.

Legally, a union is required to represent all employees fairly, without regard to their membership status. In practice, nonmembers often believe that the union is less likely to support nonmember than member grievances. Inasmuch as unions have considerable latitude in dealing with grievances, nonmembers may not wish to rely on the union's legal duty to represent everyone fairly.

As the exclusive representative, the union takes credit for all the good and blames management for all the bad features in the contract. More important, it is usually able to negotiate contractual provisions that increase membership and support the union. The most important, to be discussed in Chapter 10, are fees that nonmembers are required to pay to the union as a condition of employment. In addition, the unions typically sponsor benefit programs that are available only to union members.

The upshot is that most nonmembers join the union which becomes the exclusive representative. This fact underlies the phenomenal increases in NEA/AFT membership since 1961. In the folklore of education, teacher bargaining took off because "teachers were mad as hell and wouldn't take it any more." According to union rhetoric, management gets what it deserves; that is, poor management is a fertile ground for unionization. Unionization was allegedly a reaction to widespread maltreatment of teachers by school boards and school administrators. Though this conclusion is widely accepted in the academy and the media, what actually happened was precisely the opposite.

The teachers in Connecticut school districts have bargaining rights; the teachers in Mississippi do not. Yet the conditions of employment before the enactment of bargaining rights in Connecticut were far superior to those in Mississippi. The reality is that the bargaining laws were passed in those states which already provided the most teacher compensation and benefits. In these states, teacher and other public employee unions already exercised the most influence; politically, it is only to be expected that teacher bargaining should emerge where conditions of teacher employment were already the most favorable to teachers. Of course, this conclusion is subject to qualification and exceptions, but it is essentially valid.

In any event, both the NEA and AFT increased their membership substantially as a result of the state bargaining laws. Overall strategy in both unions was guided by leaders who recognized that it is extremely difficult to oust an incumbent union. If there had been only one teacher union in the 1960s, the pace of teacher unionization would have been much slower.

In 1961, teachers were employed pursuant to individual contracts; tenure laws, where they existed, were their main protection against arbitrary dismissal. Ten years later, more than half the teachers in the country were employed pursuant to collective bargaining contracts. Many of these contracts provided contractual protection against arbitrary dismissal by the school board; the initiative for this sweeping change came from the unions, not rank and file teachers. To be sure, the latter often agreed with or routinely accepted union rhetoric, but this had little or nothing to do with actual terms and conditions of teacher employment. What counted was (and is) subjective perception, not objective reality. Just as the unions of professional athletes strive to convince their millionaire members that the latter are being mistreated by their employers, the teacher unions persuaded the most highly paid teachers that they were being maltreated by school boards.

The foregoing comment is not intended to support employer positions, either in professional sports or public education. The point is that the NEA and AFT were not responding to a spontaneous, pre-existing climate of teacher militancy. The teacher unions created the climate much more than they simply responded to it. Collective bargaining and unionization emerged first in states where teachers enjoyed a substantial array of statutory benefits and protection;

it has yet to emerge in states like Mississippi, where teachers enjoy few or none. The big losers in its emergence were school boards and administrators, caught in the competition between two unions determined to extract maximum concessions to achieve a larger share of the teacher market.

The Impact of Collective Bargaining on the NEA

Within a few years, the substantial costs of collective bargaining necessitated drastic changes in the NEA's budget and programs. Figure 2.1 shows the existing NEA organization chart.

The contrast with its pre-union organization chart is remarkable. Prior to unionization, the NEA organization chart had included the following thirty-three departments:

Administrative Women
Art Education
Audiovisual Instruction
Business Education
Classroom Teachers
Colleges for Teacher Education
Driver Education
Educational Research
Educational Secretaries
Elementary-Kindergarten
Nursery Education
Elementary School Principals
Exceptional Children
Foreign Languages
Health, Physical Education,
    Recreation
Higher Education
Home Economics

Industrial Arts
Journalism Education
Mathematics Teachers
Music Educators
Public School Adult Education
Retired Teachers
Rural Education
School Administrators
School Librarians
School Public Relations
Science Teachers
Secondary School Principals
Social Studies
Speech
Supervision and Curriculum
    Development
Vocational Education
Women Deans and Counselors

These departments had been devoted mainly to curriculum and instruction in their respective fields. All were wiped out in the union structure that was adopted in 1972. A few groups served by the departments, such as retired teachers, higher education faculty, and education secretaries were incorporated in the new structure in some way, but their focus was changed from professional improvement to employee welfare under a union label. Most of the departments became independent organizations if they survived at all. In this respect, the NEA differs from professional organizations generally. The latter

FIGURE 2.1.

NEA Structure

Note: Does not include ad hoc internal committees of the Board of Directors and Executive Committee.

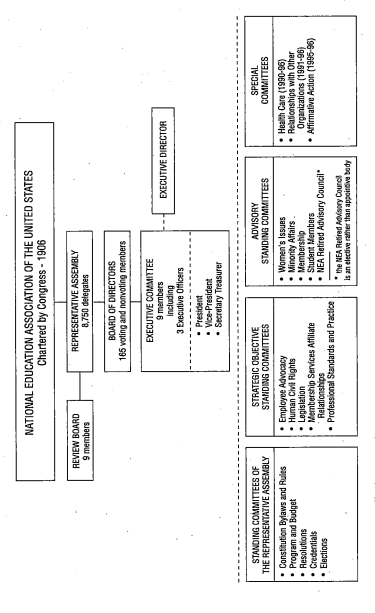

Source: *NEA Handbook, 1995–96*, p. 11.

23

include some type of organizational accommodation to serve the specialized groups in the association. For example, the American Bar Association has sections to accommodate the needs of specialists in criminal law, labor law, antitrust law, and so on. The NEA's union structure has not served its members this way since 1972, and the AFT structure never did.

The NEA did not become a union in one day; its unionization was a multi-year process characterized by internal conflict throughout the association.[8] The critical years were from 1962, when the NEA had to decide how to compete with the AFT, to 1972, when the NEA adopted unified dues and a new constitution that ensured teacher majorities in the governance structure. The sweeping nature of the change is evident from its budgetary consequences. In 1961, the NEA's budget was $8,134,163; the only expenditure for collective bargaining was $28,037 for the Urban Project, the NEA program intended to thwart unionization. In 1996, the NEA's budget exceeded $186 million; its legal position that year was that 71 percent of its revenues were devoted to collective bargaining, grievance processing and contract administration. Even after making allowances for inflation, the comparison reflects drastic changes in the NEA's role. In effect, the preunion NEA virtually disappeared. It had been the home of educational organizations devoted to curriculum, teaching methods, educational finance, and teacher education, to cite just a few; as its union needs increased, the NEA pushed out the nonunion functions and organizations that did not leave voluntarily.

In its transition to union status, the NEA discovered that "union" practices could be utilized to the NEA's benefit. Thus in 1972, the NEA required its state affiliates to adopt unified membership (local, state, and national) or a satisfactory plan to achieve it. The Missouri State Teachers Association (MSTA) refused to adopt such a plan and eventually became a separate, independent organization; all other state NEA affiliates adopted unified membership by the 1975–76 school year. NEA affiliates also sought the exclusive right to payroll deduction of dues and use of bulletin boards in the schools. Such exclusivity is intended to minimize competition from rival unions. Inasmuch as unions compete on the basis of which one can extract the most benefits from the employer, the school boards usually accept union proposals to strangle competition from other unions.

In the 1960s and 1970s, the AFT did not have local affiliates in most school districts. Since NEA affiliates had been established in most, exclusive rights to payroll deduction and access to school district facilities protected far more NEA than AFT locals from competition. NEA affiliates which had strenuously opposed "union tactics" embraced them overnight just as strenuously.

Notwithstanding their membership growth, the NEA and AFT constantly

TABLE 2.1
NEA Membership, 7/31/95

A. K-12, active and life	1,976,474
B. Higher education, active and life	76,135
C. Retired members	126,428
D. Student members	46,427
E. Substitute, reserve, and staff members	27,532
F. Total, all categories	2,252,996

Note that categories A and B, which include members who pay full dues, also include 103,000 life members who no longer pay anything. "Retired members" are a different group. They pay either $100 to be a "Retired Member for Life," $15 annually if retired after September 1, 1973, or $5 if retired before then. Thus, although the NEA asserted membership of $2.2 million in 1995, over 10 percent were life members and retirees who pay nothing or only nominal amounts, and several other membership categories paid much less than regular dues.

Source: NEA Handbook, 1995–96, p. 167.

cite membership figures which are misleading unless scrutinized carefully. Table 2.1 shows NEA membership as of July 31, 1995.

AFT Membership

In 1996, the AFT claimed a membership of 907,430, as shown in Table 2.2.

AFT membership data also must be interpreted cautiously. For example, AFL-CIO figures show AFT membership to have been only 612,000 in 1995. Why the discrepancy?

In the AFL-CIO, representation at its national convention is based upon per capita membership payments to the AFL-CIO. For this reason, its constituent unions "save" money by under-reporting their membership. At the same time, however, union leaders want to show gains in their membership; such gains impress the rank and file, ward off internal uprisings, and impress media and politicians. Inasmuch as the AFT and AFL-CIO figures are based on different criteria, both the AFT and AFL-CIO figures reflect the different criteria used for counting members.

The AFT membership figures also include employees whose dues are shared with other unions. For example, in Indiana, the AFT and United Auto Workers (UAW) formed a "Unity Team" to compete against the American Federation of

TABLE 2.2

AFT Membership, 1996

497,237	K–12 teachers
78,000	Higher education faculty
140,000	Paraprofessionals and school related personnel
14,154	Nurses and health professionals
63,039	Noneducation public employees
115,000	Retirees (author estimate)
907,430	Total, from 1996 AFT convention news release.

Source: Except for total membership, figures are author estimates from AFT officer reports to the 1996 AFT convention and other convention documents. The AFT does not release the membership figures for each of its five divisions.

State, County, and Municipal Workers (AFSCME) in four representation elections among state employees. The dues of these dual members are divided, one-third to the AFT and two-thirds to AFSCME. Both the AFT and UAW count the employees as members, giving a misleading picture of their membership. In any case, less than 60 percent of AFT members are full-time K–12 teachers.

As we shall see, the large nonteacher component of AFT membership points to some major organizational problems. Overall, AFT teacher membership has increased very little in recent years. Its membership totals show annual gains, but the new members are largely retirees, health care workers, school support personnel such as bus drivers and cafeteria employees, and 50,000 miscellaneous public employees, such as meat inspectors and drivers license examiners. Factor in about 80,000 faculty in higher education and you have a melange that may not appeal strongly to any of these constituencies.

Transition Leadership: A Commentary

To survive the challenge from the AFT, the NEA had to become a union. An astonishing feature of the NEA's transition to union status was that management labor lawyers provided the leadership for it. As surprising as this seems, some such development was inevitable at the time. To appreciate this, consider the following issues which arose in the representation elections.

1. Who is eligible to vote? In labor terminology, the issue is what positions are included in the bargaining unit. If substitute teachers were more likely to

vote for the AFT, the NEA would argue that substitutes did not share a "community of interest" with regular teachers, should not be in the bargaining unit, and therefore should not be eligible to vote in the election. Needless to say, the AFT also adjusted its positions to meet its election needs this way.

2. Where should the balloting take place? After the New York City election, the NEA feared that its supporters were not as committed as the AFT's. The NEA assumed that its supporters were less likely to vote if voting posed any inconvenience. Consequently, the NEA would often argue that voting take place .in each school, at a time when all teachers were likely to be present anyway. The AFT was more likely to argue that voting should be held at a central facility to minimize the problem of monitoring the elections.

3. Should the ballots be counted and reported school by school or only by total? If the NEA believed it would win the election, perhaps in a runoff, it would be opposed to a school-by-school count. Such a count would provide the AFT with useful information in a runoff or decertification election.

Dozens of such issues arose in the representation elections, hence the NEA urgently needed legal and strategic advice from knowledgeable parties. As so often happens when the client knows very little about the issues, the attorney's role goes far beyond merely giving legal advice; the attorneys become the strategists and tacticians as well. This was the course of events in the NEA.

In preparing for a representation election in Newark, New Jersey, the NEA employed Kaye, Scholer, Fierman, Hays and Handler, a prominent New York City labor law firm, as its legal counsel on bargaining issues. This law firm ordinarily represented management; the NEA was its only union client. In view of the NEA's lack of sophistication about collective bargaining, its labor lawyers provided the NEA's de facto leadership on collective bargaining issues during the critical early years.

Although the account was under the direction of Fred Livingston, a senior partner, the day-to-day work was handled largely by Donald H. Wollett and Robert H. Chanin. Both were very intelligent, very tough negotiators and thoroughly devoid of illusions about the situation. First of all, Wollett and Chanin were instrumental in persuading NEA leaders to drop their Hamlet-like posture on collective bargaining. They recognized how exclusive representation could be used to lock in NEA's membership superiority; since they were not responsible for the NEA's previous anti-union rhetoric, they could reject it without embarrassment. Their strategy was "to out-union the union" and it was quickly successful in dispelling the NEA's image as an administrator dominated organization.

Wollett and Chanin were also aware of the importance of the statutory framework of labor relations. They played a major role in drafting the state bargaining laws that promoted NEA's interests; for example, since the NEA enrolled supervisors and the AFT did not, Wollett and Chanin drafted legislation that allowed supervisors to be represented by teacher unions. After a bargaining statute was enacted, Wollett and Chanin sometimes negotiated the first contracts, which were then disseminated throughout the state to demonstrate that the NEA was an effective union.

Chanin was appointed NEA General Counsel and Deputy Executive Secretary in 1967; he retained only the general counsel title in 1980, when he joined Bredhoff and Kaiser, a labor law firm whose clients include the AFL-CIO and United Auto Workers. In my opinion, Chanin has had a larger impact on public education over the past thirty years than any other individual, in or out of government.

From 1961 to the 1980s, the NEA and AFT competed aggressively for the right to represent teachers. Whenever a state enacted a bargaining statute, or was about to do so, the two unions spent huge amounts of dues money on intensive campaigns to have their affiliates elected as the bargaining agents. What difference, if any, would it have made whether teachers were an NEA or an AFT affiliate? It would not have mattered; from a teacher's point of view, not the only one to be considered, the competition was largely a waste of money. Today, in advocating merger, NEA and AFT leaders agree on this, even though none expressed this point of view when the unions were competing for members.

First of all, neither union used any bargaining techniques or strategies not available to its rival; the nature of bargaining precludes any secrets about the process. In the early years, school boards and administrators often assumed that NEA affiliates would be less militant adversaries. To dispel the idea among teachers, negotiators for NEA affiliates often adopted ultramilitant strategies in collective bargaining. Of course, each union contended that it would be the better choice and occasionally one or the other was the better choice because of some local factor. Notwithstanding, the rivalry between the NEA and AFT was really to decide which union, not which teachers, would benefit. There were and are differences between the NEA and AFT, but the differences seldom affect the terms and conditions of teacher employment negotiated by their affiliates.

To sum up, teacher unions began to take off in the early 1960s. Competition between the NEA and AFT greatly accelerated the process. Each union realized the advantages of incumbency, hence each did everything possible to be elected as the exclusive representative before its rival could compete for bargaining rights. Within a decade after the New York City election, over half the nation's public school teachers were employed pursuant to a union contract. Today, the NEA/AFT enroll over three million members and their revenue exceeds $1.3 million annually. Clearly, the NEA/AFT have arrived on the national scene; the question is, where do they plan to take us?

3

NEA/AFT OBJECTIVES

U nions try to eliminate wage competition, restrict entry to the occupation, increase the demand for services provided by union members, and weaken rival service providers. These union objectives are reflected in NEA resolutions that do not mention their union implications. According to the preamble to the NEA constitution, the goals of the Association are to:

> . . . serve as the national voice for education, advance the cause of education for all individuals, promote the health and welfare of children and/or students, promote professional excellence among educators, gain recognition of the basic importance of the teacher in the learning process and other employees in the educational effort, protect the rights of educational employees and advance their interests and welfare, secure professional autonomy, unite educational employees for effective citizenship, promote and protect human and civil rights, and obtain for its members the benefits of an independent, united education profession.[1]

Resolutions adopted at the NEA's annual conventions are listed according to their preamble category. At its 1996 convention, the NEA adopted or renewed 299 resolutions as official NEA policy. Most of these resolutions are phrased in terms of the public interest, but they invariably serve union interests as well.

For example, resolution B-1 calls for "early childhood educational programs in the public schools for children from birth to eight." The NEA categorizes the resolution under the heading: "Advance the Cause of Education for all Individuals"; it could also be categorized as "expanding the market for the services

of the NEA and its members." Similarly, Resolution A-26 states: ". . . the following programs and practices are detrimental to public education and must be
eliminated: privatization, performance contracting, tax credits for tuition to
private and parochial schools, voucher plans (or funding formulas that have the
same effect as vouchers), planned program budgeting systems (PPBS), and
evaluations by private, profit-making groups." The NEA categorized A-26
under "Serve as the national voice for education"; in the union context, it is a
resolution intended to eliminate rival producers.

Italian sociologist Vilfredo Pareto observed that men find it easy to convert
their interests into principles. NEA resolutions provide a showcase example of
Pareto's observation. No matter who is supposed to benefit from an NEA resolution—the poor, minorities, the handicapped, farm workers, non-English
speaking immigrants, whoever—the resolution also protects or expands the
market for services provided by NEA members. Thus smaller class size is proposed as a benefit to pupils, not to teachers or to the NEA.

In general, the resolutions avoid any genuine issues. Resolutions urging
lower class size illustrate this point. Even if smaller classes are a benefit to
pupils, the practical issue is whether reducing class size is the most effective way
to spend the funds required. The pervasive neglect of costs and alternatives
whenever the NEA proposes pupil benefits strongly suggests that union interests underlie the proposals.

Some NEA resolutions do not even include a public policy fig leaf to conceal
the union interest. For example, Resolution A-9 states:

> Public School Buildings
>
> The National Education Association believes that closed public school buildings
> that have been deemed safe can be used effectively for public preschool, day care, job
> training, and adult education centers. The Association believes that closed public
> school buildings should be sold or leased only to those organizations that do not
> provide direct educational services to students and/or are not in direct competition
> with public schools (1982, 1987).[2]

Although its resolutions serve the NEA's interests, there is little point to criticizing the NEA for this reason; after all, the vast majority of interest groups
offer public policy rationales to promote their self-serving agendas. Criticizing
the NEA/AFT for doing so applies a double standard to the teacher unions.
Doing so may be useful politically, but it does not identify a significant difference between teacher unions and other interest groups. The NEA's self-serving
resolutions can and should be criticized if they are contrary to the public interest, not because they demonstrate a unique moral deficiency in the NEA.

The NEA's Social Agenda

The NEA supports an extremely liberal social agenda. At the risk of belaboring the point, let me quote several resolutions adopted or renewed at the 1996 convention (year of initial adoption and last amended in parenthesis).

Early Childhood Education

"The National Education Association supports early childhood education programs in the public schools for children from birth to age eight." B-1 (1975, 1995). p. 254.

Adolescent Pregnancy and Parenting

". . . The Association recommends that special programs for adolescents be implemented to include: . . .
  b. Establishment of on-site child care services." B-21 (e), (1978, 1995). p. 265.

Sex Education

". . . The Association urges it affiliates and members to support appropriately established sex education programs including information on sexual abstinence, birth control and family planning, diversity of culture, diversity of sexual orientation, parenting skills, prenatal care, sexually transmitted diseases, incest, sexual abuse, sexual harassment, the effects of substance abuse during pregnancy, and problems resulting from preteen and teenage pregnancies." B-37 (1969, 1995). B-34, p. 270.

Family Planning

The National Education Association supports family planning, including the right to reproduction freedom.

The Association urges the government to give high priority to making available all methods of family planning to women and men unable to take advantage of private facilities.

The Association further urges the implementation of community-operated, school-based family planning clinics that will provide intensive counseling by trained personnel. I-13 (1985, 1986). p. 330.

Other resolution adopted by the 1996 convention included support for:

- Comprehensive programs of AIDS education "as an integral part of the school curriculum." B-35 (1987, 1993), p. 270.
- Statehood for the District of Columbia. H-10 (1969, 1988). pp. 325–336.
- Government funding of the arts with freedom "to exercise judgement in the awarding of grants to individuals and organizations." I-22 (1990), p. 331.
- Set asides for minority contractors. I-52 (1989), p. 339.

Other NEA resolutions oppose standardized testing and English as the offi-cial language; in fact it is virtually impossible to discern any agreement between NEA positions and those widely deemed to be "conservative."

In 1995, the NEA adopted resolution B-9, which reads as follows:

Sexual Orientation Education

. . . The Association supports:

a. Accurate portrayal of the roles and contributions of gay, lesbian, and bisexual people throughout history, with acknowledgment of their social orientation.

b. The acceptance of diverse sexual orientation and the awareness of sexual stereo-typing, whenever sexuality and/or tolerance of diversity is taught.

c. Elimination of sexual orientation name-calling and jokes in the classroom.

d. Support for the celebration of a Lesbian and Gay History Month as a means of acknowledging the contributions of lesbians, gays, and bisexuals throughout his-tory. B-9 (1995) *NEA Handbook,* 1995–96. pp. 256–257.

The resolution, especially the support for Lesbian and Gay History Month, turned out to be an embarrassment. Conservative organizations criticized the NEA over B-9, and during the 1995–96 school year, several NEA members urged NEA to delete or change the resolution. Consequently, at its 1996 conven-tion, the NEA replaced resolutions B-7 (Racism in Education); B-8 (Sexism in Education); and B-9 with proposed resolution B-7, an omnibus resolution that included the following: "Discrimination and stereotyping based on such factors as race, gender, physical disabilities, and sexual orientation must be eliminated."

During the debate over resolution B-7, NEA president Keith Geiger explic-itly stated three times as convention chair that the adoption of B-7 would not change any NEA policy or program. Nonetheless, the resolution change was hailed as a "victory" by NEA critics.

Although the NEA characterizes itself as an advocate for children and edu-cation, its legislative proposals provide far more benefits for senior citizens than for young people. For example, the NEA policy on health care is as follows:

The National Education Association believes that affordable, comprehensive health care is the right of every resident.

The Association supports the adoption of a single-payer health care plan for all residents of the United States, its territories, and the Commonwealth of Puerto Rico.

The Association will support health care reform measures that move the United States closer to this goal and that achieve universal and comprehensive health care coverage, control costs while assuring quality, emphasize prevention of health care problems, and are financed by means that assure greater equity in the funding of that health care.

The Association further believes that until a single-payer health care plan is adopted, Congress should make no cuts in Medicare/Medicaid benefit levels or in federal funding of the Medicare/Medicaid program. H-6 (1978, 1994). pp. 324–325.

A 1996 study by the Alexis de Tocqueville Institution estimated that $536 billion would be required to implement resolution H-6.[3] Although the study was conducted by sources critical of both national health insurance and the NEA, the estimates seem reasonable enough. At the same time, the NEA's own polls show that 89 percent of its members have health insurance provided by the employer; an additional 9 percent have coverage through their spouses. School districts pay all of the costs of single-subscriber coverage in 50 percent of the cases; for 40 percent of the members with family coverage. On the face of it, there is no crisis facing NEA members on this issue.[4] Why then, did the NEA (and AFT) launch an intensive campaign to enact the Clinton administration's health care proposals?

Several factors explain NEA support for what would have been an extremely expensive federal program. Health insurance is a costly fringe benefit, paid from state and local funds. If the costs can be shifted to the federal government, local affiliates would be relieved of the pressure to absorb the growing costs of health insurance. Furthermore, the funds freed up this way would be available for salary increases. Thus taxes would rise, but not at the state and local levels, which provide most of the funding for public education.

Regarding social security, the NEA supports lowering the age of eligibility for benefits without any reduction in benefits; in fact, its proposals would increase federal spending on social security by $126.8 billion a year. Clearly, the NEA's legislative agenda would provide much more in benefits to senior citizens than to children. Furthermore, since increased spending for seniors would probably be paid by borrowing, not higher taxes, the NEA's proposals would impose a huge burden of debt on the young people whom the NEA purports to represent. For each new dollar in spending for children and education, NEA resolutions would spend an additional $5.24 on social security alone. Overall, NEA's legislative proposals for the 104th Congress would cost an estimated $702 billion, more than the amount supported by any member of Congress since 1991.[5]

Here again, the dynamics of union policy play a critical role. Both the NEA and AFT enroll over 100,000 retirees as members. The retirees enable the unions to show impressive increases in membership, but they also carry out valuable political tasks as well: letter writing, op-ed articles, participation in talk shows, demonstrations, telephone banks, and so on. Of course, there has to be something in it for the retirees; union support for retiree benefits serves this purpose. Understandably, there is no internal opposition to resolutions providing retiree benefits, no matter what the costs would be; everyone expects to be a retiree some day. Interestingly enough, when NEA new business items require NEA expenditures, they must be presented to the convention with estimates of their costs. No such estimates are required for resolutions calling for increased government spending. This makes it easy for the NEA to support increased government expenditures, but the cumulative effect of the process is a financial monstrosity.

NEA leaders have been concerned about the proliferation of issues coming before the Representative Assembly. At recent conventions, the board of directors has tried to change the convention rule that allows 50 delegates to introduce "new business items" up to the second day of the convention, but their effort was interpreted or at least characterized as a gag rule and defeated.

Obviously, the NEA's social agenda reflects the agenda of the most liberal wing of the Democratic Party—or vice versa. In view of the leading role the NEA plays in the Democratic Party, to be discussed in later chapters, the overlap is not surprising. Although the percentages fluctuate, the NEA's own polls show that 40 percent of its members characterize themselves as Democrats, 30 percent as Republicans, and 30 percent as Independents. How, then did the NEA become the leaders of the left wing of the Democratic party? Before I answer this question, let me comment briefly on AFT objectives.

AFT Objectives

The AFT's objectives are essentially the same as the NEA's. AFT resolutions support other unions and/or AFL-CIO positions more often, but there is very little direct conflict between NEA and AFT policies. As we shall see, the AFT's Progressive Caucus completely controls the federation. Although the caucus platform spells out dozens of objectives, the overriding one is support for "A society insuring the basic human rights of decent housing, a good job, quality education, and adequate medical care, as outlined in the AFL-CIO economic and social programs directed at those rights."[6]

The AFT's social agenda is as liberal as the NEA's, but the AFT does not publicize its social policies likely to evoke widespread criticism. For example, the NEA experienced widespread criticism in 1995 over its endorsement of gay/lesbian history month in the schools. None of the ensuing publicity referred to AFT policy supportive of gay/lesbian demands, or that the AFT contract with its staff union provides "domestic partner" benefits. Newly elected AFT president Sandra Feldman, perhaps the second most powerful leader in the AFT, is on the board of advisors to the AFT's Gay/Lesbian/Bisexual Caucus. No NEA officer has accepted such a prominent role with the same caucus in the NEA. The differences between the NEA and AFT are not so much in their objectives as in their sophistication in publicizing (or not publicizing) them.

Even the formal policy differences between the NEA and AFT are not as important in practice as they might appear to be. For instance, the AFT ostensibly supports rigorous student and teacher testing: The NEA is part of a coalition opposed to national testing for almost any purpose. Nonetheless, AFT leadership does not pursue the matter with its affiliates who adopt antitesting positions.

Caucus Functions and Operations

A state legislator once commented to me that the public schools teach the constitution and the ballot box—and leave out everything in between that determines what happens. In other words, the formal structure of an organization doesn't necessarily explain how it works. To understand how the unions function, it is necessary to understand the role of caucuses, especially in the AFT. The failure to recognize their importance is a major gap in the discussions of the two unions.

Essentially, a caucus is a political body intended to influence the election of candidates and/or the policies of a larger organization. Sometimes caucuses are simply informal meetings of organization members seeking to promote their interests or point of view. In other situations, caucuses have a formal organization, officers, and dues structure. For example, the National Collegiate Athletic Association (NCAA) enrolls all institutions of higher education participating in intercollegiate athletics. Initially, black coaches were an informal caucus within the NCAA; subsequently, they established a formal organization of their own to influence NCAA policies.

Generally speaking, caucuses are supposed to function on their own resources, not the resources of the larger organization in which they function. The reason is that organization resources are not supposed to be used to promote the views of subgroups within the organization. Some organizations assist all caucuses on an equal basis, for example, by listing their meetings in a convention program. In such cases, the parent organization must establish procedures for official recognition of caucuses. Both the NEA and the AFT have established such procedures for their national conventions.

We can categorize caucuses in two ways. First, "special interest" caucuses focus on one or a few constituencies or issues. For instance, there is a black caucus in both the NEA and AFT. In each, the black caucus supports candidates and policies deemed advantageous to blacks. In contrast, a "governance caucus" is intended to serve as a vehicle for electing organization leadership and establishing organizational policies and programs. In most organizations that have both special interest and governance caucuses, individuals are often members of a governance caucus and one or more special interest caucuses.

Caucuses play an important role in some unions. To see why, suppose an

NEA member who supports full disclosure of staff salaries and benefits is an elected delegate to the NEA convention. Inasmuch as 9,000 delegates attend, how does the individual persuade other delegates to support full disclosure? Practically, publications on the issue must be prepared and disseminated among the delegates. Since meetings are required to explain the position and to discuss strategy and tactics, help from others is essential. If a floor fight over the issue is anticipated, supportive delegates must be prepared to react promptly to parliamentary maneuvers. And so forth.

No individual can do everything that must be done to achieve full disclosure of staff compensation. An organization within the NEA is needed to perform the tasks required to achieve this objective. Caucuses are such organizations; they function as political parties within the union. Other things being equal, a caucus with a large membership and revenues will be able to achieve more union support for its positions than a caucus with fewer members and less resources. Although caucus membership and revenues are not an infallible guide to caucus influence, they are usually a useful guide on the issue.

Caucuses in the NEA

Table 3.1 lists the operative caucuses in the NEA in 1995–96. Significantly, it does not include a single governance caucus. In other words, no NEA caucus proposes a comprehensive program and tries to elect NEA officers to implement it. To be sure, candidates for NEA office seek caucus endorsements, and NEA caucuses are often active in union elections. On some issues, various caucuses exercise a de facto veto power over policies in their area of interest. Nevertheless, the absence of a governance caucus is remarkable in an organization that is so large and politically oriented. To some extent, state association meetings at NEA conventions serve caucus functions, but geography is not the most effective basis for caucuses devoted to policy development and implementation.

A brief survey of the caucuses in the NEA is instructive. Seventeen are caucuses of specialized educational groups, such as administrators or counselors. These caucuses function largely to promote the occupational interests of their members. Eleven caucuses deal with social or political causes; eight are sponsored by ethnic/religious groups; and two with other special interest activities.

As we have seen, NEA polls show that 40 percent of its members characterize themselves as Democrats, 30 percent as Republicans, and 30 percent as Independents. Even if these figures overestimate Republican membership, the absence of an effective conservative caucus in the NEA is remarkable. Only the Republican Educators Caucus (REC), the pro-life Abortion Neutrality Caucus, and the Educators for Life Caucus can be categorized as "conservative" but none is a significant pres-

TABLE 3.1

Caucuses of NEA Members

Abortion Neutrality Caucus	Irish-American Caucus
Administrators Caucus	Italian-American Caucus
Adoptive Parents Caucus	Jewish Affairs Caucus
Adult Education Caucus	Library/Information/Technology
American Indian/Alaska Native Caucus	Caucus
Asian-Pacific Islander Caucus	Men's Caucus
Black Caucus	On-Line Caucus
Campers Caucus	Peace and Justice Caucus
Counselors Caucus	Physical Education Caucus
Democratic Caucus	Physically Challenged Caucus
Early Childhood Educators Caucus	Republican Educators Caucus
Education Support Personnel Caucus	Rural and Suburban Caucus for
Educators for Life Caucus	Small Schools
Educators of Exceptional Children	School Nurses Caucus
Caucus	School Restructuring Caucus
Fine Arts Caucus	States Without a Bargaining
Gay and Lesbian Educators Caucus	Law Caucus
Greek/American/Syrian Caucus	Substitute Teachers Caucus
Green Earth Caucus	Vocational Educators Caucus
"Hands Across the Water"	Women's Caucus
Hispanic Caucus	Year-Round Schools Caucus

Source: NEA Handbook, 1996–97, pp. 405–408.

ence in the NEA. Actually, REC functions as a means of maximizing NEA influence within the Republican Party, not a means of increasing Republican influence in the NEA.[7] As a matter of fact, REC has never introduced a single resolution on any issue at an NEA convention; in 1994, it endorsed only Democratic candidates for NEA office. One such successful candidate was Dennis Van Roekel, whose supporters proudly announced that his initials stand for "Don't Vote Republican."[8]

As part of its efforts to appear bipartisan, the NEA has provided financial assistance to the Republican Educators Caucus. NEA staff members attend caucus meetings and have drafted caucus positions to ensure their conformity with NEA positions.[9] The NEA's co-optation of the caucus is also evident at state union conventions. In 1994, I attended a meeting of the state Council of Education, the governing body of the California Teachers Association (CTA). At the meeting, the CTA's Republican caucus was selling buttons promoting Kathleen Brown, the Democratic nominee for governor. Subsequently, the California Republican Party adopted a resolution declaring that the caucus was an "unwelcome organization," not to be accorded caucus privileges such as inclusion in the convention program. The resolution cited a long list of caucus actions supporting Democratic candidates and initiatives. One such charge was that "Republicans for Clinton–Gore" was a CTA front that included members of the CTA Republican caucus in the 1992 elections. The resolution withdrew caucus privileges for the CTA's Republican caucus until at least 40 percent of CTA endorsements went to Republicans. Similarly, the Republican National Committee (RNC) cut loose its ties to REC in 1995. Inexplicably, national and state Republican party organizations have not taken any initiative to foster an effective Republican caucus in the teacher unions. In fact, long before the presidential election season, the Republicans had given up on finding common ground with the unions. Months before Bob Dole singled them out for criticism in his convention speech, Republican National Chairman Haley Barbour had done so in a book setting forth the views of party leaders.[10] Meanwhile, NEA–PAC, the NEA's political action committee, had endorsed 251 congressional candidates—all but one were Democrats. Although the NEA did not endorse the Clinton–Gore ticket until July 5, 1996, NEA staff had been working on its behalf since 1995. Meanwhile, the existence of the "Republican Educators Caucus," helps the NEA foster the impression that it is a bipartisan organization.

The NEA's Educators for Life caucus also enrolls a small number of members; it is overwhelmed numerically by caucuses that support women's freedom to abort. To appreciate the numerical inferiority of these conservative caucuses, consider that the average congressional district includes about 700,000 residents of all ages. The NEA enrolls 2.2 million members. If a congressional district enrolled this many voters, it would undoubtedly include two or more political parties.

Caucuses in the AFT

In 1996, there were only four caucuses in the AFT: Progressive Caucus, Teacher Action caucus (TAC), Black Caucus and Gay/Lesbian/Bisexual Caucus (GLB). The Progressive Caucus exercises complete control over the AFT. Nothing of importance happens without its approval. The Teacher Action Caucus is a small group of left wing liberals whose presence helps the Progressive Caucus maintain a moderate image. The Black Caucus and Gay/Lesbian/Bisexual Caucus function as special interest caucuses, as they do in the NEA; however, they have less influence in the AFT than in the NEA.

During most of its history, the only caucuses within the AFT were governance caucuses. As late as the 1950s, AFT elections were contested by two roughly equal governance caucuses: the Classroom Teacher Caucus and the Progressive Caucus.

In the union movement, this situation is highly unusual. Typically, the advantages of incumbency in union office are even more influential than their advantages in elective government office. The incumbents in union office control the union publications, sponsor the news conferences, meet their constituents on union funds, arrange the convention program, and have access to helpful internal union data; meanwhile, challengers have to rely on personal resources or the resources of dissident state and local affiliates to compete against the incumbents.

The even strength of the two governance caucuses in the AFT was shattered by the massive increase in the membership of the United Federation of Teachers (UFT) in the 1960s; during that time, it became the largest local in the AFT. This increase was the direct result of the UFT's overwhelming victory over the NEA affiliates in the 1961 representation election in New York.

Within the UFT, its officers were members of the Unity Caucus, a governance caucus led by Albert Shanker; within the AFT, UFT delegates functioned as members of the Progressive Caucus. Because such a large proportion of AFT members were members of the UFT, it became practically impossible to gain a position on the Progressive Caucus slate without UFT support.

An actual case illustrates the situation. The AFT and NEA affiliates merged in New York in 1972. There were approximately 2,000 delegates at the first convention of the merged organization. The UFT sent 600 delegates. One of the issues was whether convention voting should be by open or secret ballot. The former AFT delegates supported open voting; delegates from the former NEA affiliates favored the secret ballot.

The vote outside of New York City was:

960	for secret ballot
440	against secret ballot
1,400	total votes outside of New York City

The New York City (UFT) vote was:

0	for secret ballot
600	against secret ballot
600	total votes from New York City

The total convention vote was:

1,040	against the secret ballot
960	for the secret ballot
2,000	total convention votes[11]

If the UFT sent a divided delegation to the AFT convention, candidates for AFT office might combine their votes outside the UFT with their votes from it to acquire a majority. This possibility does not exist because UFT delegates to the AFT convention are elected at large, hence the Unity slate elects every member of the UFT delegation to the state and AFT conventions.

The Suppression of Dissent in the AFT

One feature of the Progressive Caucus is its adherence to "democratic centralism." Under this principle, caucus members agree not to criticize caucus actions outside of caucus meetings. This principle is strictly enforced, hence there is no public disagreement among AFT leaders. As a practical matter, you can't be elected to the AFT's 38 member Executive Council unless you are a member of the Progressive Caucus; to be a member of the caucus, you must agree to support caucus candidates and policies and not to criticize caucus positions outside of caucus meetings.

The Progressive Caucus maintains monolithic control of the AFT through democratic centralism and slate voting. Again, the technique started in the UFT and was then applied to the state and national levels. During the 1960s, UFT elections were held annually; the elections for union officers and the executive board were held in the even numbered years; elections for divisional (elementary, junior high, senior high) vice-presidents and executive board members in odd numbered years. Under this structure, the Unity Caucus lost a few divisional executive board positions in the odd numbered years; also, the Unity candidates for divisional vice-presidents in junior and senior high schools sometimes won only by narrow margins. In contrast, the Unity candidates usually won the union wide elections by a comfortable margin (65 to 35 percent in recent years). To eliminate any organized opposition on UFT governance bodies, the Unity Caucus amended the UFT constitution to provide that all union- and division-wide elections be held in even numbered years. In 1994, the Unity Caucus eliminated divisional voting altogether, rendering it impossible for its opposition to rely on a divisional majority to elect divisional officers.[12]

In several other ways, UFT leadership has utilized legal, but highly undemocratic policies to emasculate organized opposition to leadership positions or perquisites. For example, according to the UFT constitution, its delegate assembly is the highest governing body in the union. The delegate assembly has about 2,500 delegates, but the delegates themselves do not have access to the mailing list, or even the names of the delegates. It is practically impossible to get an item on the agenda without the approval of the Unity Caucus; the elected representative of Manhattan high schools could not even place on the agenda a proposal that the union newspaper publish the salaries of union officers.[13] Furthermore, UFT publications do not carry paid political advertisements, rendering it even more difficult for opposition forces to disseminate their views to the membership.

The upshot is that the UFT sends a monolithic delegation to AFT conventions. Again, as a practical matter, if you don't belong to the Unity Caucus in the UFT, you cannot be elected delegate to the NYSUT and AFT conventions. If you are not in the Progressive Caucus at the AFT convention, you cannot be elected to AFT office. The situation reveals a masterful use of formally democratic procedures to eliminate any representation by delegates opposed to incumbent union leadership. The organizational procedures that eviscerate the dissenters are formally democratic but the outcome is a travesty, with far reaching internal and external implications.

To appreciate the national implications of slate voting in the UFT, suppose that UFT procedures provided for representation of minority positions within the UFT. Suppose also that the secret ballot forces would get 65 percent of the votes, the open-ballot causes 35 percent. Suppose further that the UFT delegation to the state convention reflected this division, which is close to the actual breakdown of caucus votes in the UFT. In that case, the convention vote on the secret ballot would have been as follows:

Vote outside of New York City:

960	for secret ballot
440	against secret ballot
1,400	total votes outside of New York City

New York City (UFT) vote:

210	for secret ballot
390	against secret ballot
600	total votes from New York City

Total convention vote:

1,170	for secret ballot
830	against secret ballot
2,000	total convention votes

Actual convention vote:

960	for secret ballot
1,040	against secret ballot
2,000	total convention votes

Although the example is from a state vote, it is a realistic portrayal of election dynamics in the AFT. Roughly one-third of AFT membership is from the state of New York and about one-third of the state membership is in the UFT.

The UFT sends a monolithic delegation to the state convention, thereby achieving complete control over all state offices. The control over the state offices is then leveraged to ensure complete control over the national organization. Candidates for AFT office from outside of New York are faced with a dilemma: join the Progressive Caucus or form a coalition to defeat it. In practice, however, any attempt to form a coalition against a caucus that controls one-third of the convention votes is virtually certain to result in exclusion from the Executive Council, the AFT's governing body. Facing insurmountable odds, the other large AFT locals join the Progressive Caucus, in effect giving up their freedom to criticize Progressive Caucus/AFT candidates and actions outside of caucus meetings.

Caucuses Under an NEA/AFT Merger

If the NEA and AFT merge, what caucus system is likely to emerge? Undoubtedly, governance caucuses would materialize in the merged organization. Nevertheless, I doubt whether governance caucuses after merger could maintain the caucus discipline that prevails in the AFT's Progressive Caucus.

The requirement that caucus members not criticize caucus positions outside of caucus meetings would be extremely difficult to enforce in a merged organization. As a caucus enlarges its membership, it is more likely to include members who must occasionally criticize or oppose caucus positions as a matter of survival in their state or local union. The United Action Caucus (UAC) in the AFT supports merger because it hopes that merger will make it possible to end the total control of the AFT by the Progressive Caucus. TAC leaders are already discussing this possibility with sympathetic parties in the NEA.

Although it commands a majority in the AFT, the Progressive Caucus would be a minority faction in the merged union. Even if the caucus remained united under a merger, which is doubtful, it would still have to attract a substantial number of NEA affiliates to achieve control of NEA key offices. This may happen but caucus discipline will not be as strict as it is in the AFT.

The rules regarding representation could have a decisive effect on the outcome. Under existing NEA convention rules, votes must be cast in person by delegates. Under this rule, the AFT locals would lose a great deal of their voting strength in a merger. Under existing AFT rules, one delegate is allowed to cast the entire vote to which a local is entitled. Furthermore, NEA allows its state affiliates representation on a more generous basis than state federation representation in the AFT. The AFT representation rules will meet strong opposition in the NEA. Whatever compromises are reached will have a major impact on the merged union, but governance caucuses seeking control of the merged union are already being negotiated.

Governance Procedures and Union Objectives

Union resolutions fulfill several functions, but stating union objectives is certainly one of the most important. In the NEA, resolutions may be submitted by any delegate. The submissions go to the resolutions committee, which is composed largely of delegates elected in each state. The number is based upon the number of NEA directors to which each state is entitled. To reach the convention floor for action, resolutions must be approved by a two-thirds vote of the resolutions committee. Resolutions are also subject to editing by a five member Internal Editing Committee appointed by the NEA president.

Inasmuch as the Progressive Caucus firmly controls AFT conventions, the procedures governing most convention business have little practical significance. Nevertheless, differences in how resolutions can be brought to the floor of the convention would have to be resolved in a merger. In the AFT, resolutions can be submitted only by locals, state federations, or the Executive Council; individual delegates cannot submit resolutions. In contrast, fifty individual delegates can jointly submit resolutions in the NEA.

In both unions, resolutions are submitted to the convention through a resolutions committee. In the AFT, the resolutions committee recommends concurrence, concurrence as amended, or nonconcurrence, but it is not supposed to prevent consideration by the convention. In the NEA, the resolutions committee must agree by majority vote to send the resolution to the convention floor. If one-third of the resolutions committee so votes, a minority report is filed with the recommendation of the resolutions committee.

The Political Dynamics of NEA Objectives

Here is a puzzle. The broader the range of NEA policies, from AIDS to day care to health care, the more internal controversy they presumably generate. Given the importance of union unity, why does the NEA get involved in so many policies not related even remotely to education?

The answer lies in union dynamics. Subgroups within the unions have non-educational objectives that are important to them. When they propose that the NEA adopt positions on their issues, it is difficult for NEA leaders to argue that doing so is undesirable. After all, union rhetoric portrays the union as a progressive force not confined to education. Union participation in noneducational policies is supposedly proof of the union's commitment to broad social goals. In the absence of any internal opposition (which is not the same thing as support), the union agenda becomes a blueprint for comprehensive social policy. Some observers see that outcome as a plot to remake our social fabric. There is no plot, but the NEA's social agenda is an extremely important matter.[14]

Like other organizations with political objectives, the NEA seeks allies that can help to achieve them. For the most part, those allies are in the liberal wing of the Democratic Party: other unions, especially public employee unions, the civil rights establishment, feminist, and gay/lesbian/bisexual organizations, and organizations that are highly dependent on government spending or government benefits of one kind or another. Reliance upon these groups as political allies results partly from the scarcity of allies based upon mutuality of economic interests. The interest groups that work for lower taxes and less government are not potential allies; neither are religious denominations seeking government funds for private schooling. Up to a point, other public employee unions are natural allies; like the NEA, they support higher taxes and government expenditures. At the point of distribution, the NEA competes with other public sector unions, but their joint struggle to increase the size of the pie usually precludes disruptive conflict over its distribution.

Inasmuch as two-thirds of all public school teachers are female, the NEA's feminist agenda is not surprising; likewise, with its substantial black and Hispanic membership, policies that appeal to black and Hispanic constituencies are only to be expected. To be sure, the NEA's social agenda is not based solely upon a political calculus or quid pro quo, without sincere supporters on policy grounds. Nonetheless, NEA policies do not necessarily reflect the convictions of most of its members or convention delegates. The convention delegates are probably more liberal than the rank and file, but we should not assume that delegates support a resolution merely because no one challenges it at the convention. The delegates are frequently indifferent to specific resolutions; it is not likely that many are deeply concerned about U.S. participation in the World Court (I-3) or the provision of desks, scissors, and other materials and instruments necessary for equity for left-handed students (B-15). Although some members have strong convictions on social issues, many others do not, even though it may be embarrassing to acknowledge the fact.

Political dynamics within the NEA also contribute to policy gaps between NEA resolutions and NEA members. Suppose you are a candidate for NEA office and the Gay/Lesbian/Bisexual Caucus introduces a resolution calling for the legalization of same sex marriages. Opposing the resolution is likely to result in loss of support, perhaps even active opposition from the caucus. Thus, even if you are opposed to the resolution you will probably avoid overt opposition to it. This scenario helps to explain why the NEA adopts so many controversial resolutions every year without controversy; from the standpoint of their union careers, NEA leaders and staff often have more to lose than to gain by opposing resolutions that have a small internal constituency.

Indeed, resolutions passed unanimously may actually be opposed by most members, even most delegates to the convention. Delegates who oppose a resolution may erroneously assume that convention opposition would be futile; if all opposing delegates assume this to be the case, no one may oppose a resolution that is against the preferences of the majority. This phenomenon is not confined to unions; it also applies to dictatorial political regimes in which no one expresses dissent. Consequently, a facade of widespread support often crumbles quickly when opposition is articulated.[15]

NEA conventions illustrate the point that individuals frequently appear to accept policies that are contrary to their private beliefs. I do not assert that a "silent majority" exists in the NEA, but a sizable minority at least is opposed to its social and political agendas. It must also be emphasized that these agendas are not the work of a conspiratorial cabal. Instead, they are the work of a large group of teachers who have never been exposed to an analysis in depth on the issues and who adopt their objectives during a hectic week of mind-numbing banalities. After all, how much serious analysis can go into hundreds of resolutions on major social issues approved during a one week convention crammed with ceremonial, housekeeping, and other nonpolicy matters?

The Impact of Collective Bargaining on NEA/AFT Social Agendas

The dynamics of collective bargaining play an important role in NEA/AFT social agendas. Two examples from author experience illustrate this point.

Example 1: I was the school board negotiator in a northern California school district. The contract provided that teachers could use their sick leave in case of illness of any member of the immediate family. "Immediate family" was defined precisely: Spouse, children, grandparents, in-laws, and so forth. Each time the contract was renegotiated, the union tried to expand the definition, and sometimes the school board agreed to the expansion.

In one particular year, however, the union proposed that teachers be able to use their sick leave in case of illness "of anyone in the immediate family or anyone living in the same household as the teacher." My inquiries revealed that the proposal was intended to enable teachers to use their sick leave when a cohabiting mate became ill.

My personal reaction was that if teachers wanted the benefits of marriage, they should get married; however, it was a school board call, and I wanted the board to have the relevant data. For this reason, I had to ascertain the cost of any concessions on the proposal. To my surprise, it appeared that about 20 percent of the teachers were cohabitating. To me, this was an additional reason to reject the proposal, but the school board agreed to it.

Example 2: The union proposal was that the district's health insurance policies should cover same sex "domestic partners." In this case, the board accepted my recommendation not to accept the proposal.

Let us consider these situations from a union perspective. The union negotiator is paid to negotiate higher salaries and more benefits for the teachers. A few teachers urge that health insurance cover domestic partners. They argue that failure to negotiate this benefit results in an "inequity," since the insurance covers the partners of married teachers.

How should we expect the union leaders to respond? Argue that treating same sex "domestic partners" the same as married couples is undesirable social policy? There are dozens of union demands that are arguably undesirable social policy; if the union tries to screen proposals on this criterion, it will be racked by constant internal conflict. In practice, the union cannot survive such conflict, hence it does not evaluate proposals from a public policy perspective. Unions are political bodies devoted to economic ends; their dynamics are similar to those in political bodies generally. If your constituents want something, you try to get it for them; let others argue that what your constituents want is bad public policy. And if, as a leader, you have to cater to subgroups within the union—or think you have to—you cater to them.

As long as there is no conservative governance caucus in the NEA, it is impossible to assess the association's political and social center of gravity. For example, the NEA has adopted rigid ethnic quotas that permeate every aspect of its operations. From the way resolutions on the subject have been adopted without dissent, one might conclude there is no opposition in the NEA to these quotas. This conclusion is erroneous, but to what extent remains to be seen.

4

BARGAINING WITH THE NEA/AFT

U nions bargain collectively; that is their raison d'être. In collective bargaining, the union is usually the driving force, and its performance in this mode is ordinarily the crucial test of its value to the employees it represents. Collective bargaining is equally important in public education but in a different way. Many issues that are resolved by collective bargaining in the private sector are resolved by political action in public education. For example, in the private sector, pensions are an important subject of bargaining, but teacher pensions are governed by state laws, not collective bargaining contracts. Collective bargaining, however, is the key to NEA/AFT political power.

In practice, bargaining varies widely from school district to school district. Bargaining for 70,000 teachers in over 900 New York City schools differs in critical ways from bargaining for twenty teachers in a rural, one-site school district. In large urban districts, teachers are often concerned about issues, such as transfers, that do not arise in small districts. Whereas private sector bargaining is governed by federal statutes and court decisions that apply everywhere, teacher bargaining is governed by state laws that often differ on important bargaining issues.

As previously noted, the National Labor Relations Act (NLRA) applies to private sector unions but not to unions of state and local government employees. Nevertheless, in most states that have enacted bargaining laws applicable to teachers (Table 4.1), collective bargaining is defined in ways that are similar to the definition in the NLRA.

TABLE 4.1

State Tacher Bargaining Laws

---

1. States that have enacted bargaining laws: Alaska, California, Connecticut, Delaware, Florida, Hawaii, Idaho, Illinois, Indiana, Iowa, Kansas, Maine, Maryland (only in Baltimore City and four counties), Massachusetts, Michigan, Minnesota, Montana, Nebraska, Nevada, New Hampshire, New Jersey, New Mexico, New York, North Dakota, Ohio, Oklahoma, Oregon, Pennsylvania, Rhode Island, South Dakota, Tennessee, Vermont, Washington, and Wisconsin, also the District of Columbia.

2. States without a teacher bargaining law but that allow collective bargaining as a school board option: Alabama, Arkansas, Colorado, Kentucky, Louisiana, Missouri, and West Virginia.

3. States that prohibit teacher collective bargaining in public education: Arizona, Georgia, Mississippi, North Carolina, South Carolina, Texas, Utah, Virginia, and Wyoming.

The legal definition of collective bargaining sheds very little light on the actual process. A broad view of the process includes but is not limited to:

- Drafting collective bargaining legislation and lobbying for its enactment;
- Organizing teachers to be represented by a union;
- Winning elections to decide what union, if any, will represent teachers;
- Negotiating labor contracts;
- Participation in impasse procedures: mediation, fact-finding and arbitration of interest disputes;
- Filing and processing grievances;
- Research on terms and conditions of teacher employment;
- Litigating unfair labor practice charges;
- Monitoring and attempting to influence legal/judicial developments affecting union/employee rights, privileges, responsibilities;
- Publications concerning events and developments related to collective bargaining;
- Union governance costs: conventions, conferences, committees, and so on;
- Training programs for negotiators, union leaders.

The NEA/AFT participate in all of these activities. Let us assume that an NEA affiliate has been elected exclusive representative, that is, has been authorized to bargain on behalf of teachers in an appropriate bargaining unit. Let me first illustrate how teacher bargaining functions, so that the discussion is based on the realities, not legal abstractions or idealized versions of the process. No example or set of examples can encompass all the bargaining situations that arise, but the following comment may help to dispel the mythology that prevails on the subject.

The teacher unions bargain on "terms and conditions of employment." Although defined differently in various state laws, the following topics would be included under most definitions:

Agreement, scope and purposes

Class schedules

Duration of the agreement

Evaluation procedures

Health insurance

Layoff

Number of paydays

Pay for special duties
  (coaching, etc.)

Promotions

Recognition of the

bargaining unit

Safety provisions

Savings clause

Seniority

Suspension and discharge

Time off for professional meetings

Travel pay and allowances

Definitions of terms used

Dues deduction

Duty free lunch

Grievance procedure

Hours of work

Military service credit

Parental complaints

Preparation periods

Pupil discipline

Sabbatical leave

Salary schedule

School calendar

Sick leave

Termination and
  renegotiation

Transfers

Union rights

Vacations[1]

Most of the above items involve a multiplicity of issues. For example, in negotiating grievance procedures, the following issues have to be resolved:

Access to grievance files

Appeals to higher levels

Costs of arbitration

Definition of grievance

Expedited arbitration

Information required on
  grievance forms

Terminal point of the
  procedure

Time limits to respond
  to grievances

Who can represent the grievant

Binding or advisory arbitration

Exceptions to the grievance
  procedure

Group grievances

Released time for
  processing grievances

Time limits for submitting
  grievances

Who can grieve

Classroom teachers are not likely to know how these matters are resolved elsewhere or the legal considerations affecting them. As a result, full-time union negotiators usually control the union bargaining team, even when the team members are teachers.

Teacher contracts of employment usually run from July 1 to June 30 of the following year. The union will want an agreement by early June so it can be ratified by the teachers before they leave on summer vacation. The bargaining schedule must take into account the possibility of an impasse and the necessity to submit the disputes to mediation, possibly fact-finding as well. Inasmuch as these procedures can take one to three months, bargaining is scheduled to begin early in the spring. Supposedly, this ensures that the parties will have adequate time to explain their proposals, and consider the other party's.

So much for the theory. The reality is more like the following. The negotiations begin March 1. Since the existing contract expired June 30, the union presents several inflated demands. After all, the worst thing the union can do is ask or settle for less than what might be achieved; to ensure this does not happen, the union proposals have to be sufficiently high so there is no chance they will be accepted. Furthermore, no matter what the school board offers, the union has no reason to accept it promptly; school boards rarely lower their offers. Union negotiators who accept board offers long before a deadline are likely to be criticized for doing so; arguably, if they had "hung tough," they would have gotten this or that additional concession.

Since the union must justify its extravagant initial demands to teachers and the public, it is difficult for the union to retreat from its initial negotiating positions. Meanwhile, the school board has a problem. If it makes its best offer prior to any impasse procedures and the offer is not accepted, the board will be disadvantaged in the impasse procedures. The mediators and arbitrators in these disputes tend to show their impartiality by recommending concessions by each party. Parties that make their best offer prior to the impasse procedures appear intransigent by refusing to make additional concessions in the impasse procedures. Making your "best offer" implies that further concessions will not be forthcoming, but it is difficult not to make them if a supposedly impartial third party recommends them. The more the district holds back, however, the less likely there will be an agreement prior to the impasse procedures.

Legally and practically, the school board ordinarily cannot offer less during the impasse procedures than it offered beforehand. By invoking the impasse procedures, the worst the union can do is get the same agreement that it could have gotten previously, along with having demonstrated that it has done everything possible to get a better one.

And so the dispute goes to impasse and cannot be resolved until the fall, perhaps October or November. In the meantime, the delay has generated new problems, such as whether the agreement will be retroactive to July 1. During this time, the union is conducting a campaign denigrating the school board's offer. Obviously, the union's position must be that the impasse is due to the board's intransigence; the union cannot concede that its unreasonable demands are responsible for the impasse.

If the agreement is only for one year, negotiations on the successor contract begin a few months after an agreement is reached for the current year. If the contract is for two or more years, grievances and unfair labor practice charges may be filed, thus continuing the conflict even after there is a contract.

The dynamics of bargaining foster a highly adversarial culture in another way. The union negotiator usually tries to convince the school board that more concessions are essential to avoid poor morale, even an uprising among the indignant teachers. To be credible, the teachers must demonstrate how determined they are to see that justice is done. The outcome is a high-wire act, from which many an actor has slipped.

The union negotiator must raise the level of teacher militancy to achieve the maximum level of board concessions. However, if the teachers' expectations are too high, the teachers will not be satisfied with reasonable board offers. The union must raise teacher expectations but convince them on the day of reckoning that less constitutes an excellent contract. Many a time, in an effort to squeeze out an additional last minute concession, the union negotiator tells the district negotiating team what a penurious contract it is offering; within a few minutes, the teachers will be told what a terrific contract they are getting. Unfortunately, in their efforts to persuade the school board that it should offer more, the unions sometimes convince only teachers of this point. When this happens, our example does not end with a rosy scenario.

Union Business Agents a/k/a/ UniServ Directors

In the private sector, negotiators employed by the union are "union business agents." In the NEA, they are "UniServ directors." Legally, most UniServ directors are employed by state and local associations but as shown by Table 4.2, the NEA contributes significant amounts to the program.

In fact, the UniServ program is the largest single item in the NEA budget. According to NEA Bylaw 2-7, NEA dues (national only) for members engaged in "professional educational employment" shall be .00225 times the national average annual salary of classroom teachers in public schools, plus .00055 of this average to be allocated to the UniServ program. For 1996–97, NEA estimated the average annual salary of classroom teachers to be $37,712, resulting

TABLE 4.2

NEA Support for UniServ, 1996–97

5.214	UniServ Grants	$ 40,516,815
5.21	UniServ Training	$ 1,993,460
	Total UniServ	$ 42,610,275
	Total 1996–97 NEA Budget	$192,767,400
	UniServ percent of total	22.1

Source: NEA *Strategic Focus Plan and Budget Fiscal Year: 1996–97* (Washington: National Education Association, 1996), pp. 19, 41.

in national dues of $107; for support personnel the average was $19,247, resulting in annual dues of $54.50.[2]

Let us follow the money trail. The NEA's UniServ grants are made to state and local associations according to guidelines established by the NEA Board of Directors. The guidelines authorize a UniServ grant for every 1,200 NEA members and agency fee payers, but 1,400 is considered a more viable figure. Special circumstances may justify a lower one; for instance, if the members/agency fee payers are dispersed over a wide geographical area in several school districts, fewer than 1,200 may be required for a grant. The state affiliates contribute most of the UniServ funding at rates set by the state associations. These rates are based upon the contracts that the state associations negotiate with the unions representing UniServ directors; the states must make up the difference between the grant from NEA and the total cost of the UniServ directors on their payroll. In a small number of situations, the UniServ grant goes directly from the NEA to the local, and the local funds the remaining costs of the UniServ director.

Although most UniServ directors are employees of the state associations, local associations participate in the funding in one of three ways. One way provides a UniServ director who serves a local or group of locals as chief negotiator and grievance representative. Another level of funding, usually one-third of state dues, provides a UniServ director to represent the local association in grievances that culminate in binding arbitration. Grievance arbitration is a quasi-judicial process that may require more time than it takes to negotiate the contract. The state associations cannot afford to have UniServ directors represent every grievant in every case in the absence of a minimum level of local support for UniServ directors. If the local associations do not contribute anything to UniServ support, the UniServ director is available as a consultant but not necessarily in person in bargaining or grievance procedures.

The AFT's approach to collective bargaining differs from the UniServ program. The AFT assumes that since collective bargaining is the union's raison d'être, elected union leaders should be the negotiators. Instead of appointed negotiators, as in the UniServ program, the elected union officers bargain for AFT locals. Of course, locals have to enroll a large enough membership for this to happen.

When collective bargaining emerged in the 1960s, the NEA contended that its system of governance assured teacher control. The contention was intended to discourage teachers from voting for AFT affiliates in representation elections. When NEA and AFT affiliates were competing for the right to represent teachers, the NEA repeatedly raised the specter of permanent union leaders, such as are present in the AFT and most unions.

As we shall see in Chapter 11, the NEA is moving away from term limits toward normal union practice of unlimited terms of office.

The structure of the UniServ program raises an interesting question. Why do state and local associations pay NEA $107 in dues when $24 is returned to state and local associations for the UniServ program? Why don't the state and local associations pay less in NEA dues, and use the difference to fund their full-time staff as they see fit?

The reason is partly historical. The NEA established the UniServ program in 1970. At the time, the NEA's urban affiliates enrolled relatively few members and generated relatively low revenues. Start-up financial support from outside the local districts was essential, especially in view of the NEA's weak presence in urban areas. The UniServ program was immediately successful; within two years, the NEA was supporting 600 UniServ directors. The UniServ program has been a major factor in the NEA's growth since 1970.

In any event, the UniServ rebate has a significant public relations advantage for the NEA. The NEA and some of its state/local affiliates are required to file Department of Labor form LM-2. The LM-2 requires the union to list the salaries and expenses of officers and union staff. Because the LM-2 need not be filed by unions unless they represent some private sector employees, most NEA affiliates do not file an LM-2; the NEA files only because it represents some private sector employees.

The NEA's 1995 LM-2 lists the salaries and expenses of 581 NEA officers and staff. If the NEA were the legal employer of the UniServ directors, it would be required to list over 1,500 additional employees; as will be pointed out in Chapter 8, most UniServ directors receive over $100,000 annually in salaries and fringe benefits. By having its state and local affiliates employ the UniServ directors, the NEA avoids rank and file discontent over the issue. And since most state associations are not required to disclose UniServ compensation, the NEA's state affiliates are also able to avoid such discontent.

Typically, the UniServ director serves as the chief negotiator for several local associations that are too small to employ full-time union staff. In some situations, a central city or large suburban school district will employ a full-time director while the other suburban and rural districts share a UniServ director. The latter serves under a council composed of representatives from the participating local associations. The council can remove the director, but because most of the funding is from the state association, the replacement is usually another member of the union representing UniServ directors. The local association, or the Uni-Serv unit in the case of a group of associations, is free to employ whomever it wishes, such as a teacher from their own ranks with bargaining experience.

The UniServ director typically serves as the chief negotiator, but this is up to each local association. If the local prefers, the UniServ director serves only as a member of the negotiating team or is simply available as needed; the local association negotiating team may caucus to call the UniServ director for advice on a situation or proposal. In most cases, however, the UniServ director serves as the chief negotiator. The director has the experience, knows what has been or is being negotiated in nearby districts, and has received up to date training on state aid and other matters related to negotiations.

Technically, each local association is free to accept any agreement it finds acceptable. In practice, the UniServ director tries to persuade the locals to accept coordinated objectives. Notwithstanding the rhetoric about teacher control, the UniServ director usually exercises decisive influence on negotiating objectives, strategy, and tactics. For instance, because the UniServ director is informed on a daily basis about the prospects for state aid to local districts, the director is in the best position to decide whether to reject a school board offer, accept it, or simply play a waiting game.

Coordinated goals are simple but very important strategically. The following list recommended by a California UniServ director serving fifteen local affiliates in 1995, is typical:

1. Settle for no less than 5 percent.
2. Accept no bonuses. [A bonus is a one-time payment of salary that does not increase base salaries in future years. The purpose of the recommendation is to pressure school boards to increase teacher salary schedules—ML].
3. Negotiate agency fee. Don't settle for a multiple year agreement without it.
4. Negotiate binding arbitration.
5. Continue with the county-wide calendar with winter break after Christmas, spring break after Easter.
6. Maintain or improve the district's contribution to health benefits.
7. Settle early if you meet the goals; postpone settlement if you don't.[3]

The "bread and butter" nature of these goals merits comment. Despite all the rhetoric about the union's interest in "professional issues," teacher and union welfare objectives set the bargaining agenda. At the same time, the bargaining objectives, like the legislative ones, are not publicized as teacher welfare. Higher salaries are necessary to attract good teachers. Reducing class size is essential to individualize instruction, and so on. Even the union security objectives are characterized as desirable public policy; for instance, union proposals to prevent competition from other unions are supposedly said to be essential for "labor peace." The identification of teacher union interests with the public interest is obviously self-serving. In the culture of public education, "What's good for teachers and teacher unions is good for the country" is irrefutable public policy, challenged only by the religious right, greedy corporations, and antidemocratic extremists.

The UniServ memorandum also illustrates a major union advantage in collective bargaining. Implicitly or explicitly, labor negotiators must continually decide what justifies a concession. In most cases, comparability is extremely important, often decisive. If a union seeks a concession that no one else enjoys, its burden of justification is likely to be insuperable. Conversely, if a particular local is the only one which does not enjoy a certain benefit, there is a correspondingly heavy burden on the employer to provide the benefit.

The teacher unions, therefore, try to have the most generous agreements completed first; the union then cites these "lighthouse settlements" as justification for generous settlements from the school districts that follow. Naturally, school boards prefer that the least generous agreements be completed first, so that school boards can cite them as reason not to make concessions sought by the union. The union advantage results from the fact that the UniServ directors typically represent teachers in all school districts in a given area. In contrast, the school boards are often represented by different negotiators, no one of whom has the backup data or control available to the UniServ director.

Granted, the asymmetry in information is not always quite so sharp. For example, several school boards in an area might employ the same negotiators, perhaps a law firm specializing in labor relations. State or regional school board organizations sometimes track certain items for comparative purposes. Overall, however, the UniServ directors usually operate with a significant information and tactical advantage over school board negotiators at every step of the process.

In addition to serving as chief negotiator, the UniServ director usually represents local affiliates in grievance procedures, unfair labor practice charges, mediation, and fact-finding. The upshot can be a very uneven work load, especially when new contracts must be negotiated. The tendency to negotiate multiyear contracts eases the load even if the contracts include wage reopeners in the second or later years. Usually the resolution of wage issues in multiyear contracts depends on state aid and districts tend to settle along predictable lines. When several contracts in the same area are about to expire, the UniServ directors are extremely busy; to negotiate at the table day after day, they must first meet with their negotiating teams to discuss issues and positions. If negotiations lead to impasse, the UniServ director must usually devote at least a few days to mediation. If fact-finding is involved, more time is required to prepare and present the union's case, and to critique the school district's.

In all of these procedures, however, the UniServ directors enjoy information advantages over school board negotiators. For example, suppose the UniServ director represents ten local associations, and one of the impasse issues is how much the school district should pay for health insurance. The UniServ director has the data on line for the entire region, often the entire state. Meanwhile, the school boards must generate the data on an ad hoc basis.

The Contractual Status of UniServ Directors

Essentially, four contracts govern the UniServ program:

1. The contract between the NEA and the state association.
2. The contract between the state association and the local association or group of local associations (UniServ Unit).
3. The contract between the state association and the union representing UniServ directors.
4. In the case of local associations which employ their own UniServ director, the contract between the local association and the UniServ director.

Despite the complexities, the contracts are generally successful in avoiding internal controversy. For example, most UniServ directors are employees of the state association, yet they work under the direction of a UniServ Unit Council consisting of representatives from the participating local associations. The responsibility for evaluating the UniServ directors can be a controversial issue. The practice is for the state association, which is the legal employer, to delegate the authority for evaluation to the UniServ Unit Council. Not surprisingly, the contracts between local, state, and/or national unions, or between the NEA affiliates as the employer and unions representing UniServ directors, rely on binding arbitration to resolve disputes over alleged violations of the contract.

Like other NEA activities, the UniServ program explicitly requires both affirmative action and quotas. The affirmative action goal is a UniServ staff that is at least equal to the proportion of minorities in the state. "Minorities" are defined in the NEA's governance documents, which include explicit quotas for them. A state association that does not have an affirmative action program acceptable to NEA or that does not comply with an acceptable affirmative action program may be denied funding for that reason.

Interestingly enough, it is NEA's goal that the percentage of female UniServ directors be 50 percent—and also that "local and state affiliates are required to consider women on an equal basis with men." It is doubtful whether these policies can be reconciled with nondiscrimination against male candidates. For instance, the NEA reimburses a local association or UniServ unit up to $500 for interviewing a female or minority candidate for a UniServ position. To be reimbursed, the association(s) must inform the state UniServ coordinator of the expenses incurred and the ethnic and gender identity of all individuals interviewed for the position, including the person hired. In contrast, there is no such reimbursement for interviewing white male candidates.

Significantly, the UniServ contracts allow the state association and NEA to utilize the services of UniServ directors for twenty days (ten outside the state at the request of NEA, which pays the expenses involved). In strike situations or crucial election contests, NEA and/or the state association can mobilize a small army on short notice to assist a state or local association; the contractual option is frequently invoked to assist associations in critical political campaigns.

Building Representatives/Chapter Chairpersons

In larger districts, especially in large schools, the UniServ director cannot handle all the day-to-day matters that require union attention. Common practice is to delegate routine union responsibilities to the officers of the local; in the larger schools especially, the union designates "chapter chairpersons" or "building representatives" to monitor contractual affairs. Essentially, these individuals function as shop stewards; they are the front line representatives of the teacher union. The larger the school, the more likely it is the union will negotiate some released time with pay for its building representatives. This can be a period or more per school day, depending on the number of teachers and the contract between the union and the school district.

In the private sector, the rights and responsibilities of shop stewards have been an acrimonious issue. For instance, companies have agreed to allow shop stewards a certain amount of released time to represent employees in grievance procedures. Subsequently, the companies may find, or at least allege, that the shop stewards are stirring up grievances in order to justify their released time. This issue also arises in public schools. In practice, school boards often agree to union demands concerning building representatives that would not be acceptable to private sector companies. To illustrate, the contract between the United

Teachers of Los Angeles (UTLA) and the Los Angeles Unified School District includes the following provisions relating to chapter chairpersons:

Right to consultation before any bell changes. (Art. IV, Sec. 8.0)

Right to exclusive use of school bulletin boards. (Art. IV, Sec. 20 and 80e)

Right to post announcements on school bulletin boards. (Art. IV, Sec. 8.0f)

Right to represent employees in disciplinary meetings upon request. (Art. IV, Sec. 8.0a)

Right to view and receive copies of documents in personnel files. (Art. IV, Sec. 8.0g)

Right to attach comments before forwarding certain documents. (Art. IV, Sec. 8.2d)

Right of faculty review and disclosure of documents. (Art. IV, Sec. 8.2a)

Right to decide whether to sign certain documents. (Art. IV, Sec. 8.2c)

Rights of consultation concerning documents forwarded to certain offices. (Art. IV, Sec. 8.2b)

Rights relating to documents forwarded. (Art. IV, Sec. 8.2)

UTLA right to serve as exclusive representative. (Art. IV, Sec. 7.0, 8.0, 8.0j)

UTLA right to use facilities. (Art. IV, Sec. 1.0)

Right to be grievance representative upon request. (Art. IV, Sec. 8.0a)

Right to notification in cases of inquiry and assault. (Art. IV, Sec. 8.0b)

UTLA right to use mailboxes. (Art. IV, Sec. 1.0)

UTLA right to use school mail system. (Art. IV, Sec. 3.0)

Right to meet with site administrator. (Art. IV, Sec. 8.0h)

Right to propose items for faculty agenda. (Art. IV, Sec. 8.0i)

Right to speak within first 45 minutes, or 15 minutes before end of faculty meeting. (Art. IV, Sec. 8.0i)

Right to hold union meetings in school buildings during off-duty time. (Art. IV, Sec. 8.0d)

Right to serve as official on-site exclusive representative. (Art. IV, Sec. 7.0 and 8.0)

Right to use school public address system. (Art. IV, Sec. 8)

Right to be sole exclusive representative. (Art. IV, Sec. 7.0, 8.0, 8.0j)

Rights relating to shared decision making and school based management. (Art. IV, Sec. 8.01, Art XXVII)

Right to reasonable use of school telephone. (Art. IV, Sec. 8.0c)

Prohibition of district meetings on Wednesdays after school. (Art. IV, Sec. 8.0d) (Union meetings are scheduled on Wednesday afternoons).[4]

Regarded individually, none of these rights might be unduly onerous, but their collective impact is another matter. The school principals may not remember or be sure of building representative rights on every issue; the inevitable tendency is to consult the contract before taking action, a mindset that leads inexorably to union control. If union rights are not clear, the building representative will adopt the position most favorable to the union; not wanting to risk losing a grievance arbitration, the principals often defer to the building representatives even when they would not be contractually required to do so.

Readers might dismiss these rights as much ado about nothing, and this conclusion may be appropriate with respect to some items. Nevertheless, others set forth rights that have significant implications not widely appreciated. Thus Article IV of the UTLA contract includes four items providing UTLA with "exclusive rights"; in conjunction with references to exclusive rights elsewhere in the contract, they preclude an effective challenge to UTLA from any other union. If a group of teachers or another organization seeks to decertify UTLA, but cannot use the district mail system or hold meetings in school facilities, its chances of waging a successful campaign to decertify UTLA are slim indeed.

The union rights in the UTLA contract highlight the hypocrisy of union rhetoric on school reform. This rhetoric features criticisms of school bureaucracies, restrictive rules, and Mickey Mouse forms. What is overlooked is that school management is the victim, not the perpetrator, of most of these evils. Collective bargaining has imposed an enormous bureaucratic burden on school management—a burden monitored daily by building representatives eager to pounce on any deviation from the contract in the name of "policing the contract." The UTLA contract provides a notable example of the gap between the rhetoric and the reality of school bureaucracies. While UTLA's contract adds substantially to management burdens, UTLA is promoting legislation and a constitutional initiative that would severely limit school expenditures on administration.

The NEA Role in Litigation

As previously emphasized, the legal environment for teacher bargaining is a critical factor in its effectiveness. In practice, the laws relating to teacher bargaining must often be interpreted judicially. This is one reason why both the NEA and its state affiliates have large budgets for legal services; the NEA's 1995–96 budget for legal services was almost $24 million, 12.9 percent of the total NEA budget.[5] Although the budget for legal services was presented in a different format in the 1996–97 budget, it appears that comparable amounts were budgeted for 1996–97.

When a case has national implications, the NEA is likely to provide the legal services. For example, *Perry Education Association* v. *Perry Local Educators Association* was an Indiana case involving access to the district interschool mail system.[6]

Prior to 1977, both the Perry Education Association (PEA), the NEA affiliate, and the Perry Local Educators Association (PLEA), an independent association, had equal access to the system. In 1977, PEA won a collective bargaining election and was certified as the exclusive representative of the Perry teachers. In the first contract between the PEA and the Perry Board of Education, the PEA was accorded access to teacher mailboxes and the district mail system. These rights were explicitly denied to any other "school employee organization." PEA's exclusive access was carried over into the contract renewal when it was challenged by the PLEA.

The PLEA's legal argument was that the contract between the PEA and the Perry Board of Education denied PLEA's constitutional right to equal access to the district mail system. The federal district court held that PEA's exclusive right to use the district mail system did not violate the 1st and 14th Amendments; upon appeal, the Court of Appeals for the Seventh Circuit reversed and the PEA appealed the reversal to the U.S. Supreme Court. In a five to four decision, the Supreme Court reversed the decision of the Court of Appeals. Its rationale was that the district mail system was not a public forum; inasmuch as the school board could have denied both the PEA and PLEA access to the district mail system, granting the PEA access to it as the exclusive representative did not violate any basic right of the PLEA to similar access.

The Perry case illustrates how the NEA and AFT systematically weaken their opposition to the point of extinction. The four dissenting justices argued, I believe correctly, that the public forum issue was irrelevant. The dissenters conceded that the school district mail system was not a public forum. However, once the district granted access to it, the issue was one of equal access. Since the school board had granted access to the PLEA and PEA prior to certification of the PEA as the exclusive representative, the issue was whether such certification was grounds for denying access to the PLEA. The minority opinion held that as long as the school board allowed its mail system to be used to discuss matters of employment, it could not deny access to it on the basis of the viewpoints expressed. Inasmuch as the purpose of PLEA communications was to express its differences with PEA, denial of access to PLEA constituted viewpoint discrimination by the school board. The PLEA was not asserting a right to use the district mail system because it was a public forum; it was asserting a right not to be discriminated against if the district did allow access to the mail system.

NEA/AFT affiliates typically justify their demands for exclusive rights to district facilities as a way of facilitating "labor peace." Realistically, "labor peace" is merely a rhetorical cover for stifling criticism of the incumbent union. Presumably, school boards would want "labor peace," yet it is the incumbent unions that rely on the "labor peace" argument to justify exclusive rights of one kind or another. Actually, many teacher union provisions on exclusivity are probably illegal, regardless of the validity of the Perry decision. Consider the following provision in a Pennsylvania contract.

D. *Exclusive Rights to CATA/PSEA/NEA*

During the life of this Agreement the School Board agrees not to permit any teachers' organization not affiliated with PSEA/NEA to hold meetings on school property nor to utilize school bulletin boards, mail boxes or buildings for the purpose of distributing literature pertaining to that organization. However, these rights shall be guaranteed to the Coatesville Area Teachers' Association and its State and National affiliates.[7]

On its face, the foregoing provision applies even to teacher organizations such as Phi Delta Kappa that are not interested in representing teachers on terms and conditions of employment; in fact, even organizations that explicitly deny such an interest are prohibited from having meetings on school property. The teacher unions, ever alert to defend teacher freedom in the classroom to present conflicting points of view make sure that teachers are not exposed to any bearing on the union's role.

The NEA's Legislative Role in Collective Bargaining

The NEA is very active at both the federal and state levels on collective bargaining legislation. Let me cite a personal experience on this topic.

In 1991, I was invited to testify on collective bargaining legislation in West Virginia before a commission appointed by the governor. While waiting to testify, I had the opportunity to listen to Robert H. Chanin, the NEA's general counsel, explain the merits of the public employee bargaining law proposed and endorsed by the West Virginia Education Association, the West Virginia Federation of Teachers, and other public employee unions in West Virginia.

Chanin pointed out that the proposed legislation explicitly prohibited strikes by public employees; as he phrased it, the proposed legislation gave up "labor's most important weapon." And sure enough, the proposed legislation explicitly declared that strikes by public employees were prohibited.

West Virginia has a part-time legislature with very little staff support. The commission members were obviously impressed by Chanin's presentation, as I was. However, they were impressed by its substance, whereas I was impressed by its hypocrisy. For starters, the proposed legislation did not include any penalties for violating the prohibition against strikes. In order to end a strike, public employers had to find a judge who would issue an injunction against the strike. Consequently, striking public employees would not be subject to any penalties unless and until they violated a restraining order.

Judges in West Virginia are elected. If and when a school board managed to find a judge who might issue a restraining order against striking teachers, the union would argue that the school board did not appear before the court with "clean hands." For example, the union would argue that the school board had not bargained in good faith, hence was not entitled to equitable relief.

The union's appearance in court would be preceded by a barrage of unfair labor practice charges to the public employment board; the union attorneys would urge the court not to restrain the strike until the unfair labor practice charges were resolved. In any event, most teacher strikes do not last more than a few days; by the time the legal maneuvering was over, so would be the strike. As a matter of fact, NEA and AFT leaders have instigated successful strikes in states in which strikes were illegal by emphasizing that no teacher in the state had ever been penalized for going on strike. The outcome in West Virginia was a commission report split along party lines, followed by legislative stalemates in which Democratic majorities supporting collective bargaining legislation could not override gubernatorial vetoes of the legislation.

As we have seen, collective bargaining greatly enhances union membership and revenues. Consequently, both the NEA and AFT seek federal legislation that avoids the necessity of enacting bargaining laws on a state-by-state basis. The NEA's strategy was to enact federal legislation that rendered federal aid to the states contingent upon the enactment of state bargaining laws comparable to the National Labor Relations Act. Under such legislation, a state that had not enacted such a bargaining law would not be eligible for federal aid to education. As improbable as such legislation appears to be now, it has been a high priority in the NEA since the Carter administration. The NEA's 1996–97 Legislative Program includes the following in its Legislative First Tier:

> . . . Legislative issues developed and *initiated by NEA* that require continuing high activity levels to accomplish the goal.

> *II. Collective Bargaining*

> NEA supports a federal statute that would guarantee meaningful collective bargaining rights to the employees of public schools, colleges, universities, and other postsecondary institutions. This statute should allow for the continued operation of state statutes that meet federally established minimum standards. The federal statute should, in addition, assure that employees will not be denied bargaining rights solely because they participate in a site-based decision making program, a faculty senate, or other system of collegial governance.[8]

NEA efforts to enact a federal statute providing bargaining rights for unions of state and local public employee unions raises a basic constitutional issue which is the subject of considerable political and scholarly debate. Congress cannot constitutionally require the states to enact public sector bargaining laws. Should Congress be allowed to achieve this result indirectly by requiring such legislation as a condition of receiving federal aid? On the one hand, it is argued that Congress can set whatever conditions it deems appropriate to federal aid to the states; if the latter do not like the conditions, they can always refuse the federal aid. The contrary view is that this is a backdoor way of allowing Congress to enact unconstitutional impositions on state governments.[9]

Of course, in different circumstances, the constitutional issue could work to the NEA's detriment. Suppose it is proposed that federal appropriations for education require school districts above a certain size to adopt competitive bidding for delivery of certain instructional or support services. Undoubtedly, the NEA/AFT lobbyists would become ardent federalists overnight.

Teacher Unions and the Civil Rights of Teachers

Most teachers regard the NEA/AFT as protectors of teacher rights as citizens; in the real world, the teacher unions are a threat to civil liberties when union interests are threatened by their exercise. This conclusion can be illustrated by a Wisconsin case involving the 1st Amendment rights of teachers.[10]

The case arose out of a 1971 bargaining impasse between Madison Teachers, Inc. (MTI), an NEA affiliate, and the Madison Board of Education. One of the issues in dispute was a union proposal that nonmembers of the association be required to pay a service fee to the association for its services as the bargaining agent. Failure to pay the fee would result in termination of employment with the district. The school board refused to accept the proposal, and eventually a contract was reached without it. However, prior to reaching agreement, the school board had held a regular open meeting at which teacher opponents of agency fees were allowed to speak against it.

About a month later, MTI filed an unfair labor practice charge against the school board. The substance of the charge was that by allowing the teachers to express their opposition at the school board meeting, the board had violated its statutory duty to bargain only with the MTI, that is, the exclusive representative of the Madison teachers.

The unfair labor practice charge was upheld by the Wisconsin Employment Relations Commission (WERC) and the Wisconsin Supreme Court. Upon appeal to the U.S. Supreme Court, the decision was unanimously reversed. The Supreme Court decision pointed out that the school board could not restrict the expression of views on the basis of their content at an open meeting of the school board. Allowing teachers to express their views at an open board meeting did not constitute "negotiations," but prohibiting them from doing so violated their constitutional rights to free speech and to petition the government. The NEA argument was that rights to free speech could be restricted if a clear and present danger was involved; the NEA alleged that allowing the teachers to address the school board on the union's agency fee proposal would endanger the collective bargaining procedures enacted by the Wisconsin legislature. As the Wisconsin Supreme Court asserted, the restriction on teacher rights to address the school board was necessary "to avoid the dangers attendant upon relative chaos in labor management relations."

Note that if nonteachers had expressed the same views as the teachers who objected to the agency fee, there would have been no unfair labor practice charges. In other words, if the MTI had prevailed in this case, the teacher rights as citizens would have been diminished. And this would have been true of all teachers in the states which have enacted bargaining laws, not just the Madison teachers who opposed the agency fee proposal. All teachers would have been prohibited from addressing the school board on any matter subject to negotiation between the board and the union. In view of the wide scope of "matters subject to bargaining," the NEA's legal position would have resulted in a major diminution of teacher citizenship rights.

Interestingly enough, NEA by-law 2–1 provides that "active membership is limited to persons who support the principles and goals of the Association and maintain membership in the local and state affiliates where eligible." Legally, the quoted section cannot be enforced. If a teacher is represented in collective bargaining by an NEA affiliate, the teacher cannot be denied membership even if the teacher opposes everything the NEA stands for. Apart from this, if interpreted as written, the by-law would exclude from membership teachers who do not support racial quotas, abortion on demand, domestic partner benefits, public school monopolies, and other NEA "principles and goals." The section quoted is not enforced, but its presence is a threat to members who try to change NEA "principles and goals."

Reflections on Collective Bargaining in Public Education

Teacher salary schedules are "terms and conditions of employment." They are also public policies, as are the other provisions in teacher collective bargaining contracts. In political terms, collective bargaining in public education constitutes the negotiation of public policies with a special interest group, in a process from which others are excluded. This is contrary to the way public policy should be made in a democratic representative system of government.[11] I will elaborate on this objection in Chapter 12, but a different one merits discussion here.

To justify collective bargaining in public education, the NEA/AFT argued that the statutory approach to terms and conditions of teacher employment was too cumbersome and too inflexible. Working conditions should be settled at the local level by parties familiar with local conditions. Ironically, teacher bargaining has led to a system in which teacher unions pursue statutory benefits more than ever.

In response to proposed teacher bargaining statutes, legislators might have said: "If you want to negotiate conditions of employment at the local level, you shall have this right. As part of the deal however, we are also repealing the state laws on tenure, sick leave, retirement, and other terms and conditions of employment. We'll provide some protection for teachers in the transition period, but after a reasonable time, terms and conditions of employment shall be settled at the local level through collective bargaining."

As it happened, the legislatures said nothing of the kind. Instead, most simply ignored the existing state legislation on terms and conditions of teacher employment. Inevitably, the statutory benefit became the floor for union bargaining proposals. Furthermore, the states made no effort to limit union efforts to enact more statutory benefits for teachers. As a result, and greatly strengthened by the dues and PAC revenues resulting from collective bargaining contracts, NEA/AFT affiliates devoted more resources than ever to enacting statutory benefits.

There is really no private sector counterpart to this dual system of benefits. The private sector unions try, and occasionally succeed, in enacting statutory benefits. Federal statutes provide various benefits for railroad workers, coal miners and other groups of private sector employees. Nevertheless, despite these situations, private sector benefits are normally achieved through collective bargaining or through federal legislation that applies to all employees. In education, however, the NEA/AFT rely on state legislation as an independent source of benefits and to ratchet up their bargaining demands.

When California enacted its collective bargaining law in 1975, teachers already enjoyed the following statutory benefits:

Salary protections
Sick leave
Tenure protection
Layoff and reemployment rights
Pension benefits
No involuntary assignment to extracurricular duty or summer employment
Military leave
Job protections in district mergers
State civil rights protections

These benefits exceeded the benefits available to most private sector employees, yet the state's bargaining law explicitly provided that collective bargaining contracts could not eliminate or reduce any statutory benefit.

In short, teachers enjoy a dual system of benefits (contractual and statutory) that has no counterpart in the private sector. In the next chapter, therefore, we turn to the NEA/AFT political operations that pave the way for the statutory benefits.

5

UNION POLITICAL OPERATIONS

Since 1976, when the NEA began endorsing political candidates, it has invariably endorsed Democrats for president. In congressional races, its support goes overwhelmingly to Democrats. In races for the U.S. Senate in 1992, NEA-PAC endorsed thirty-nine candidates in primaries and general elections. The only Republican to receive NEA support was Senator Arlen Specter, who received NEA support in the Republican primary. In the general election, the NEA supported Lynn Yaekel, his Democratic opponent. In the 1996 election, the NEA supported 251 congressional candidates, of whom only one was a Republican. At the 1996 Democratic convention, more delegates (405) were NEA members than the number of delegates from any state except California. Thus the NEA combines an extraordinary level of political activity with an overwhelming tilt toward the Democratic party.

As will soon be evident, the AFT is even more closely tied to the Democratic party than the NEA. Together, the NEA/AFT form a political machine of unparalleled size and sophistication. Despite their effectiveness, however, the public knows very little about union political operations. These operations are as important as collective bargaining in achieving union objectives. I begin with an example of how the NEA/AFT utilize collective bargaining to enhance their political power.

In campaigns for elective office, the teacher unions spend heavily on direct mail. Their direct mail campaigns often experience substantial losses due to incorrect addresses. The solution: Negotiate school board agreement to provide updated address lists of union members, thereby increasing the accuracy of the lists while relieving the unions of the costs of keeping them up to date. The lists can be utilized in elections for local, state, and national office. They can also be utilized to pressure school boards to make concessions in collective bargaining or to accept a fact-finder's recommendations in a bargaining impasse. Thus a union objective achieved in collective bargaining at the local level is very valuable at all levels of political activity.

As the NEA/AFT approach to mailing lists illustrates, NEA/AFT political operations are inextricably tied to their collective bargaining activities, and vice versa. Payroll deduction of dues and PAC contributions is essential to union viability in both collective bargaining and political action. In most states, payroll deduction is negotiated at the local level. In some states, however, local unions have a statutory right to payroll deduction, thus rendering it unnecessary to negotiate the issue at the local level. In short, the NEA/AFT are geared to political action, not as a supplement but as a primary focus of union activity.

NEA Political Action Committee (NEA-PAC)

Political action committees emerged in the 1940s when labor unions were prohibited from spending regular union funds for candidates for federal office. Since 1945, the practice of pooling political contributions from members for distribution to the candidates has become the usual way to contribute cash to union endorsed candidates. This practice was initiated by the Committee on Industrial Organization, which merged with the American Federation of Labor in 1955 to become the AFL-CIO. Even though federal restrictions discouraged many groups from setting up their own committees, the idea appealed not only to labor unions, but to business and ideological groups as well. With the establishment of NEA-PAC in 1972, the NEA became the first national educational organization to organize a political action committee; twenty years later, it contributed over $2 million to congressional candidates; an additional $2 million went to state and national political parties for voter registration and related activities.

In 1974 when 608 PACs were registered with the Federal Election Commission, Congress passed several amendments to the Federal Election Campaign Act. In addition to sanctioning the concept of political action committees, the amendments permitted labor unions to use dues revenues to establish and administer PACs and pay the cost of soliciting contributions from members and their families. Soon thereafter, the great PAC rush began, and endorsements, contributions, and volunteers began flowing to favored candidates and causes. By July 1996, there were 4,033 federal political action committees which had raised nearly $248.6 million from January 1, 1995 to March 30, 1996.[1]

NEA-PAC was established in 1972 with personal contributions of $2,225 from NEA's elected officers and staff members and $28,000 from other NEA members. Also in 1972, the NEA's Representative Assembly authorized payroll deductions to NEA-PAC. Since then, NEA-PAC has emerged as one of the very largest and most influential PACs in U.S. political affairs.

NEA-PAC is governed by a council on which every state affiliate is represented. State affiliates receive additional representation in proportion to their membership. In addition, the council includes representation from the Board of Directors, the Executive Committee, the Higher Education Caucus, the Women's Caucus, the Caucus of Educators of Exceptional Children (CEEC), and the National Council of Urban Education Associations (NCUEA). The NEA Executive Officers hold the same positions in NEA-PAC as they hold in the NEA. NEA-PAC is administered through NEA's Office of Government Relations. Its procedures emphasize incumbency and affiliate support; much of the preliminary work is done by state and local affiliates that interview candidates, using questionnaires from the national office. (See Appendix A). If an incumbent has generally supported NEA positions, NEA-PAC does not elicit the views of opposing candidates. The NEA refused permission to reprint the questionnaire on the absurd ground that they were intended for internal use only.

NEA-PAC Revenues

Table 5.1 shows NEA-PAC expenditures and rank among federal PACs since 1983. The NEA absorbs the costs of PAC administration, thus enabling NEA-PAC to contribute more cash directly to candidates. Inasmuch as the AFT's Committee on Political Education (AFT/COPE), the AFT's PAC, almost always contributes to the same candidates (if AFT/COPE contributes at all), teacher union support clearly plays a significant role in federal elections.

Most NEA-PAC revenues are raised from teacher payroll deductions. Generally speaking, the forms on which teachers authorize payroll deductions of dues also allow teachers to authorize PAC deductions in amounts designated by the teachers. The forms also include statements to the effect that the PAC deduction is voluntary and refusal to contribute does not affect teacher rights as a union member.

To facilitate PAC fundraising, the NEA disseminates a highly sophisticated manual on the subject.[2] Although payroll deduction is the preferred mode, the manual sets forth detailed guidelines on fund-raising by other means: PAC Week (or PAC Day); telephone campaigns, special events such as dinners, dances, auctions and giveaways, and direct mail. Members are encouraged to hold fund-raisers around payday; one of their attractions is that NEA can pay the costs of these events from dues, as long as the costs do not exceed one-third of the contributions.

TABLE 5.1

NEA-PAC Expenditures Compared to Other PACs. 1983–1994

Federal PAC Rankings	1993–94	1991–92	1989–90	1987–88	1985–86	1983–84
MAXIMUM RANK IN FEC LISTING	50	50	50	50	50	50
Democratic Republican Independent Voter Education Committee[a]	1	1	1	2	12	38
Emily's List[b]	2	11	na	na	na	na
Campaign America[c]	3	30	29	7	9	na
American Federation of State County & Municipal Employees—P E O P L E	4	7	7	16	31	28
NRA Political Victory Fund[d]	5	4	9	5	7	5
Association of Trial Lawyers of America Political Action Committee	6	6	6	10	15	46
National Education Association Political Action Committee	7	3	5	12	17	14
American Medical Association Political Action Committee	8	2	4	4	6	7
Machinists Nonpartisan Political League	9	12	12	17	26	19
UAW-V-CAP (UAW Voluntary Community Action Program)	10	8	10	15	19	16

[a]International Brotherhood of Teamsters. AFL-CIO

[b]A liberal feminist PAC

[c]Senator Robert Dole

[d]National Rifle Association

Source: Federal Election Commission.

The legal requirements and suggested techniques relating to each type of event are spelled out, along with the detailed responsibilities of officers and union staff. The manual also includes model posters and model language for telephone calls.

In addition to the funds raised by state and local PAC operations, NEA-PAC sponsors several fund raisers at the NEA's annual convention. Lottery type drawings are common with the state associations taking turns providing the prizes. At the 1996 convention in Washington, the prizes were:

July 3, —$1,000 in cash donated by Idaho Education Association;

July 4, —An around the world trip for two or $5,000 cash, donated by Indiana State Teachers Association

July 5, —A new 1996 Ford Escort or $10,000 cash donated by the state affiliates ($1,000 each) in Alaska, Arizona, California, Louisiana, Minnesota, Nevada, North Dakota, Ohio, Pennsylvania, and South Carolina

July 6, —A 1996 Pontiac Bonneville or $20,000 cash donated by the Illinois Education Association.

At the convention, NEA-PAC also sponsored "Running for Office," a race with two age divisions; the entry fee of $25 was a contribution to NEA-PAC. From its inception in 1981 to 1995, "Running for Office" has generated over $4.0 million for NEA-PAC. In toto, NEA-PAC raised $720,000 in five days at the 1996 convention, an average of $77.60 per delegate. This was the 16th consecutive year in which NEA-PAC had exceeded its fundraising goal. Awards were given for the highest average contribution per delegate and per state association member; the highest total state contribution; and the highest percentage increase by states. Stickers, flags, and pins are attached to delegate badges to be a constant reminder of the success or failure of individual and state efforts.

The "Reverse Checkoff"

Initially, NEA-PAC was supported by a "reverse checkoff." Under the reverse checkoff, a certain amount is deducted from teacher paychecks for the union PAC. The teacher who does not want to contribute to it must take some action to avoid the deduction or to have the money refunded. In other words, instead of requiring teacher assent to a deduction from teacher paychecks, the reverse checkoff forces unwilling teachers to take action to avoid the PAC deduction.

At the time NEA-PAC was established, unions were prohibited from using the reverse checkoff. The NEA, however, claimed that it was a "professional" organization, not a union, and was therefore free from the restrictions placed on unions with regard to PACs. However, on July 20, 1978, the Federal Elections Commission brought suit against the NEA, NEA-PAC, and eighteen of NEA's affiliates to enjoin them from collecting political contributions for federal office by means of a reverse checkoff. Not surprisingly, the NEA was held to be a union, therefore, not eligible to utilize the reverse checkoff.

In his oral argument before the U.S. District Court, NEA General Counsel Robert H. Chanin asserted:

> . . . [I]t is well recognized that if you take away the mechanism of payroll deduction you won't collect a penny from these people, and it has nothing to do with voluntary or involuntary. I think it has to do with the nature of the beast, and the beasts who are our teachers who are dispersed all over cities who simply don't come up with money regardless of the purpose." Transcript at 12–20.

Federal district judge Oliver Gasch commented on Chanin's candid assertion as follows: "In this Court's view, 'Knowing free-choice' means an act intentionally taken and not the result of inaction when confronted with an obstacle."[3]

The NEA was fined $75,000 and ordered to refund $800,000 taken illegally from members. Despite this setback, however, NEA-PAC has been extremely successful in raising campaign funds for its endorsed candidates. It should be emphasized that some states still allow the reverse checkoff for state and local PACs. Where it is allowed, NEA/AFT affiliates continue to utilize it, thereby adding substantially to PAC funds from payroll deductions.

Some idea of the value of the PAC payroll deduction is evident from its 1995 prohibition in the state of Washington; the number of PAC contributions dropped from 45,000 to 8,000 within a short time. Thereupon, the Washington Education Association (WEA) increased its dues for a "community outreach" program (COP) to compensate for the loss of the PAC deductions. The WEA also forgave repayment of loans made from dues revenues to the WEA-PAC. On February 12, 1997, Washington Attorney General Christine Gregoire filed suit against the WEA for collecting, spending, and reporting violations of state campaign finance laws. The attorney general's suit charged that the WEA's COP was a second political action committee, and that the WEA had failed to comply with state laws requiring teacher consent for payroll deductions for political purposes; also that the WEA had failed to meet the reporting and disclosure requirements required of contributions to political action committees. When the WEA moved for partial summary judgment, the attorney general's reply included the following statements:

- "It is simply not believable that there are no mechanisms in place to control the use of over $300,000 dollars a year of member assessments taken specially out of their paychecks for a program created by their representative assembly." (p. 12)
- "The evidence noted above shows that the state portion of COP spent over one-third of its money on contributions to political committees, and nearly two-thirds of its money on politically related activities. There is no doubt that one of the primary purposes of COP is to influence governmental decision making by supporting or opposing candidates or ballot measures." (p. 19)
- "The WEA's interpretation of the statutes at issue . . . would lead to the absurd result that a common method of funding political campaigns would not have to be disclosed. It would also defeat the public's right to know who is funding political campaigns." (p. 25)
- "The facts presented to the Attorney General do not even faintly resemble the facts in the instant case." (p. 26)
- "The WEA states in its brief that 'out of WEA's total budget of more than thirty million dollars for the two year period at issue, only $5,000 was in support or opposition to a candidate or ballot propositions.' . . . This state-

TABLE 5.2

NEA Campaign Priority Classification

I. A marginal or special circumstance district with a pro-education incumbent

II. A marginal or special circumstance district with an anti-education incumbent

III. An open seat (no incumbent running) considered marginal or special circumstance with a pro-education candidate running

IV. A race in which a pro-education incumbent does not face a difficult reelection campaign

V. An open seat in which a pro-education candidate would have an extremely difficult time winning

VI. A District in which a pro-education challenger would have an extremely difficult time defeating an anti-education incumbent

VII. A District in which the incumbent's support is mixed and endorsement is temporarily withheld pending additional evaluation.

Source: Office of Government Relations, *How to Endorse Candidates* (Washington: National Education Association, 1989), p. 18.

ment is ludicrous. The reports on file with the PDC from the WEA and its registered lobbyists reveal that in 1996 alone it made $741,247.67 in contributions just to NO on 173 & 177 Committee." (pp. 29–30) ("PDC" is the Public Disclosure Commission, State of Washington) (Defendant's Memorandum in Opposition to Plaintiff's Motion for Partial Summary Judgment (Doc. No. 96-2-04395-5) Thurston County Superior Court, March 20, 1997)

Regardless of the outcome of the charges against the WEA, the critical role of the payroll deductions is obvious.[4]

The NEA Budget for FY 1995–96 included $532,547 for NEA-PAC administration, and another $146,477 allocated to accounting services for NEA-PAC and state affiliate PAC accounting services. The 1996–97 budget provided $114,340 for NEA-PAC administration; other PAC expenses were lumped together with other budget items in such a way as to obscure the amounts spent for PAC activities. Services to state PACs are provided by NEA's Government Relations department and funded from members' dues. Using dues revenues for PAC administration is legal but it demonstrates the futility of the prohibition against using dues revenues for political purposes.

NEA-PAC Endorsement Procedures and Priorities

The NEA naturally tries to elect lawmakers who will support its objectives. The NEA's endorsement procedures play a crucial role in this process. For Congressional candidates, these procedures are spelled out in the NEA-PAC Endorsement Kit, which is sent to interview teams in every congressional district.

The endorsement kit includes interview instructions, questionnaires, a profile of the district, reports of the Government Relations staff, a district profile, and a summary of NEA positions. No mathematical formula is rigidly used to assess candidates nor are the candidate positions scored in any particular way. Information about candidates is generated from several different sources, such as the party congressional campaign committees, state affiliates, political newsletters and journals, and meetings with legislative allies, such as AFL-CIO/COPE. It would be difficult to identify any aspect of the procedures that is underfinanced or neglected.[5]

Recent NEA conventions have adopted over 300 resolutions on a wide variety of subjects. Resolutions supporting equity for incarcerated persons and left-handed students suggest the need for priorities if the resolutions are to guide NEA's political program. In effect, NEA-PAC establishes the priorities through a series of position statements in the NEA candidate questionnaire. Candidates are requested to "agree or disagree with NEA's position." Candidates are also asked to spell out their top five priorities for the national agenda. Appendix A shows eight of the first ten NEA positions in the 1996 candidate questionnaire proposed maintenance or increases in federal funding.

Nevertheless, noneducational issues also play a major role in NEA-PAC endorsements. NEA-PAC operating procedures state that candidates recommended for endorsement should support NEA positions on the following "Profile of Selected Issues: Equal Rights Amendment, increased federal funding for education, federal funding of nonpublic schools, collective bargaining, civil rights, health care, employer benefits, and campaign finance reform. Any state affiliate that recommends to NEA-PAC endorsing a candidate who opposes NEA's position on any of these issues shall provide a written explanation of the candidate's position and rationale for why the endorsement is in the compelling interest of the NEA."[6] The written explanation must be followed up by additional information at the NEA-PAC Council meeting.

Conceptually, one might commend the NEA for including noneducational issues in its endorsement criteria. After all, the fact that endorsements are usually made only on special interest criteria is one of the negative aspects of U.S. politics. Realistically, however, it would be misleading to praise the NEA for considering noneducational issues in its endorsement criteria. Its positions on noneducational issues are either crucial to the Democratic coalition of which the NEA is a major component, or promote NEA's special interests even though not characterized as "educational issues." For instance, adoption of the Clinton administration's health care program would free up substantial state and local revenues for higher teacher salaries.

The NEA-PAC endorsement kit includes a "Report Card" showing how the candidate voted on issues of importance to the NEA. "Friendly incumbents" are candidates who support NEA backed legislation 80 percent or more of the time, generally the minimum acceptable for endorsement. Interview teams are cautioned against accepting candidate statements of support for NEA positions without checking their actual voting records before endorsement

As Table 5.2 demonstrates, NEA-PAC guidelines emphasize the importance of districts in which association support can be the margin of victory or defeat.

Endorsement teams are cautioned against supporting candidates who support NEA positions but have no realistic chance of winning the election. NEA-PAC rarely disagrees with a state PAC; such disagreements are almost always confined to situations when friendly candidates endorsed by NEA-PAC and the state association PAC are running for the same office. For example, if there is an open Senate seat and two NEA friendly candidates are running against each other in the primary, NEA might opt for neutrality while the state PAC wishes to support a particular candidate.

NEA-PAC: Endorsements and Distributions

From the outset, NEA-PAC was ostensibly a bipartisan effort. The NEA position was that education should be a bipartisan effort, above "partisan politics." In keeping with this stance, NEA publications emphasize the importance of a bipartisan approach in every phase of NEA-PAC operations. As one NEA publication emphasizes, "Repeat, repeat, repeat the bipartisan theme of our political program. Make sure that anyone with eyes and ears knows that our Association and our members are involved with the activities of both political parties."[7] In implementing this approach, NEA-PAC encourages NEA members in both Democratic and Republican parties to be active as candidates for office or delegates to party conventions. This includes financial support to NEA members who are delegates or alternates to national party conventions.

In 1996, NEA-PAC support included round trip coach fare to the convention city. Delegates who attended NEA caucus meetings received an additional $400. All were eligible for interest free loans up to $500 and those filling out an NEA delegate survey received convention memorabilia that could be auctioned to offset expenses. Delegates were requested to wear yellow NEA jackets, and such jackets were very prominent at the Democratic convention. Note, however, that NEA encourages members to be delegates long before the national conventions; this effort includes state and regional meetings in which NEA endorsement procedures, convention schedules, critical issues, and strategies are thoroughly reviewed.

Local Political Operations

To appreciate the political impact of the teacher unions, it is necessary to recognize the similarities between unions and political parties. William Form has summarized these similarities as follows:

> Both (1) are organized at local, state, and national levels and are loosely coordinated; (2) are run by elected officers; (3) conduct conventions to hammer out legislative objectives; and (4) screen candidates for nominations; (5) solicit contributions to finance campaigns of candidates; (6) use volunteers to mobilize voters at elections; and (7) have difficulty disciplining volunteers.[8]

Form then goes on to compare unions and political parties from the standpoint of political effectiveness. The union advantages are as follows:

- Unlike party leaders, labor leaders communicate regularly with their members.
- Unions have facilities that are easily converted to political use.
- Unions have a steady income, whereas political parties must rely on voluntary contributions.
- Unions focus on specific political goals, whereas political parties must appeal to more amorphous benefits.
- Unions can usually recruit volunteers for political activities more readily than political parties.

To be sure, some differences, such as the availability of patronage, favor superior party effectiveness; nonetheless, Form concludes that "On balance, labor's political structure is superior to the party's."[9]

Prior to becoming a union, the NEA was not a very potent political force. The reason was that local associations did not have the full-time staff and facilities that are so critical in political campaigns. Teacher unionization, however, has resulted in thousands of full-time union staff who participate in political campaigns; also, an enormous expansion of data, facilities, and equipment that can be used in such campaigns. It is not surprising that NEA political operations are often superior to political party operations, especially at the local level.

In practice, it is commonplace for candidates to utilize teacher union facilities in political campaigns. This is sometimes arranged at nominal rent to avoid the appearance of illegal contributions. In any case, it should be evident that teacher union support at the local level plays a major role in political campaigns. This is especially true in "nonpartisan" school board elections, where union opposed candidates cannot rely on weak party structures for help in running against candidates supported by teacher unions.

Bipartisanship: Rhetoric and Reality

Like any interest group, the NEA seeks and welcomes support from Republicans as well as Democrats. Certainly, the percentage of endorsed candidates in the Democratic and Republican parties need not be equal to justify the claim of "bipartisanship" and the NEA has supported some Republicans and an occasional independent candidate for federal office. For most practical purposes, however, the NEA (and AFT) are adjuncts of the Democratic Party. Their overwhelming support for Democratic candidates is not limited to cash and campaign contributions, but also involves close coordination of union staff with Democratic party operations long before any formal endorsements are made. For example, by February 1996, the NEA was working closely with the Democratic National Committee to reelect the Clinton–Gore ticket. Instead of developing its own list of target states, NEA-PAC was using the list provided by the Democratic National Committee (DNC). In addition, NEA-PAC had begun to work with the DNC to slot delegates to the Democratic convention.[10]

As a matter of fact, in 1996 NEA-PAC was finding it difficult to identify any Republicans to endorse. Prior to 1996, NEA and NEA-PAC had contributed soft money overwhelmingly to Democratic Party organizations. As "conservative" Republicans replaced "moderates" in the 1994 elections, no Republicans in Congress could meet NEA-PAC's criteria for endorsement. To avoid a total absence of support for Republicans, NEA and NEA-PAC began to contribute more "soft money" to Republican party organizations, a practice permitted under the rules of the Federal Election Commission (FEC).

The overwhelming tilt toward Democratic candidates in 1996 simply reflected the pattern that NEA-PAC has been following since its inception. For example, in 1984, the NEA endorsed twenty-six candidates for the U.S. Senate, all Democrats. Only sixteen of the 304 candidates NEA-PAC endorsed for the House of Representatives were Republicans.

The NEA explanation for its lopsided tilt to Democratic candidates is as follows:

> The Democratic Party is not nearly as well funded as the Republican Party. The Democratic Party does bestow a considerable amount of power to its larger financial contributors, but the Democrats depend more heavily on the organizational strength of large membership organizations, like NEA, for the "people power" they bestow.
>
> The Democratic Party has traditionally been more receptive to NEA, in part be-

cause the Democrats cannot pay for the time and services provided for free by hundreds of thousands of Association members. In addition, Democratic Party policy on the issue of federal support for education tends to be closer to NEA's goals than Republican Party policy.[11]

To say the least, the NEA's explanation is rather disingenuous. NEA-PAC is part of the labor union family of PACs that gave over $40 million (94 percent) to Democrats in the 1992 elections and only $2.4 million to Republicans. Democrats also received more funds from business PACs in 1992; indeed, Democrats collected nearly two-thirds of all PAC contributions. Labor PACs supported 64 percent of incumbents and risked 19 percent on open seat candidates. In their efforts to reduce the number of Republicans in Congress, labor PACs gave 18 percent to challengers. Public sector unions contributed 92 percent of their funds to Democrats.[12]

The low percentage of NEA-PAC funds going to Republicans actually overstates the support given to Republicans. One reason is that the higher the office, the lower the percentage of PAC funds to Republicans. Thus at the presidential level, no Republican candidate has received support from NEA-PAC, and the proportion of Republican senatorial candidates receiving NEA-PAC support is much lower than the proportion of candidates for the House of Representatives. Similarly, at the state level, the proportion of teacher union Democratic candidates endorsed for governor is higher than the proportion of endorsed candidates for the legislature.

Another critical factor is that the cash contributions do not take into account the value of "in-kind" contributions, that is, volunteers who serve on telephone banks, transport voters to the polls, put up signs and posters, turn out for demonstrations and rallies, stuff envelopes, and so on. Obviously, the value of in-kind contributions varies a great deal, but it is often more valuable than the cash contributions.[13]

Whatever the usual ratio of in-kind contributions to cash contributions, it is higher for candidates supported by teacher unions. Typically, teachers have summers, weekends and more time generally that can be devoted to political campaigns. Their work day during the school year tends to be less than most; as will be pointed out in Chapter 6, teachers provide campaign services on election days more often than most voters. Furthermore, teachers tend to be better educated than the voting population as a whole; the teacher ranks include valuable campaign skills which can be put to good use.

The high proportion of NEA-PAC funds going to Democrats understates NEA-PAC's support for them for still another reason. NEA-PAC contributes to several PACs that support only Democratic candidates. Two examples are

Emily's List, a PAC that supports female Democrats running for Congress, and IMPAC 2000, a Democratic affiliated organization involved in redistricting issues. When contributions to such organizations are factored in, the percentage of NEA-PAC support for Democrats is even higher.

Not surprisingly, the NEA is sensitive to criticisms of its close ties to the Democratic Party. A recent NEA publication asserts:

> *Fallacy:* The NEA is a captive of the Democratic Party. Variation of fallacy: The Democratic Party is a captive of the NEA.
>
> *Fact:* Neither of the above! The NEA is bipartisan and encourages its members to be active in the political process. Its positions on political issues and candidates are based on a legislative program that is adopted annually by the NEA Representative Assembly.
>
> The NEA and its affiliates support and work for proeducation candidates regardless of party affiliation. We endorse both Republican and Democratic candidates at all levels of government. NEA representatives attend both the Democratic and Republican conventions.
>
> The NEA is one of many interest groups that seek to persuade Democratic and Republican candidates for office to take positions in support of public education. Like all other such groups, we win some and we lose some, and that's the way it works in a diverse and democratic society.[14]

First of all, the statement is false; the NEA has never supported a Republican candidate for president. Apart from this, the absence of data in the quotation is a clue to its misleading nature. If there were persuasive data supporting the NEA's claim to bipartisanship, the NEA would undoubtedly feature it in any defense of the claim. Furthermore, the references to diversity and democracy are patently irrelevant to the criticism that the NEA is allied with the Democratic Party.

Why do more Democrats than Republicans support NEA positions? In NEA terminology, why are more Democrats "proeducation" or "propublic education?" For the NEA to say that it supports more Democrats because more Democrats support NEA positions raises more questions than it answers. After all, the Republican Party was the propublic education party until the 1950s. The Democratic Party included a much higher proportion of ethnic and religious groups, especially Irish and Italian Catholics, who supported government assistance for denominational schooling.

One need not be a partisan for either party to realize that conflict between the NEA/AFT and Republicans may be long term with no obvious solution in sight. On the other hand, Republicans are emphasizing lower taxes, downsizing government, and increasing resort to private sector alternatives to government delivery of services. Perhaps the rhetoric is often overdone, but the party orientation is in the general direction of the rhetoric. On the other hand, the NEA/AFT, like public sector unions generally, have a stake in higher taxes, higher levels of government spending, and the avoidance of competition from the private sector. It is difficult to see how conflict over these opposing positions can be avoided; here and there, it can be, but the conflict seems more likely to intensify as long as "proeducation" is defined as support for larger federal appropriations for education, health care, senior citizens, and a variety of other social services and entitlements.

Developments on the Republican side reinforce the conclusion that the NEA is on a collision course with Republican legislators. The Republican party in California withdrew convention privileges from the Republican Educators Caucus of the California Teachers Association in 1995 until at least 40 percent of CTA endorsements went to Republican candidates. Another significant recent development was the 1995 publication of *Agenda for America, a Republican Direction for the Future*.[15] Although the book includes a disclaimer that it is not a Republican party project, the editor was Haley Barbour, chairman of the Republican National Committee at the time. Remarkably, *Agenda for America* explicitly identifies the NEA and AFT as the major obstacles to educational reform and proposes specific measures to weaken the unions financially. The turning point in NEA/Republican relations was Bob Dole's speech accepting the Republican nomination for the presidency. Before a national television audience, Dole asserted:

> The teachers unions nominated Bill Clinton in 1992, they are funding his reelection now, and they, his most reliable supporters, know he will maintain the status quo. I say this not to the teachers, but to their unions: If education were a war, you would be losing it. If it were a business, you would be driving it into bankruptcy. If it were a patient, it would be dying. To the teachers unions I say, when I am president, I will disregard your political power, for the sake of the children, the schools, and the nation. I plan to enrich your vocabulary with those words you fear—school choice, competition and opportunity scholarships—so that you will join the rest of us in accountability, while others compete with you for the commendable privilege of giving our children a real education.[16]

Notwithstanding Dole's explicit statement to the contrary, the NEA and AFT presidents immediately issued news releases alleging that Dole had attacked teachers. Nonetheless, Dole's criticisms have largely undermined NEA efforts to maintain a bipartisan image. Its practice of sprinkling a few dollars on a few Republican moderates will no longer suffice to justify its claim to be "bipartisan."

The overwhelming preponderance of endorsements for Democratic candidates is not the only data that calls this NEA claim into question. According to NEA, 365 of 4,288 delegates to the 1992 Democratic convention were NEA members. In contrast, only 25 NEA members were delegates (14 regular, 11 alternates) to the 1992 Republican convention. In 1996, 405 NEA members were delegates to the

Democratic convention; only 34 members to the Republican convention. The NEA's close ties to the Democratic Party are evident in personnel as well as endorsements and delegate counts. For instance, Debra DeLee, the NEA's manager of government relations, was appointed in December 1993 to be the Executive Director of the Democratic National Committee. As Executive Director, DeLee supervised day to day activities with Congress and the White House. Subsequently, DeLee was appointed Chief Executive Officer of the 1996 Democratic Convention in Chicago, the position she held through the convention. At the NEA, DeLee had been responsible for NEA's lobbying efforts and all political advocacy and NEA-PAC activities; according to NEA's 1992–93 Program Accomplishment Report:

> Program 5.41, expenditures $108,723
>
> Ongoing liaison was provided to the Democratic and Republican National Committees (DNC, RNC) as appropriate. In 1993, Government Relations Director, Debra DeLee was elected as a vice-chair of the Democratic National Committee. In addition, 15 NEA members are also DNC members. As a result, NEA's involvement with the DNC has significantly increased. The Association now participates in all political and senior staff meetings held by the Democratic Party. Since the beginning of the Clinton Administration, NEA involvement with DNC/White House initiatives has been substantial. . . . The Association works closely with the Association of State Democratic Chairs on a regular basis.[17]

The foregoing quotation is followed by a recital of NEA's efforts to work with the Republican party. The recital begins by noting NEA's efforts to work with the NEA's Republican Educators Caucus, an organization that has done more to promote the NEA in the Republican party than to promote the Republican Party in the NEA.

Last but certainly not least, the 1996 NEA convention was completely oriented to the election of the Clinton–Gore ticket. The NEA's "Friend of Education" award went to President Clinton as a preliminary to his endorsement, which had been a foregone conclusion for a long time. It is interesting that the campaign materials such as signs, flyers, buttons, and bumperstickers were made and distributed long before the official endorsement; in a convention with over 9,000 delegates, no one challenged this flagrant violation of association protocol.

NEA's Political Operations

Endorsements for elective office are one thing; effective action during legislative sessions is another. Of course, these processes are closely related, but electing friendly members of Congress is only part of an effective political program. Legislation must be drafted, introduced and publicized; research conducted to support it, and to counter the opposition; prompt responses to amendments may be crucial, and so on. Consequently, we must consider NEA's legislative as well as its campaign operations.

The NEA's Strategic Plan and Budget for fiscal year (FY) 1995–96 is based upon support for six organizational centers, each of which serves one or more strategic objectives. Political activities are a major responsibility of the Center for Public Affairs; Its budget for FY 1995–96 was over $25.7 million, over 13.8 percent of the NEA's budget. Of this amount, almost $10.4 million was allocated to the Office of Government Relations, which includes a staff of six lobbyists on congressional issues.[18]

Another $2.4 million is budgeted for two field offices that assist state and local associations on political matters.

In practice, the allocations to Government Relations constitute only a small portion of NEA financial support for its political operations. For example, "publishing" and "communications" are also political expenditures. Table 5.3 illustrates this point.

The NEA budget includes scores of other political expenses which are listed under nonpolitical headings. Certainly, the Republicans under attack in NEA publications, news releases, and advertisements would be astonished to discover that the NEA's attacks are not "political" expenditures.

Realistically, the issue boils down to the difference between the legal definitions of political activity and its practical meaning. The regulations of the Federal Election Commission (FEC) allow unions to spend dues revenues for political education of their members and for issues advocacy. Thus the unions can pay for advertisements that "educate" their members about the fact that candidate A has voted against union positions X, Y, and Z, but they are not allowed to use dues revenues to urge members to vote for A instead of B. This issue is further complicated by the need to avoid the appearance of dictating to union members; in communications to the media, the NEA "endorses" candidates, but it only "recommends" in communications sent to the membership.

NEA/AFT publications pay great deference to the idea that NEA members resent being told how to vote. Supposedly, the publications simply provide information so that members can make up their own minds on the issues. NEA references to the author illustrate its approach to information. In discussing an article I wrote, NEA On-Line referred to me as "a Bowling Green State University Scholar," which I have never been. My affiliation was and is with the Social Philosophy and Policy Center, a separate organization on the university campus. NEA On-Line then went on to assert: "Lieberman is a former union activist who once ran for AFT office. He then switched his loyalties to favor management and the right wing." The NEA description fails to point out that the author:

TABLE 5.3

Budget, NEA Center for Public Affairs, FY 1995–96

COMMUNICATIONS	$ 3,535,470
Program 1.11 NEA/State Media Co-op Program	$ 1,400,000

Production and distribution of broadcast spots for state affiliates
who decide their placement.

Program 1.12 Opinion Leader Advertising	$ 450,000

Op-ed pieces by the NEA President in publications such as *New
York Times, Washington Post,* and *Education Week.* Copies are provided to affiliates. This budget also helps to underwrite "news
programs" on National Public Radio.

Program 1.13 New Media Services	$ 1,236,121

Essentially, this program funds NEA's efforts to promote public
education in the media, also to counter its critics. Other objectives are to "develop positive working relationships with the news
media, both print and electronic," and secure media coverage of
NEA activities and policies and programs.

Program 1.14 Writing Center	$ 449,349

The Writing Center prepares "speeches, articles, editorial columns,
reports on issues, and messages for internal and external audiences."

Source: National Education Association, *Strategic Plan and Budget, Fiscal Year: 1995–96* (Washington: National Education Association, 1995), pp. 1–3.

- Is a life member of the NEA.
- Never held full-time union employment.
- Was employed by NEA as a consultant and expert witness several times since
  1962, when he ran for AFT president.
- Established and directed teacher leadership programs in 1972–74 officially
  praised by NEA.
- Published his first article critical of teacher bargaining in 1979, seventeen
  years after his candidacy for AFT office.
- Was a frequent delegate to NEA and AFT conventions from 1956 to 1975.
  The above errors, misleading statements, and omissions illustrate the kind
  of "information" in NEA communications to its members when union interests are at stake.

From a practical point of view, this distinction between "educational" and "political" expenditures is absurd, but in fairness to the NEA/AFT, their critics also rely upon it to justify political spending without violating federal election laws.

How much does NEA spend for political purposes? This is an exceedingly important issue that best awaits consideration in Chapters 9 and 10; however, the expenditures explicitly identified as "political" in the NEA budget are much less than the actual amounts. Even at a cursory level of analysis, the NEA's political program leaves nothing to chance—if an activity is important for political success, there is support for it in the NEA budget.

For instance, in some jurisdictions, there is growing interest in mail balloting. Obviously, this issue raises a host of strategic and tactical questions: Under what circumstances will mail balloting help or hinder NEA's political objectives? What kinds of voters tend not to vote? Is there time to identify and reach them before the deadline to return the ballot? What are the organizational savings and what are the new expenditures required? The NEA has the resources to research such issues, and it does so extensively.

Congressional Contact Team (CCT)

Quite frequently, the scale of NEA political activity goes far beyond conventional support activities. The NEA's Congressional Contact Teams (CCT) illustrate this point. The NEA encourages its members to volunteer for service on the campaign staff of congressional candidates. Obviously, these volunteers are likely to have excellent access to winning candidates. With this in mind, the NEA sponsors the Congressional Contact Team (CCT) program. The program is designed to encourage NEA members to serve as volunteers for congressional candidates. If the candidates win, NEA members will be in a strong position to promote NEA positions. As part of the program, NEA subsidizes the expenses of volunteers for winning candidates to travel to Washington for a CCT conference. At the conference, the volunteers are briefed on the issues from an NEA perspective before meeting with their congressional representatives. Naturally, the volunteers urge support for the NEA positions during their presence in Washington.

The trip to Washington is only the highlight of an impressive operation. NEA's Office of Government Relations publishes *How to Conduct the NEA Congressional Contact Team Program.*[19] The publication covers every aspect of the CCT program, including the criteria for selecting CCT members, how CCT members should dress and act in Congressional offices; and CCT member relationships with the state CCT coordinator, UniServ directors, NEA staff, members of Congress and their staffs, and association members. NEA reimburses the state affiliates for the costs of the program; in addition, NEA pays the expenses of

CCT members who travel to Washington to lobby for NEA's legislative objectives. A monthly newsletter, *Grass Roots,* informs CCT members of recent developments and urges them to take action as appropriate. In high stakes situations, the NEA communicates immediately with CCT members in selected districts so as to maximize pressure on members of Congress whose votes are in doubt. Of course, the NEA is not the only organization that brings members to Washington to lobby, but few, if any, can bring supporters from every congressional district for this purpose. The NEA also operates a telecommunications network with grassroots supporters that is probably unmatched by any other special interest.

AFT Political Operations

AFT/COPE funds, like NEA-PAC's are raised primarily by means of payroll deduction and are allocated by top level AFT officers who serve as officers of AFT/COPE. At its 1996 convention, AFT staff announced the availability of the following materials supporting the Clinton–Gore ticket:

- Fact sheets on various issues.
- Endorsement guides to be used whenever possible.
- Issue flyers.
- Model forms for campaign stickers, buttons, pins, etc.
- Get out the vote (GOTV) flyers.
- Letters from local/state federation presidents to various constituencies.
- Direct mail flyers comparing Dole and Clinton.
- Flyers on contingencies such as the nomination of Colin Powell for vice-president.

These materials had been developed on the basis of extensive polling and prepared with considerable sophistication. Since polls showed Clinton to be weak on character and consistency, the AFT materials emphasized Clinton's character and consistency in vetoing budgets passed by Congress. The materials prepared this way were tested with focus groups before dissemination. In like fashion, environmental flyers emphasized Clinton's support for more environmental safety and health regulation, a strategy intended to appeal to government employees whom the AFT hopes to organize.

The AFT is even more pro-Democratic than the NEA; less than two percent of AFT/COPE funds has gone to Republicans in recent years. The NEA's slightly greater support for Republicans is due to the fact that the association functions in more areas controlled by Republicans. Assessing the AFT's political effectiveness, however, is difficult because AFT's political activities are coordinated with the AFL-CIO's Committee on Political Education (COPE). Prior to

1996, AFL-CIO COPE employed about twelve to fifteen professionals, a field staff of twenty and a clerical staff of about twenty. All together, the international unions based in Washington probably employed ten times as many professionals.[20] As this is written (June 1997), the AFL-CIO is making a major effort to upgrade its political effectiveness, hence its previous record is not necessarily a guide to its future effectiveness. Union effectiveness in getting members to vote in accordance with leadership preferences is a much debated issue; it appears, however, that COPE support increases member support from 7 to 12 percent.

Operationally, COPE has been most successful when it focused on "labor issues," such as defeating right to work laws. It has not been very persuasive among union members when it goes beyond these issues; union members disagree among themselves on gun control, abortion, and affirmative action, to cite just a few. Nonetheless, the Clinton–Gore ticket won 55 percent of the labor vote in 1992, an impressive margin in view of the fact that independent candidate Ross Perot received 24 percent of the votes.

Except for clearly defined labor issues, the AFL-CIO has not followed a highly consistent legislative position. It supports consumer legislation that does not adversely affect any of its unions. Similarly, its opposition to taxation of fringe benefits would obviously help most union members, but would not be in the interests of low income groups that do not receive fringe benefits. As one sympathetic observer commented, "labor behaved predominantly as a special interest lobby as well as a lobby for consumers and other class segments when their economic interests overlapped."[21] It should be noted, however, that the overall decline in union membership has not necessarily resulted in a corresponding decline in union political influence. Union success in raising dues and PAC funds may have compensated for the weakening effects of declining membership.

AFT elected officers and staff also play a prominent role in Democratic Party affairs. Prior to his death in 1997, AFT President Albert Shanker had been active in Democratic Party politics since the 1970s, and AFT political directors also have had close ties to the Democratic Party. Elizabeth M. Smith took office as director of AFT/COPE in January 1995. Prior to accepting this position, Smith held positions with prominent Democratic members of Congress and served as legislative and political strategist for the Amalgamated Clothing and Textile Workers. Smith had also been a member of the Rules and Bylaws Committee of the Democratic National Committee and of the Board of Directors of the National Democratic Party.

Smith's involvement in Democratic Party affairs merely continues frequent practice for AFT staff members. To cite just one additional example, Scott Widmeyer, the AFT's director of public relations, took a leave of absence in 1984 to serve as Deputy Press Secretary for Walter Mondale's presidential campaign. Essentially, the only difference between the NEA and AFT on "bipartisanship" is that the AFT does not even bother with the figleaf.

Like the NEA, the AFT had been working hard to elect Democratic candidates, presidential and congressional, long before the AFT's endorsement of the Clinton–Gore ticket at its 1996 convention in August. A convention workshop on the 1996 elections featured the DNC's director of political affairs, a prominent Democratic polling firm, and the AFT political staff. All took for granted, as did the audience, that the issue was how, not whether to elect the Democratic ticket. The total absence of a conservative presence of any kind in the AFT convention is remarkable since only 25 delegate signatures are required for caucus recognition in the AFT.

The NEA and AFT: Policy Conflict and Convergence

The NEA and AFT have disagreed from time to time on important issues. For example, the NEA opposed collective bargaining during the early 1960s while the AFT was highly supportive of it. After the NEA endorsed collective bargaining, it supported state bargaining laws that applied only to teachers, whereas the AFT supported state legislation applicable to state and local public employees generally. The NEA opposed comprehensive coverage because the AFT had closer ties to the labor relations agencies that would administer the labor laws. To avoid this disadvantage, the NEA sought bargaining laws that would be administered by educational personnel. Today, both unions support what was formerly the AFT position.

Still another disagreement was over the establishment of the U.S. Department of Education, a high NEA priority opposed by the AFT. Again, the differences were due to union maneuvering to achieve insider status. The AFT wanted education to remain under the jurisdiction of the House Education and Labor Committee, where the AFT's allies in the AFL-CIO enjoyed close relationships with committee leadership. The NEA's thinking was that if Congress established a Department of Education, the NEA would be the dominant interest group in the new congressional committee to be established.

The sharpest existing differences are on race and gender relations. The NEA has been supportive of ethnic and gender quotas since the early 1970s, more so than any other major nonethnic organization in the United States. The two unions filed opposing briefs in the *Regents of the University of California* v. *Bakke,* the leading case on affirmative action.[22] The AFT brief opposed preferential treatment for disadvantaged minorities in admissions to the University of California-Davis medical school; the NEA brief supported it. Although the differences on affirmative action are important, they are likely to diminish or even be eliminated by judicial decisions that strike down the ethnic and gender quotas that run rampant in the NEA.

There have also been foreign policy differences, especially on nuclear disarmament, but the other major policy difference between the two unions concerns affiliation with the AFL-CIO. This issue is likely to be resolved during the ongoing merger talks on the basis of mandatory national affiliation with an option to affiliate at the state and local levels. Another difference, which is gradually diminishing, relates to the status of nonteacher employees. The AFT always accepted them as full members, whereas they were not allowed to vote in NEA elections or hold NEA office until 1980. A 1993 AFT brochure alleges that as of September 1989 some NEA affiliates accepted dues from support employees who were not allowed to vote or hold union office; excluded classified employees from policy-making bodies in the union; and allowed only associate membership that provided publications but no services. Or they made no provision at all for support personnel.

Most of the AFT criticisms have diminished or been eliminated; as Chapter 7 shows, the NEA is moving toward full inclusion of support personnel. In any event, the policy differences between the NEA and AFT have had little, if any impact on union support for congressional candidates. From 1988 to 1994, NEA-PAC allocated 4.1 percent of its PAC funds to Republicans; AFT/COPE allocated only 1.9 percent. Republican candidates received 4.8 percent of AFT/COPE endorsements, but the average contribution was $7,348 for Democrats, $2,778 for Republicans.

NEA/AFT political convergence is especially evident from the small number of contests in which the unions supported opposing candidates. In elections to the U.S. House of Representatives from 1988 to 1994 (four election cycles), the NEA and AFT supported candidates from different parties in head-to-head contests only 14 times. With 435 seats at stake in each election, this works out to only one such disagreement in every 124 races. Also in these four election cycles, there were only eight occasions in which the NEA and AFT supported opposing candidates in Democratic primaries. In some instances, the union that supported the loser in the primary supported the winner in the general election.

Three factors explain most of the differences in NEA/AFT endorsements. The AFT is more influenced by AFL-CIO endorsements; the AFT rarely deviates from AFL-CIO positions on anything. Second, the NEA is more willing to support incumbent "moderate" Republicans; the AFT finds it more difficult to support any kind of Republican, because it has less to spend and has fewer local/state affiliates in jurisdictions controlled by Republicans. Also, NEA-PAC is much more willing to support candidates who are not favored to win; the AFT supports a higher percentage of favorites. Also, the AFT's close ties to Jewish groups and "neoconservatives" have no parallel in the NEA. AFT president Albert Shanker and several members of his closest associates emerged from a Jewish, democratic socialist milieu in New York City. The AFT and UFT have always been active in Jewish affairs through pro-Isreal demonstrations, heavy purchase of Israel bonds, and support for free emigration of Russian Jews. Several AFT/UFT officers are active in the Jewish Labor Committee, an AFL-CIO front that is active in Jewish communities.

An interesting example of NEA's willingness to support "moderate" Republicans over unfriendly Republican incumbents occurred in 1976; in that year, NEA-PAC contributed $2,000 to Newt Gingrich's unsuccessful campaign to unseat John J. Flynt in Georgia's 6th Congressional District. In 1990, the NEA supported Republican Herman Clark against Gingrich in the Republican primary. In contrast, the AFT is rarely involved in Republican primaries.

To summarize, most of the policy and political differences between the NEA and AFT have disappeared or are likely to disappear under an NEA/AFT merger. Some issues have been resolved by events over which neither union had much to say. Others result partly from demographic differences or from historical factors that are losing their salience with the passage of time. The AFT tried to eliminate the NEA's tax exemption before the merger talks; it is avoiding the issue during the talks and will probably continue to do so, regardless of their outcome.

Historically, the NEA has emphasized term limits for its elected officers. During the years of intense rivalry, the NEA was highly critical of the AFT's organizational structure, which permits elected officers to run for reelection as often as they wish. In recent years, the NEA has been moving away from term limits, and merger will accelerate the process. After all, AFT officers who have been elected to highly paid positions are not going to adopt rules that preclude their staying in office. At the same time, incumbent association officers who would like to get rid of term limits can appear to be doing so in order to effectuate merger, not for personal gain.

The NEA/AFT convergence on political candidates and policies is the bottom line. First, it is strong evidence that the differences between the two unions are far less important than their similarities. Especially among conservatives, it is naively assumed that the AFT is more reform oriented, more innovative, or more hostile to a liberal social agenda. NEA/AFT convergence on candidates and public policies suggests the differences are greatly exaggerated. Furthermore, their convergence suggests that political and/or policy differences will not hold up a merger between the two unions.

Perhaps the basic implication is that NEA/AFT policies and political objectives are driven much more by union imperatives than by views of union leaders. For instance, the hope that enlightened union leaders will move away from conventional union opposition to teacher tenure or merit pay must be recognized as an illusion. NEA/AFT may be forced to accept changes that are contrary to union imperatives, but they will do so only under heavy pressure. This conclusion underscores the importance of recognizing union imperatives; otherwise, one hopes in vain that union leaders will change their positions.

6

STATE TEACHER UNIONS

S ince the rise of teacher bargaining, the state education associations (SEAs) have emerged as political powerhouses in virtually every state. To be sure, most were influential before then, but their political influence has reached un-precedented levels under collective bargaining. To understand how and why this happened, we need to review briefly the state association role prior to teacher bargaining.

Constitutionally, education was not included among the purposes of the federal government. Libertarians and some religious denominations believe that education should not be a governmental function at all, but the main-stream view is that it should be provided by state and/or local government. Since school boards are legally agencies of the state governments, the boards have as much or as little authority as the states allow. Not surprisingly, since the rise of public education in the mid-1880s, most of the key actors, such as Horace Mann, have been state officials.

Although legally a state function, education was financed largely from local taxes until the 1970s. The reliance on local taxes resulted in severe inequalities in per pupil spending within states. In some states, the inequalities were struck down judicially; in other states, political pressures led to state efforts to reduce inequality of school spending. These efforts led to higher levels of state support as a percentage of school revenues. In the 1990s, state governments and local communities each provided about 46.5 percent of school revenues, with the federal government paying the rest.[1]

In seeking more state aid to education, the state teacher unions also try to tie it to other union objectives. In 1982, Mario Cuomo won a close primary against New York City mayor Ed Koch for the Democratic gubernatorial nomination. Cuomo went on to win a close race for governor in the general election. In his account of these activities, Cuomo explicitly credited the support he received from AFT President Albert Shanker and the New York State United Teachers as the turning point of his campaign.[2] After his reelection in 1986, Cuomo signed "Excellence in Teaching" legislation that provided state aid to New York schools, but only for teacher salaries. At one time, the amounts appropriated reached about $160 million. At the time, the New York City schools were in wretched physical condition. An even larger payoff emerged in 1992 when Cuomo signed legislation that required all teachers to pay service fees to the union as a condition of employment. In other words, teachers (and other state and local public employees) had to pay fees to a union from the first day of their employment in a New York school district; the local unions did not even have to bargain for this concession. With one-third of its membership in New York State, the legislation led to substantial increases in AFT revenues at local, state, and national levels.

Federal legislation also tends to increase the role of the state education associations. In education, the federal government deals with local school boards primarily through the state departments of education. Because the states administer most federal educational programs, the state associations play a key role in their administration. Most important, the strength and militancy of local associations depend upon what state laws allow them to do; in turn, the latter depends on the influence of the state associations. A state association that is successful in legalizing teacher strikes will generate more militant local action than a state association that has not been able to legalize them.

Within the NEA itself, state association officials are not as dominant as they were prior to collective bargaining. The reason is that teacher bargaining led to more powerful local associations. Before the bargaining era, the state associations dictated to the locals; the latter were mainly social organizations that were subordinate to school administrators. Furthermore, the local associations did not have the resources to sustain an independent course of action. This is not the case when the local associations have the resources to organize politically, as many do now.

The foregoing comments are not so applicable to state federations of the AFT. First, state federations that include teachers exist in only forty states. With the exception of New York and Rhode Island, the state federations are much smaller in members and revenues than the state NEA affiliate. AFT teacher membership is mainly drawn from large urban school districts in the northeastern United States and the Middle West plus a few such districts in the remaining states. Consequently, my analysis of "state teacher unions" relates mainly to the state education associations affiliated with the NEA.

State Association PACs

The first state association PAC was established in Utah in 1965. By 1972, when NEA-PAC was established, at least twenty-two state associations had established a PAC, and all of the others did so shortly thereafter. The state laws regulating state PACs vary widely, but the common tendencies are clear enough.

Again, let us follow the money trail. Appendix D shows the 1994 expenditures for twenty state association and one state federation PACs and their rank among all PACs in its particular state. Obviously, the state association PACs are typically among the very largest. Because teacher contributions are made monthly by payroll deduction every year, their state PACs accumulate substantial amounts for distribution during the election years. Like federal PACs, the state PACs spend regular dues income for PAC expenses. As a result, state association spending for political candidates is much higher than the amounts distributed to candidates.

NEA/AFT affiliates raise more per teacher in states that allow the reverse checkoff than in states that prohibit it. In all states, however, the amounts distributed by state PACs vary from year to year, and from primary to general election. Differences in rank order may or may not reflect significant differences in the amounts of the contributions; for example, the highest ranking PAC may contribute very little more than the second highest, but the differences between the second and third ranking PACs may be very substantial.

Taking such variables into account, it appears that the state association PACs are among the top three in most states, and among the top six in virtually all (see Appendix D). Inasmuch as AFT-PACs almost invariably support the same candidates in areas where both NEA and AFT-PACs are active, NEA/AFT-PACs jointly would be the very largest in almost half the states. And since in-kind contributions are often worth several times the cash contributions, and teachers contribute more in-kind than any other interest group, state teacher unions are understandably major political players in most states.

Generally speaking, the larger regional and local affiliates of the NEA/AFT also have their own PACs. A 1996 survey by the Education Policy Institute identified 232 local teacher PACs, but the actual number is much higher. The survey identified a total of fifty-seven local PACs in Michigan and thirty-three in Indiana, mainly in the larger school districts. Some local PACs raise all of their funds from their members; others rely partly on contributions from the state teacher union PACs.[3] It is also the case that some large local PACs in the AFT contribute more than the PACs of their state affiliates.

Like NEA-PAC and AFT/COPE, the state PAC expenditures do not fully reflect the state union political contributions. For example, I-PACE, the Indiana State Teachers Association PAC, is a leading Indiana PAC in terms of cash contributions. In 1994, it contributed $335,000 to candidates for state office; however, I-PACE funds do not include ISTA expenditures for I-PACE administration, the expenses for the ISTA government relations office, and the political activities of ISTA Uni-Serv directors. Nor do they include the expenditures of the local and regional PACs of ISTA affiliates. As would be expected, ISTA's distribution pattern is heavily skewed in favor of Democratic candidates. The small ISTA support for Republicans goes overwhelmingly to prolabor Republicans who are heavily favored to win reelection; the ISTA supported Republicans tend to be winners by comfortable margins. This is typical of teacher association PAC contributions to Republicans.

In addition to political expenditures that are reported, the teacher unions engage in deliberate deception to avoid full disclosure of their spending for political purposes. This issue is discussed in more detail in Chapter 10, but it should be noted here that large sums are involved. The California Teachers Association's (CTA) 1993 campaign against Proposition 174 illustrates this point. Proposition 174 was a voucher initiative opposed by CTA. The initiative lost by a 7-to-3 margin after intense opposition from every state-wide public school organization in California.

CTA reported cash and in-kind contributions of $12.6 million in its campaign against Proposition 174. In fact, CTA's early polling—a costly item in its own right not reported as a political expenditure—revealed widespread dissatisfaction with public education. The CTA recognized that this dissatisfaction was a major reason 70 percent of the voters supported vouchers in preelection polls.

Aware that a voucher initiative would be on the 1993 ballot, the CTA launched a television program on forty-six television stations in every television market in the state. The spots were produced to demonstrate something positive about public education. They were shown repeatedly, usually twice within a thirty second span to drive the message home. The advertisements were shown in close proximity to news and information programs which attract high percentages of likely voters. Frequency was such that the average voter would see the CTA spots (up to 100 times for typical viewers) from January 14 to February 21, 1993, an extremely high saturation level.

Internal CTA documents make it absolutely clear that the entire television campaign was "a direct and conscious prelude to our campaign against the voucher initiative." Although CTA recognized that the spots would not be as popular among teachers as early advertisements on class size, CTA leaders pointed out that the spots were "aimed much more directly at nonteachers, specifically at the people who will decide the future of education when they vote on the voucher initiative."[4]

Inasmuch as the CTA television spots did not mention the voucher initiative, their costs were not included in the CTA's official statements on its expenditures to defeat Proposition 174. These costs would include CTA staff time and expenses as well as the costs of production and television time. Because the expenditures were not categorized as "political," many California teachers who are not members of CTA were required to share the costs of these expenditures. Supreme Court decisions have held that forced political contributions are unconstitutional, hence the CTA interest in failing to characterize the expenditures accurately is understandable.

The data on CTA's in-kind contributions is especially impressive. According to the CTA's political consultant, the CTA volunteer phone bank against Proposition 174, was the largest "in state history and the history of American politics." A total of 24,579 volunteers completed 943,149 calls, 101,000 on the Monday before the election. The campaign against the voucher initiative utilized more than 1,000 trained speakers of whom more than 40 percent were CTA members. Abstract arguments for vouchers are not enough to overcome these statistics.

Endorsement Procedures and Distributions

As we might expect, state endorsement procedures are very similar to NEA's. Questionnaires emphasize state issues, which vary widely. In states without a bargaining law, support for it is likely to be the critical issue; in states which have already enacted such a law, support for agency fees or raising school revenues may be the litmus test for an endorsement.

Typically, the state questionnaires cite state association legislative objectives and request a response indicating support or opposition thereto. Issues pertaining to union revenues rank very high. For example, the first question in the 1994 questionnaire of the Virginia Education Association was as follows:

The VEA supports legislation granting statutory protection of the right of its members to have dues collected through voluntary payroll deduction.

Background information: Payroll deduction of dues allows public employees to make convenient payments for insurance, retirement programs, charitable contributions and membership in employee organizations and professional associations. Payroll deduction does not require membership in any organization, deny employees's right to work or constitute any form of collective bargaining.

The vast majority of VEA affiliates (85%) and VEA members have had voluntary payroll deduction through cooperative arrangements with their school boards. Some arrangements have been in place for as long as 50 years.

The VEA would view support for any legislation which would deny or restrict voluntary payroll withholding of dues for its members as *an unfriendly act.*

[   ] Agree with VEA   [   ] Disagree with VEA

Comments:

The tally sheet for the interview exam includes the following instructions:

PAYROLL DEDUCTION OF DUES (Question #1 on the Questionnaire)

If the candidate answers "Disagree/VEA" they will not be eligible for endorsement (by action of the VEA-PAC Executive Committee 3-6-93).

Out of the eighteen questions in the questionnaire, support for the VEA position on payroll deduction of dues was the only issue on which agreement with the VEA position was stated to be essential for an endorsement.[5]

The state association PACs support Democratic candidates by an overwhelming margin. After all, the same state association PACs that recommend federal candidates to NEA-PAC also recommend the state candidates for state association support. As a practical matter, deviations from the pattern of Democratic endorsements are more likely to happen at the state than the federal level. There will be more marginal districts in which association support can affect the outcome, hence more districts in which Republican as well as Democratic candidates vie for association support. Also in Republican districts, the state associations may have reason to support some candidates over others in Republican primaries.

Case studies from widely disparate states confirm the close ties between the state associations and the Democratic Party. A recent example from California is instructive.

California enrolls one of every nine pupils in U.S. public schools. The state is rather evenly divided politically and includes many highly competitive elections for local, state, and federal office. For these reasons, it provides several opportunities to observe state association relationships to the Republican and Democratic parties. The following letter from Bill Press, Chairman of the California Democratic Party, to CTA President Del Weber, provides an interesting perspective on the issue. After noting that "the CTA and the Democratic Party are two different organizations with two different agendas," Press went on to say:

> The Democratic Party's main goal in 1994 is to defeat Pete Wilson and elect a Democrat as California's next Governor. We hope you will join us in that crusade, because we firmly believe that's the best way to serve our public schools.
>
> But I assure you that, in pursuing our goal of getting rid of Pete Wilson, we will never do or say anything that is critical of California's public schools, students or teachers. And we count on you to hold us true to that promise.
>
> Having "cleared the air" I look forward to a close partnership in 1994.[6]

The Press letter seems a bit weak on logic; how could Press assure Weber that the Democratic Party "will never do or say anything that is critical of California's public schools, students or teachers"? Despite the absence of an explicit reference to the CTA, Press's pledge supports the conclusion that the California Democratic Party exerts considerable influence over the CTA. After all, to pledge never to criticize the public schools, students or teachers is to imply nothing about them will ever justify criticism. CTA could not ask more.

To be evenhanded about it, we should also consider the Democratic Party's influence over the CTA, at least in California. During the 1994 gubernatorial campaign, Alice A. Huffman, the CTA's Director of Government Affairs, also headed a political consulting firm, A C Public Affairs, Inc. The latter had a $170,000 contract with the campaign office of State Treasurer Kathleen Brown, the leading candidate for the Democratic nomination. Prior to CTA's vote on an endorsement in the gubernatorial race, Huffman had supported Brown for the nomination; after the latter's contract with Huffman's consulting firm was publicized, Brown received a majority of the CTA's State Council votes for the nomination but not the 60 percent required to win the CTA's endorsement.

Subsequently, widespread sentiment surfaced in the CTA for firing Huffman, who had violated CTA's prohibition against management ownership of an outside business. The problem was that Huffman had close ties to influential black leaders in the California assembly; for example, Barbara Lee, chairperson of the legislature's Black Caucus, sent a letter to CTA President Del Weber, asserting that "we do not intend to see such an advocate and leader be smeared in a political battle between gubernatorial candidates." In addition, Lee requested "an immediate explanation of your organization's understanding of these allegations and CTA's response to them." An even more threatening comment came from Willie Brown, the Assembly Speaker, who let it be known that "anyone who messes with Alice Huffman messes with Willie Brown." The spectacle of prominent Democratic leaders in the assembly interfering openly in CTA's internal affairs raised widespread doubts about CTA's independence from the Democratic Party. In this particular case, Huffman was reassigned and eventually resigned her position with CTA.

Payroll Deduction of PAC Funds: The Public Policy Issue

Payroll deductions for PAC funds raises some troubling public policy issues that are widely overlooked. The teacher unions invariably propose, and school boards usually accept, a payroll deduction form that authorizes and directs the board to deduct and transmit a teacher designated amount for the union PAC. The contractual provision almost always maintains the payroll deduction in effect from year to year unless revoked in writing by the teacher. In states that allow the reverse checkoff for state and local PACs, the school boards collect and transmit

PAC funds to the association without any authorization from individual teachers; the latter must ask for their money back in order to receive a refund. Frequently, the collective bargaining contract stipulates that the board will not grant payroll deduction for any other teacher organization or PAC. Even where this is not explicitly stated, the overwhelming practice in the thirty-four bargaining law states is to restrict the PAC deduction to the union sponsored PAC.

How this happens merits attention. Payroll deduction of union dues is a mandatory subject of bargaining in the bargaining law states. Inasmuch as payroll deduction of dues is essential to union viability, NEA/AFT affiliates accord it their highest priority. To the school board, however, payroll deduction of dues and PAC funds is merely a technicality—a union proposal that can be accepted promptly to demonstrate reasonableness or good faith, or entitlement to brownie points from the union. School boards rarely oppose union demands for the exclusive right to payroll deduction. In most school districts, there is no rival teacher organization requesting payroll deduction of dues, hence there is no organized constituency opposed to exclusivity. Even NEA and AFT locals do not object to it when they are in the minority; to do so would undermine exclusivity when their affiliates are the bargaining agent. The upshot is that the incumbent union usually negotiates the exclusive right to payroll deduction of dues, hence of PAC funds also.

In most school districts, payroll deduction and transmittal of PAC funds never surfaces as an issue. The contract merely states that the school district will deduct dues upon submission of a signed authorization from individual teachers. The dues authorization form, which is usually prepared by the union, routinely includes the PAC deductions. In any case, school boards rarely challenge the PAC deduction.

In political terms, school boards, public agencies, are collecting political funds for a private organization (the union PAC), at no cost to the union, which also exercises a veto power over any other PAC deduction. Regardless of its legality, the practice is unfair to teachers who wish to contribute to other PACs. One solution would be to prohibit government collection of political funds for private organizations; probably this cannot be achieved unless the Republicans hold the governorship and legislative majorities in both houses of the state's legislature. This situation prevailed in fifteen states after the 1994 elections, but legislation on PAC issues was introduced in only two states. One reason was the Republican lack of sophistication about the teacher unions; another was union support from a small but critical number of Republican legislators. Indeed, if the state association PACs contribute more to Republicans, more Republicans will join Democratic legislators to oppose the prohibition. Furthermore, the NEA/AFT are not the only public employee unions with a stake in payroll deduction of PAC contributions. If it is not feasible to prohibit payroll deduction of PAC funds, individual teachers should have the right to payroll deduction of PAC funds for the teacher's choice of PAC. As matters stand, only teacher union PACs enjoy the benefits of payroll deduction of PAC contributions.

As long as Democrats receive the overwhelming share of NEA/AFT PAC funds, we can anticipate more Republican bills to prohibit school board collection of PAC contributions. Even if unsuccessful, these bills reflect a basic strategic change among union opposition. Instead of a constant struggle to prevent union gains, prohibiting the PAC deductions would roll back their prerogatives and resources. Second, the strategy would force the NEA/AFT to devote more resources to protecting their revenue stream instead of expanding it. It frequently costs very little to introduce a bill but a great deal to oppose it successfully. In addition, bills to prohibit school boards from collecting union PAC funds could be a bargaining chip in the state legislatures. Legislators fearful of union opposition might be able to neutralize it by sunsetting agency fees or forcing the unions to reenact these statutory rights periodically instead of having to be concerned only about their repeal. Having to reenact the rights would force the unions to avoid opposition to legislators who could block reenactment. Similarly, more school boards are likely to propose elimination of PAC deductions in future negotiations, perhaps anticipating that the proposal will be dropped for union concessions. The unmistakable trend, however, is toward school board and legislative efforts to prohibit PAC deductions or to enable teachers to contribute to whatever PAC they wish.[7]

Government Relations (Lobbying)

All the state associations employ staff lobbyists. The California Teachers Association (CTA) sponsors about twenty bills a year but scrutinizes and follows every bill that relates to education. This can be several hundred bills a year, far more than any other organization can monitor. CTA sponsored legislation is categorized as follows:

Tier 1   CTA will exert maximum effort to pass. Example: Early retirement to be a permanent option.

Tier 2   CTA supports, but bill does not require maximum effort. Example: Accumulated sick leave to be credited to longevity for computing retirement benefits.

Tier 3   Limits use of credential fees for credential activities.[8]

Legislation introduced by others is reviewed by CTA's State Legislation Committee. The committee categorizes such legislation as follows:

Support	CTA supports the bill as vigorously as possible.
Approve	CTA supports but will not commit substantial resources to enactment.
Oppose	Defeat of bill is a high CTA priority.
Disapprove	CTA opposes but does not commit substantial resources.
Neutral	CTA has no position.
Watch	CTA will track the bill; future action dependent on amendments.[9]

Once its State Legislative Committee adopts a position, CTA's nine lobbyists orchestrate the effort to line up support for it. The acceptability of proposed changes, or of legislative deals, is the responsibility of the CTA president or board of directors. These legislative processes are aided and abetted by an impressive array of services that have whatever it takes to get the job done. A brief history of Proposition 98 illustrates this point.

In 1978, California enacted Proposition 13, an initiative that drastically reduced the availability of property taxes for school revenues. CTA had not been adequately prepared to oppose Proposition 13 or to deal with its consequences; perhaps the most important consequence was to shift most of the tax burden for education from local school boards to the state legislature. In the next ten years, CTA beefed up its political operations in order to circumvent Proposition 13 and assure education funding without a protracted legislative struggle every year. The eventual solution was Proposition 98, an initiative that committed about 40 percent of the state's revenues, other than special purpose funds, to public education.

The CTA campaign for Proposition 98 began in the fall of 1987, when CTA ran television spots on most California stations as well as some in Arizona and Nevada that reach California communities. The television spots emphasized class size because CTA polling revealed that only 11 percent of the California voters deemed large classes to be a problem. Within a few weeks, 42 percent of the voters perceived overcrowding as a major problem; subsequently, the campaign for Proposition 98 emphasized the urgent need to reduce class size.

Proposition 98 passed on November 8, 1988, by a margin of 128,000 votes out of a total of 9,128,000. The initiative drastically altered the state budget process by guaranteeing that 40 percent of state revenues would be allocated to public education. Naturally, other public employee unions and interest groups recognized that Proposition 98 would probably decrease their share of state revenues. Thus Proposition 98 was enacted over the opposition of other public employee unions facing the prospect of a shrinking pie. Its passage was a stunning display of political muscle.

The predictable sequel materialized soon thereafter. One month after the enactment, legislation was introduced to allocate half of new Proposition 98 funds to reducing class size. CTA successfully opposed the bill, arguing that it was an undesirable restriction on school board flexibility. Despite the CTA television campaign emphasizing the need to reduce class size, most of the new money from Proposition 98 was spent for higher teacher salaries and benefits.

Since enactment of Proposition 98, controversies over the California state budget have focused largely on efforts to suspend or weaken its provisions, such as by including child care in the services covered by the 40 percent allocation. When these efforts failed, California Governor Pete Wilson was unable to avoid a tax increase. The increase was a major factor in Wilson's inability to gain conservative support for his 1995 presidential campaign.

The Politics of "Nonpartisan" Elections

At the federal level, citizens do not vote on ballot initiatives or candidates for nonpartisan offices. In most states, they do, or at least the possibility exists. Furthermore, voters often vote for state officials, such as state treasurer, who exercise decisive influence on educational issues from time to time. Although no one can predict when the actions of such officials will be critical, state association support serves as a sort of insurance policy in this regard.

A remarkable example of how this pays off occurred in California in 1993. Educational voucher supporters were able to place Proposition 174, an initiative entitled "Parental Choice," on the November ballot. By law, the California Secretary of State must approve the initiative heading as reflective of its contents. After the CTA initiated legal action to require changes in the heading, March Fong Eu, the CTA endorsed candidate for Secretary of State, ordered that the heading be changed from "Parental Choice" to "Education Vouchers." In polling immediately thereafter, support for Proposition 174 dropped ten points—an outcome obviously anticipated by CTA strategists.

In fourteen states, the state superintendent of education is elected on a nonpartisan ballot. In these states, however, the teacher unions play an extremely important electoral role. For example, in California, the CTA has consistently supported "nonpartisan" candidates drawn from the ranks of the Democratic Party. In 1982, Bill Honig changed his registration from Democratic to no party affiliation before running successfully for state superintendent of public instruction. After ten years of office, he was forced to resign over conflict of interest charges in 1992. The nonpartisan posture of the department of education he left behind was an issue in 1993 when California voted on Proposition 174. In the critical three month period before the election, department staff made over 300 telephone calls to the antivoucher forces. About one-third (113) were made to paid legal and political consultants to the antivoucher campaign; almost as many to the CTA. During this period, there were only four calls from the state department of education to the campaign office of the provoucher forces.[10]

As anyone knowledgeable about politics can attest, most "nonpartisan" state officers are anything but. Delaine Eastin, the "nonpartisan" state superintendent of education in California in 1996, also turned out to be the cochairman of the credentials committee at the 1996 Democratic convention. In an earlier day, the state superintendency was held by Republicans just as partisan as the Democratic office holders. The point is that to appreciate the full range of state education association political influence, we cannot overlook elections to nominally nonpartisan offices.

In this connection, one other union political target is virtually overlooked in the media but constitutes an extremely important source of union influence. I refer to elections to the state teacher retirement boards. In 1995, these boards controlled the investment of $342 billion of teacher retirement funds. Most of the boards include a few state officials but a majority of board members are elected directly by the states' teachers. The teacher unions have demonstrated repeatedly their support for "social investing," that is, investing to fulfill the unions' social objectives instead of maximizing the return on the investments. In practice, this leads to disinvestment in companies that are involved in privatization efforts, or pursue some other practice opposed by the unions.

Because the state unions have access to the teacher address lists, it is practically impossible to elect teacher representatives not endorsed by the state teacher unions. In view of the underfunding of the pension funds, and the fact that the returns on investment are inversely related to the proportion of teacher elected members on the boards, the union role in these matters deserves a great deal more attention than it has received thus far.[11]

Political Training

The state associations spend substantial amounts for training on collective bargaining and political action. The CTA's major political training effort is an annual one week workshop for teacher political leaders and activists. Teachers are charged, but most costs are subsidized by the CTA. A comprehensive curriculum covers the main aspects of political campaigns:

candidate identification	recruitment and training
coalition building	right-wing extremists
local PACs	school board elections
recruiting, organizing and managing volunteers	targeting voters
	telephone banks

Workshop faculty include legislators, consultants, and lobbyists. No other state organization trains such a large group of political activists every year; in fact, the CTA effort overshadows the training efforts of both political parties in California. Thus, over a period of years, the CTA trains an impressive number of sophisticated political operatives, with considerable time to utilize their skills in political campaigns. These activists are backed up by equally impressive technological capabilities; for example, CTA maintains state-wide voter registration records enhanced with phone numbers and demographic data. With the ability to reach a voter pool of 500,000 teachers and retirees, including their spouses, CTA can conduct an impressive grassroots campaign on short notice.

The Political Role of UniServ Directors

Chapter 4 pointed out that UniServ directors are union business agents under a different label. Their political role is at least as important as their bargaining role; as Chapter 11 will show, the allocation of UniServ time between collective bargaining and political matters is a frequently litigated issue. In court cases involving the allocation of UniServ time, the CTA asserts that more than two-thirds is devoted to collective bargaining, that is, activities chargeable to nonmembers. With this in mind, it is instructive to see what internal union documents have to say about the matter.

The UniServ funding agreements between the NEA and the state associations, and between the state and local associations, emphasize the political responsibilities of UniServ directors. These responsibilities include directing local association political activities. Where multiple local associations are served by the same UniServ director, the latter is supervised by a "UniServ Council" as well as a state association manager. State association model bylaws for UniServ councils call for four meetings every year. In California, the suggested agenda for the first meeting is as follows:

First Meeting Agenda

1. Endorsement of school candidates;
2. Adoption of unit policies as appropriate;
3. Consideration of bylaws amendments;
4. Bargaining update;
5. Political action activities.

The recommended schedule for UniServ units' political program is as follows:

Political Action Program

Goal I: Unit will actively participate in campaigns of Unit endorsed candidates and issues.	September–November
Goal II: Unit will work cooperatively with CTA in the statewide priorities.	Ongoing
Goal III: PAC will design and implement biannual fund raising drives.	Fall and Spring
Goal IV: Unit will endeavor to implement payroll deductions for Unit PAC.	By February and ongoing thereafter
Goal V: Unit will prepare for upcoming elections by interviewing candidates.	August–September
Goal VI: Unit will support lobbying efforts of CTA and NEA.[12]	Ongoing

In California, every local association is assigned to a state association staff member; the latter has primary but not exclusive responsibility for monitoring the effectiveness of the local associations. This oversight function includes the following:

E. Political Action

1. *Development and implementation of effective local political action programs,* including organization of local chapter/unit mechanisms for political activity and integration of local political programs with organizing and bargaining priorities of the local unit.
2. *Organization of local chapter/unit participating in CTA/NEA political action arms,* including all programs which incorporate legislative advocacy, legislative contact systems, and candidate endorsement procedures.
3. *Promotion of and recruitment for individual memberships in CTA/NEA political action arms,* including organization of participation and recruitment campaigns for CTA-ABC and NEA-PAC.[13]

The NEA's *Series in Practical Politics* also refers frequently to the political assistance provided by UniServ directors. For instance, the guide to the Congressional Contact Team program points out that "UniServ staff help coordinate, advise, and assist with member lobbying activities on a Congressional District basis." CCT members are advised that UniServ directors can help with newsletter production, flyer production, bulletin boards, association meetings, telephone campaigns, and association caucuses. Decisions to involve the public "should be made in cooperation with UniServ staff." Also, according to NEA guidelines, UniServ directors are supposed to supervise all fundraising for NEA-PAC.[14]

NEA-PAC guidelines also recommend that UniServ directors participate in the interview of candidates for elective office. Because of their experience, training, longevity, and the fact that they are the custodians of the union's political memory, the UniServ directors play a major role in all political activities at the local level.

It would be difficult to overestimate the significance of this fact. In nineteen states, all or some nonmembers of teacher unions are required to pay the union for collective bargaining services. Legally, nonmembers are not required to pay for union political activities. Therefore, the amount of UniServ time devoted to political activities is a matter of intensive legal and financial controversy, with hundreds of millions of dollars riding on the outcome.

Chapter 10 will argue that UniServ directors devote most of their time to political matters. Estimating conservatively, the NEA and the its affiliates employ about 1,800 UniServ directors and managers. On the basis of NEA publications discussing the political tasks and achievements of UniServ directors, I estimate that at least one-third of UniServ time is devoted to political action. This means that the UniServ program employs the equivalent of 600 full-time political professionals, not counting their support staff, such as secretaries. Bear in mind, however, that the UniServ program does not include the NEA and state affiliate staff in lobbying and related political activities. Regardless of the precise numbers, the NEA and its affiliates employ more political operatives on a full-time equivalent basis than the Republican and Democratic parties combined. When we add AFT staff who perform the same tasks as UniServ representatives, and with the same political duties and orientation, the NEA/AFT political presence is impressive indeed.

The Political Effectiveness of State Education Associations

Assessing the political influence of a state education association is a complex task. Knowing how much the association contributed to political campaigns is not very helpful unless we know how much other parties have contributed. Furthermore, campaign funds can be spent foolishly or wisely. Win/lose records are suspect; the endorsements may have gone to candidates who would have won without the endorsements. In short, we cannot assess influence realistically apart from consideration of several complex factors that bear on the issue.[15] Before addressing SEA political influence directly, let me cite some anecdotal evidence I observed at first hand.

Since his election in 1993, Jersey City Mayor Bret Schundler has been considered a rising star in national Republican circles. Because of corruption and academic deficiencies, the Jersey City schools were being administered by a state appointed superintendent when Schundler took office. Elected mayor in a Democratic city with large minority populations, Schundler proposed a school choice plan applicable only to Jersey City.

Schundler's school choice plan received widespread national attention. With a Republican governor and both houses in the New Jersey legislature controlled by Republicans, it was widely assumed that the New Jersey legislature would enact Schundler's school choice plan, especially since New Jersey Governor Christine Whitman had expressed support for it. For about two years, Schundler delivered speeches all over the United States on the merits of his proposal. In addition to Schundler's staff, the Heritage Foundation assigned a staff member to work with him on legislation and coalition building. Schundler even established a national organization to create grassroots support for it.

Since the plan would have applied only to Jersey City, it was hardly a threat to public education in New Jersey. Nevertheless, the New Jersey Education Association, aided by a million dollar contribution from the NEA, crushed the plan in the New Jersey legislature. After initially expressing support for school choice, Governor Whitman held off support, suggesting that it should be introduced only one to two grades a year in Jersey City. A school choice plan that can expand only one to two grades a year in a single school district is about as feeble as such plans can get, but not a single member of the New Jersey legislature would introduce the required legislation. While Schundler and Whitman supporters argued over the Governor's tepid support, the NJEA and NEA initiated a million dollar media campaign to improve the image of public education in New Jersey. Eventually, Whitman appointed a fifteen member commission to study school choice; the commission's recommendations merely replaced one cosmetic school choice plan with another cosmetic plan.

Alabama, which is a nonbargaining and right-to-work state, provides another remarkable example of state association political power. In the first state senate after adoption of the 1901 constitution, lawyers cast 71.5 percent of the votes. Forty years later, it was not unusual for twenty-five of the thirty-five senate seats to be filled by lawyers; meanwhile, only a handful of legislators listed teaching as their occupation. By 1984, however, the Alabama legislature was much more responsive to legislators controlled through and by the Alabama Education Association. By 1985, there were only twenty-two lawyers out of a total of 140 legislators; teacher membership was up to forty. In 1987, 58 of 140 members were active or retired teachers, former teachers, or spouses of teachers. A 1991 survey by the Alabama Alliance of Business and Industry showed that 35 of 140 state legislators were recipients of income from school districts or colleges. The AEA executive director twice narrowly missed being elected governor in the 1990s. AEA power slipped a bit from its peak in the 1980s, only because its dominance in the 1980s led business and agricultural interests to seek more balance in Alabama politics.[16]

Apart from such examples, and there are several, what conclusions, if any, can be drawn about the political effectiveness of the state education associations? The simple, unassailable answer to the question is as follows: In a large majority of states, the state education association affiliated with the NEA is one of the three most effective interest groups active in state politics. There is overwhelming agreement on this point among political scientists who have studied interest group participation in state politics. The leading study of the topic was conducted by dividing the United States into four regions which included all the states and applied the same criteria to all. Seventy-eight political scientists participated in the study over a five year period. The results in the thirteen midwestern states were typical.

State teacher associations were included among the most effective lobbies in eleven of the thirteen states. In fact, they were categorized as the most effective in ten states, which is more than any other interest group. As Hrebenor and Thomas point out:

> The rise of public sector groups representing state and local employees and public school teachers has changed the balance of power in state legislatures across the region. Public employee associations and education groups have in some states become the most powerful lobbies.
>
> Teachers and, to a lesser extent, public employees are the new face of labor in the Midwest. Overall, in the Midwest the top ranked interest groups or interests are not surprising: Teachers, bankers, labor, business, lawyers, and doctors. Perhaps most interesting is the fact that teachers rank as the most effective interest group in three of the four regions; they are supplanted by business groups only in northeastern states ... all in all, a wealth of subtle differences exists among the various states in the Midwest, the fifty individual states, and the four regions. But in the final analysis (at least in this regional study) what is remarkable are the growing similarities among quite different states and regions as well as the increasing consequence of interest group politics on the state level with those on the national level.[17]

As impressive as this evaluation is, it understates NEA/AFT political influence. It does not touch upon their enormous influence in local politics, especially in school board elections. Nor does it convey their influence at the national level, or among private organizations, such as the National PTA, People for the American Way, and Americans United for Separation of Church and State. It does not convey the heavy influence of the state teacher unions over the investment policies of the state teacher pension funds; this influence often leads to making investment decisions involving several billion dollars on the

TABLE 6.1

Most Effective Midwestern Interests, by number of states

Interest	Number of Midwestern states where interest is judged to be most effective	Number of Midwestern states where interest is judged to be of second level of effectiveness	Total Rank
1. Schoolteachers' organizations	10	1	21
2. Bankers' associations (includes savings and loan associations)	8	5	21
3. Labor associations (includes AFL-CIO)	8	2	18
4. General business organizations (chambers of commerce)	7	4	18
5. Lawyers (bar association/trial lawyers' organization)	4	7	15
6. General farm organizations (mainly farm bureaus)	3	9	15
7. Doctors	4	4	12
8. Labor (individual unions, Teamsters, UAW, etc.)	5	1	11
9. Manufacturers	4	3	11
10. Retailers (companies and associations)	4	3	11
11. Utility companies and associations (electric, gas, telephone, and water companies)	3	5	11
12. Health care groups	2	7	11
13. Individual banks and financial institutions	2	6	10
14. Realtors' associations	3	3	9
15. Insurance	1	6	8
16. K–12 education interests	3	1	7
17. Universities and colleges (institutions and personnel)	2	3	7
17. General local government	2	3	7
19. Antiabortion groups	2	2	6
20. State and local government employees	2	1	5
21. Liquor, beer, and wine	1	3	5
22. Mining companies and associations	1	3	4
23. Agricultural commodity organizations (stock growers, grain growers, etc.)	1	2	4
23. Oil and gas companies and associations	1	2	4
25. Environmentalists	1	1	3
25. Taxpayers' groups	1	1	3
28. Truckers/Private transportation	1	0	2
28. State agencies	1	0	2
28. Sporting, hunting and fishing, and antigun control groups	1	0	2
31. Senior citizens	0	2	2
31. Railroads	0	2	2
33. Gaming interests (racetracks, casinos, and lotteries)	0	1	1
33. Newspapers/Media	0	1	1
33. Tourist industry	0	1	1

Note: Scores were calculated by allocating 2 points for each "most effective" ranking and 1 point for each "second level of effectiveness" placement and adding totals. Where a tie in total points occurs, interests are ranked according to the number of "most effective" placements (where possible). Placement of interests in "most effective" and "second level effectiveness" categories was determined by authors of the individual state studies.

Source: Ronald J. Hrebenor and Clive S. Thomas, *Interest Group Politics in the Midwestern States* (Ames: Iowa State University Press, 1993), p. 348.

basis of union social or political agendas, not the maximum return to retired teachers.[18] Indisputably, the state teacher unions are a major political force whose influence extends far beyond educational policy.

Political Effectiveness: The NEA Perspective

In view of their close relationships, the NEA and its state affiliates frequently evaluate their political efforts jointly. In 1993, the NEA and its National Council of State Education Associations (NCSEA), commissioned a study of their political effectiveness in the 1992 elections. The purpose of the study was "to evaluate the strengths and weaknesses of the Campaign '92 activities of both the NEA and the state affiliates."

The study was carried out by Mellman, Lazarus, and Lake, a Democratic political consulting firm. It included interviews with NEA's Government Relations staff at NEA and the two NEA field offices. The field work included interviews with state affiliate staff, candidates, party caucuses, chairpersons or members of party central committees, and various interest groups in six states (Colorado, Florida, Indiana, Ohio, Pennsylvania and Washington). In this way, the assessment included one state from each NEA region, including four states targeted by the Clinton–Gore Campaign. Interviews were also conducted with two focus groups of NEA members in three states (Colorado, Florida, and Ohio). One focus group was composed of Clinton voters; the other of Bush–Perot voters. These interviews were the main source of feedback from NEA members.

On the "success" side, five features of the NEA campaign were identified:

- The dollar amounts raised for the campaign.
- The commitment of NEA staff was "a vital resource" for the state associations, and in some instances, for the coordination with the Clinton–Gore campaign.
- The Rapid Response Team at NEA headquarters was so effective that NEA's state affiliates often had campaign materials before the state Clinton–Gore offices.
- Coordination with the Clinton–Gore Campaign maximized effective use of NEA resources.
- The early date to assemble the state directors (June 1992) was crucially important to success; the report recommended an even earlier date for future campaigns. Every state and NEA staff concurred in this recommendation.

The most important of fourteen recommendations for future action was for more and better training for members, UniServ and Government Relations staff, and state leadership. Some other highlights were as follows:

- An earlier start would help to get key personnel to buy into the program earlier.
- The need for a mechanism to resolve disputes over multijurisdictional endorsements.
- The state affiliate, jointly with NEA or by itself, should deliver the NEA contribution to the party or coordinated campaign. This will help the state affiliate claim credit, and "have a seat at the table" during the campaign and after the election of successful candidates.
- Several daily LAN-mail updates should be used in the 1996 campaign for instantaneous transmission in the final stages of the campaign. ("LAN" refers to Local Area Network, an electronic communication system-ML.)
- A new materials distribution mechanism at NEA headquarters is needed, but compliance with state laws should be assured. When there is uncertainty about the priority of distribution, the materials are not distributed down to the building level.
- In communicating with members, use "recommendation"; with the public at large, "feel free to call it an endorsement." Be sure to provide members with backup that explains the rationale for the "recommendation."
- The list of issues discussed in mailings should be short and easily followed.

The focus group findings emphasized that members tend to view state and local issues as the most important, since most funding decisions are made at these levels. Information from state and local associations was also regarded as more reliable and useful.

Despite the elaborate endorsement process, many members felt that their views had not been sought, and resented having NEA "dictate" their choice of candidate. The report points out that these reactions are common among national labor unions and professional organizations. Finally, to validate the endorsement process, the report recommends more feedback on what candidates have done to justify the endorsement. This would help to avoid the view that endorsements are worthless because candidates don't keep their promises.[19]

The NEA/NCSEA study confirms what is already evident; the teacher unions are one of the most powerful interest groups in U.S. politics.

7

THE WAR AGAINST COMPETITION
AND CONTRACTING OUT

The tremendous power of the teacher unions raises several questions. How do the unions maintain their power? What are the threats to it, and how do the unions deal with these threats? In this chapter we address these questions with respect to the biggest threat to union power, to wit: competition.

First, a few definitions, "contracting out" refers to school board decisions to purchase services instead of providing them through school board employees. "Outsourcing" and "subcontracting" are other terms used to denote this practice, but they are not commonly used in education. "Privatization" is frequently used, but it denotes much more than contracting out. For example, educational vouchers are a form of privatization but they raise a host of issues different from those involved in contracting out per se. Thus, when used here, "privatization" will be synonymous with contracting out even though the terms are not synonymous in other contexts.

Prefatorily, we should note the pervasive importance of contracting out. In deciding whether to eat in a restaurant or at home, we are deciding whether to contract out cooking and washing dishes or perform these tasks ourselves. The right to choose among such options is extremely important; being deprived of it would destroy effective management of our personal affairs. Similarly, contracting out issues arise in companies as well as individuals. Should the company hire full-time legal counsel or employ outside counsel? Should the company print its annual report or should it contract with a commercial printer to do so? And so on.

In both the public and private sectors, employers face intense opposition to contracting out from the labor unions representing employees adversely affected by the practice. As unions, the NEA/AFT try to control teacher labor markets by (1) requiring all teachers to be employed pursuant to a union contract, (2) increasing the market for member services, (3) restricting access to teacher employment except on terms acceptable to the union, and (4) minimizing internal conflicts that might threaten group solidarity on basic objectives. Unions everywhere pursue these objectives. What distinguishes teacher from private sector unions is the way the fact of public employment affects their efforts to prevent contracting out. In the private sector, unions have gone on strike over the issue, but strikes in public education are a different ball game for these reasons:

1. The outcome of teacher strikes depends on the mobilization of public and political opinion. The outcome of private sector strikes depends on the economic pressures on the parties.

2. In a private sector strike, union pressure is based upon union ability to inflict economic losses on employers; in teacher strikes, school boards often save money.

3. Teacher unions frequently play a major role in electing management, that is, the school board members. With few exceptions, no such opportunity exists in the private sector.

4. Ordinarily, school management cannot lock out teachers in an impasse whereas this is legally possible in the private sector. Teachers are required to work a certain number of days each school year. If teachers are locked out, the days have to be made up. In the private sector, there is no legal requirement to make up time lost as the result of a strike.

5. There is no legal duty of loyalty to the employer in public education. The reason is that public employers may not discipline teachers for exercise of their First Amendment rights. A teacher can safely assert: "We have the worst educational program anywhere." A private sector employee who said publicly, "We make the worst widgets on the market," in order to achieve concessions in bargaining might be subject to disciplinary action.

6. Inasmuch as they can't be locked out, teachers may threaten to strike. If the school district hires substitutes, the teachers show up for work. If the district does employ substitutes, a small number of teachers on strike can disrupt a school district. In contrast, private sector employers can protect themselves against such tactics, by building up their inventories to fulfill orders during a complete shutdown of manufacturing operations.

To be sure, there are exceptions and qualifications in these differences. Certainly, not every difference between teachers and private sector bargaining enhances the bargaining power of teacher unions. In the private sector, employers are legally free to pass on the costs of concessions to their customers. Competitive pressures may limit what employers are willing to do, but they have the legal freedom to pass costs on to consumers. In education, there are no competitive pressures on employers, but school boards seldom have untrammeled legal freedom to pass on higher costs to the taxpayers. The school board may need voter approval to raise taxes, or increased appropriations from the city council, or more state aid.

Because they are unions, the NEA/AFT try to prevent school districts from contracting out work performed by union members. In practice, school districts seldom contract out instruction, so it is not obvious why the NEA should be so concerned about the issue.[1]

In the NEA, opposition to contracting out is a consequence of its transformation from an association dominated by school administrators to a public sector union. The NEA was founded by school administrators, and until the 1960s, administrators were in de facto control over association policies. Obviously, school administrators had no interest in restricting their rights to contract for services. In conjunction with the widespread attitude that teachers were "professionals," hence not to be combined organizationally with school bus drivers and cafeteria workers, most state education associations ignored contracting out until the 1980s. Let us see why their earlier indifference has changed to all-out opposition in recent years.

The NEA and AFT are producers of representational services. And like producers generally, the NEA and AFT seek to find other markets for their services. What might these other markets be?

The AFT has always tried to organize support personnel, but its opportunities to do so are severely limited by the fact that it does not have a presence in most districts. Nevertheless, because the AFT is primarily a large city union, and large cities tend to employ large numbers of support personnel, the latter are an important constituency in the AFT. This constituency resulted partly from the increase in paraprofessionals funded by federal programs; when the author was a candidate for AFT president in 1962, support personnel were virtually invisible in both the AFT and NEA, and there was no program, actual or proposed to address their problems. Indeed, there was considerable opposition in both unions to recruiting support personnel even though it was permissible under the AFT constitution. This attitude changed in the late 1960s, partly for defensive reasons; AFT leaders feared that if the federation did not organize support personnel, AFT ability to shut down school districts during a strike would be severely impaired.

Unlike the AFT, the NEA has not tried to organize employees outside of educational institutions and school districts. For this reason, school support personnel constitute the major growth area for the NEA in the near future. First, U.S. school districts employ about two million educational support personnel. Second, the NEA is advantageously situated to organize these employees. Since the NEA already has a local affiliate in most school districts, its organizational structure needs only minor changes to accommodate educational support personnel. Although some of its state and local affiliates are not enthusiastic about enrolling support personnel, the NEA is now making an all-out effort to organize them. NEA governance documents now require or facilitate representation from support personnel; NEA publications feature their problems and the services they receive.

Clearly, educational support personnel can shore up the unions' revenue base. The question is: What can the NEA and AFT do for the support personnel? The NEA/AFT answer is loud and clear: "We can protect you from privatization." Whether such protection is needed is not as important as whether the NEA/AFT can convince support personnel that it is. And, as we have seen, the unions are well prepared on this point; to put it bluntly, they do very well in the fear business.

In 1995, the NEA established the Center for Educational Support Personnel as the organizational focus for this group. Prior to this, the NEA had already published two manuals on how to prevent contracting out. *The People's Cause* had been published by the NEA's Center for the Preservation of Public Education; *Contracting Out: Strategies for Fighting Back* by the Affiliate Services Division.[2] Both demonstrate the scope and intensity of the NEA campaign against contracting out.

According to *The People's Cause*, the "Warning Signs" that privatization may be imminent include school board members or administrators who are members of "far right" organizations; support the introduction of competition or market forces to the public school system; are heavily supported by business; are being criticized for poorly run schools; and are facing severe budget problems.

If the administrator is new to the district, local union leaders are urged to check with the union in the previous district for signs of the malignancy. Board meetings should be monitored carefully "for any talk of privatization or schools for profit"; likewise so are meetings of the "Chamber of Commerce, Rotary Club or other business organizations."

Another warning sign is "unknown visitors or representatives from private companies conducting tours of school grounds." Management visits to other school districts that have adopted some form of privatization are another; and meetings with private company representatives are still another warning sign. School district employees are warned not to fall into the trap of accepting privatization that doesn't affect them directly; in fact, all efforts to privatize public services are to be regarded as a warning sign.[3] One can only wonder whether local leaders have any time left for teaching, negotiating, or home life after they run down all these "warning signs."

After a similar list, *Contracting Out* points out that "Many locals approach the problem as they would an organizing, contract, or political campaign." The guide then suggests an organization plan that includes a steering committee and two groups—one for strategy and internal communications, the other for community outreach.

Under "research," *Contracting Out* recommends investigation of administrators encouraging contracting out and suggests that "The local may want to meet with these people immediately and bring to bear whatever political pressure it can." Other suggestions include identifying local merchants who may lose contracts to provide equipment or supplies, efforts to tie a board member or administrator to a bidder, and careful scrutiny of the procedures for soliciting and reviewing bids. Locals are advised to make all requests for information in writing and to request assistance from the UniServ staff. The guide also includes several suggestions for investigating the companies which may be involved; for example, "The goal is to find information that casts doubt on the company's . . . social responsibility. For instance, you might uncover investments in South Africa or poor environmental practices." A list of references and resources to help locals find negative information about contractors is included under "Research Materials."

The advice on tactics is not very pleasant reading for school boards and contractors. It includes:

- Suggestions to contractors that "bidding may not be worthwhile";
- Ideas for rallies, demonstrations, picketing, buttons, billboards, leaflets;
- Signs with "a catchy slogan or a question such as "Why does (board of education member's name) want to give our jobs away?";
- Refusing voluntary overtime or optional assignments;
- Following a supervisor's instructions to the letter;
- Taking no responsibility for solving problems that arise;
- Following all administrative rules strictly;
- Refusing to "make do" with inadequate or inappropriate equipment and supplies;
- Referring all questions and complaints to whoever came up with the idea for contracting out or the main office of the contractor being considered.

No mention is made of the fact that union sponsorship of these activities would normally constitute violation of a no-strike clause in a collective bargaining contract or of a statutory prohibition of strikes. Instead, *Contracting Out* pays extensive attention to media relations; the NEA is well aware of the fact that controversies over contracting out are struggles for favorable public opinion.

An entire chapter is devoted to how to use collective bargaining to prevent contracting out. The guide includes model contract language to ensure that no employee loses a job or overtime or any other benefit of any kind. The following model language is proposed as the most desirable protection: "The duties of any bargaining unit member or the responsibilities of any position in the bargaining unit shall not be altered, increased, or transferred to persons not covered by this agreement."

To say the least, *Contracting Out* is thorough. It suggests six possible legal strategies to block contracting out:

1. Filing unfair labor practice charges over school district failure to bargain on contracting out issues.
2. Violations of civil service laws, state constitutions, and city and county charters.
3. Challenges to school board authority to contract out.
4. Violations of prevailing wage requirements.
5. Violations or neglect of affirmative action/minority set asides. The guide suggests that "the association may need to file the suit jointly with a minority contractor or group of contractors."
6. Violations of residency requirements.

Contracting Out also suggests that school district employees who become employees of a private contractor may have bargaining rights under the National Labor Relations Act. In the states without a bargaining law, this possibility has deterred some school districts from contracting out; they prefer to deal with school district employees who do not have bargaining rights instead of a private sector labor force which might obtain them. Notwithstanding the fact that the contracting company, not the school district, would have to bargain with the union, school management sometimes fears that the presence of a private sector union would be an undesirable precedent in district affairs. To take advantage of these fears, UniServ directors are urged to help the newly privatized employees exercise their NLRA rights. By doing so, they increase the pressures on school districts not to contract out in the first place.

The company that manages to negotiate a service contract despite NEA opposition may discover its troubles have just begun. At least, that is the message *Contracting Out* delivers—loud and clear. To be blunt about it, *Contracting Out* includes several suggestions on how newly privatized school district employees can sabotage company operations. In fact, even when a district contracts only for management services, *Contracting Out* advises various actions intended to weaken the contractor's viability.

To facilitate campaigns against contracting out, *Contracting Out* provides model language for billboards, newspaper advertisements, radio and television spots, collective bargaining contracts, letters to the editor, and the like. These messages are drafted on the basis of extensive polling and experience in opposing contracting out. Some are even available in foreign languages to insure complete penetration of target audiences.

AFT Opposition to Contracting Out

The AFT's antiprivatization program does not differ materially from the NEA's. Pro forma, the AFT's public position was that contracting out should be considered on a case-by-case basis. In practice, the AFT rarely if ever identifies a case in which it approves contracting out. Furthermore, the goal statement of the AFT's Paraprofessional and School Related Personnel Division includes the following: "We also consider privatization a violation of democratic principles since it places in the hands of private industry the responsibility the public has entrusted to its public officials thereby lessening the degree to which voters can hold these officials accountable for the proper administration of public services. Therefore, we are committed to keeping school services in the public sector by fighting efforts toward privatization."[4] Obviously, this is not a case-by-case approach to contracting out.

The AFT maintains a hotline on privatization and publishes a variety of brochures and pamphlets denigrating it in every way imaginable. AFT training programs and publications on how to block contracting out would be virtually interchangeable with the NEA's; a 1995 AFT five day "Privatization Workshop" was designed to provide participants with:

- a detailed campaign calendar;
- models for developing alternative plans;
- strategies to identify and mobilize allies in the community;
- volunteer recruitment plans;
- effective media strategies; and
- campaign literature plans, with one flyer or newsletter in the works.

Locals were urged to send two representatives who would participate with AFT staff "to develop a strategic campaign plan" based on previous campaigns.

Historically, the AFT's antiprivatization efforts preceded the NEA's. On a bulletin board of AFT on-line, the AFT's members-only forum on the Internet, the following message appears:

"Although touted as a new education reform, privatization has a long history. Twenty years ago, for example, a strategy called 'performance contracting' was sponsored by the federal Office of Economic Opportunity (OEO). In this scheme [sic], private firms were hired to raise student achievement in public schools, with their payment dependent on higher student test scores. The effort was a disaster. Classrooms were in chaos, and student achievement did not improve. One contractor admitted to trying to raise student test scores by teaching the students answers to specific test questions."[5]

It is instructive to compare the AFT's version of the project with the following analysis of it published by the Brookings Institution:

> . . . The United Federation of Teachers was as opposed as its parent to performance contracting, and its president, Albert Shanker, announced on the radio that he believed the OEO Bronx program to be illegal and threatened action to prevent its continuation. The teachers in the experimental schools took this cue and were continually at loggerheads with the contractor, Learning Foundations. There were reports that they threw some of the Learning Foundations equipment out of second-story windows and told students to throw away their parent questionnaires. Discipline in the junior high schools involved in the experiment became so bad at one point early in the fall that all testing and instruction were halted and a full-time policeman had to be stationed in one of them. Instruction could only be resumed when the president of Learning Foundations, Fran Tarkenton, at that time also quarterback of the New York Giants football team, was able to rally community support around the project. Even so, records from the project are very incomplete. The tests at the end of the school year were given in a ballroom a few blocks from the school and a new form of attrition was introduced as students walked from the school to the testing room. Moreover, some of the ninth grade control students were not post-tested because the school principal assigned Battelle a testing date that was after the school year was over, the parent questionnaires and student information cards were never filled out, and the project director kept very poor records of who was and who was not in the program. . . . The situation in Hartford and Philadelphia was almost as disorganized.[6]

Parenthetically, the AFT also represented teachers in Hartford and Philadelphia at the time. Whether or not the AFT sabotaged the experiment in New York City (and the evidence is overwhelming that it did), the UFT under Shanker's leadership clearly did everything it could to block and then to disrupt the experiment in order to ensure its failure. Not surprisingly, a report on the "experiment," if one can call it that, by the General Accounting Office (GAO) concluded that:

"Because of a number of shortcomings in both the design and implementation of the experiment, it is our opinion that the questions as to the merits of performance contracting versus traditional educational methods remain unanswered."[7]

Another independent evaluation by the Battelle Institution reached essentially the same conclusion.[8] With no shame, the AFT repeatedly cites the OEO project as proof that contracting out instruction has been tried and found to be unsuccessful.

Strategic Considerations

If necessary, the unions will spend huge amounts to thwart contracting out in specific situations. In Hartford, Connecticut, the AFT conducted an intensive campaign to terminate the school board's contract with Education Alternatives, Inc. (EAI). The school board's interest in contracting out was partly due to the fact that the average 1994–95 teacher salary in Hartford was $58,800, not including an additional 28 to 33 percent of salary for fringe benefits. Meanwhile, academic achievement in the district was dismal indeed; just prior to the primary election in October 1995, the state revealed that only four of 771 Hartford students "fulfilled grade level expectations" in all four subject areas of the Connecticut Academic Performance Test. Such data had led the Hartford school board, a nonideological board that was predominantly Democratic, to consider contracting out.

Notwithstanding these considerations, the AFT went ballistic in its efforts to terminate the EAI contract. The AFT:

- Assigned union staff to foster community opposition to the contractor;
- Repeatedly criticized the school board and EAI in expensive advertisements in the *New York Times;*
- Published and disseminated flyers opposed to contracting out generally and to EAI specifically;
- Used teacher leave benefits to campaign against supporters of contracting out;
- Subsidized travel to Hartford by parents allegedly dissatisfied with EAI's performance in Baltimore;
- Contributed to purchase of a $50,000 bus used by the Hartford Federation of Teachers for "community outreach." The bus was used to help register sympathetic voters with fifty Hartford teachers serving as election registrars. In addition, it was used to transport union supporters to school and school board meetings where they could support Hartford Federation of Teachers positions.
- Sponsored and supported anti-privatization candidates in the Hartford school board elections.[9]

The foregoing by no means includes all the AFT efforts to oppose contracting out in Hartford. Despite the massive union effort, however, a board majority after the election was willing to continue the contract with EAI, provided that disagreements over costs could be resolved. When the board and EAI were unable to resolve the disagreements, the board, weary of the unending controversy, terminated the contract on January 16, 1996. As in the New York City case, the AFT proclaimed the termination a vindication of its foresight and the evils of contracting out. School boards elsewhere might draw a much different conclusion, to wit: that it is much easier to terminate an independent contractor than highly paid, but unsatisfactory, tenured teachers protected by a union willing to engage in sabotage if need be. One year after the contract was terminated, the Connecticut legislature enacted a state takeover of the Hartford schools, replacing the board with seven trustees appointed by the governor and legislative leaders. The "experiment" that was never really tried was indeed the last chance for the Hartford board of education to reverse the abysmal state of public education in Hartford.

It is ridiculous to regard EAI's experience in Baltimore and Hartford as "experiments" or even as evidence on most contracting out issues. If an "experiment," what hypothesis was being tested? Whether privatization in a large urban district over the all-out opposition of the AFT can succeed? The AFT's sabotage of the "experiments" in the 1970s should have been sufficient to discover that the answer is negative. Even in the absence of union opposition failure would not constitute persuasive evidence on the issue. Dozens of automobile companies were unsuccessful and went out of business in the early days of the automobile industry. We could hardly conclude, however, that these failures demonstrated the imperative need for the government to manufacture automobiles.

In addition to its own antiprivatization program, the AFT draws upon the AFL-CIO's Public Employee Department (PED) for assistance. PED membership consists of the thirty-five AFL-CIO unions that enroll some public employees. Prior to his death in 1997, AFT President Albert Shanker had served as PED president and had been one of its eight executive vice-presidents for several years.

Understandably, PED is a major center of antiprivatization activity. One of its publications is the *Human Costs of Contracting Out: A Survival Guide for Public Employees,* a highly sophisticated antiprivatization manual.[10] The manual includes a list of union publications opposed to privatization and strategies for intimidating potential contractors; for example, the AFL-CIO's Food and Allied Service Trades Department publishes *The Manual of Corporate Investigation,* a detailed procedure for investigating companies providing services to public employers.

The Good Faith Issue

NEA/AFT/AFL-CIO efforts to prohibit contracting out emphasize public policy reasons, not employer or union benefits, as the rationale for the prohibitions. Paradoxically, these unions have embraced contracting out when it was in their interest to do so. For instance, AFL-CIO unions insisted upon contracting out in the 1950s when the federal highway program was under consideration. At that time, the unions feared that the federal government would utilize federal employees instead of private contractors to build the interstate highway system. To preclude any such eventuality, the construction unions, which dominated the AFL-CIO, insisted that highway construction be contracted out.

In their own operations, both the NEA and AFT and their affiliates frequently utilize service companies, including nonunion ones, instead of their own employees to provide various services.[11] As a matter of fact, well over 10 percent of NEA expenditures are for contracted services.[12]

A striking example of union inconsistency on the issue relates to Robert H. Chanin, the NEA's general counsel. As general counsel, Chanin had been an NEA employee from 1968 to 1970, when he became a partner in Bredhoff and Kaiser, a law firm that represents labor unions. Through Bredhoff and Kaiser, Chanin continues to serve as NEA's general counsel as an independent contractor. Although the NEA now employs ten staff attorneys, Chanin very probably earns much more money as a contractor than he did, or would have, as an NEA employee. In this connection, NEA and AFT contracts with unions representing their employees allow the NEA and AFT to contract out—perhaps another reason why the NEA/AFT do not publicize these contracts.

The state NEA affiliates frequently employ part-time negotiators—and do so partly because the part-time negotiators do not receive the fringe benefits paid to UniServ directors. The bizarre outcome is that part-time negotiators without fringe benefits try to negotiate contracts that would prohibit school districts from employing part-time employees without fringe benefits. They justify their proposals on the grounds that school districts should not be allowed to save money this way!

Another example of NEA/AFT inconsistency on contracting out is their support for arbitration of labor disputes. Ordinarily, the courts are the appropriate forum in which to pursue claims that a party has violated its contractual obligations. Not so in education, at least in the labor relations field. The NEA/AFT, like unions generally, demand binding arbitration of union claims that school districts have violated their labor contracts. The typical labor contract in education provides that such disputes be settled by private arbitrators selected pursuant to the procedures of the American Arbitration Association, a private organization. As a result, most teachers work under contracts that provide for private resolution of contractual disputes.

Ironically, the union arguments for utilizing arbitration instead of the courts are identical with the conventional arguments for privatization. The NEA/AFT negotiator invariably asserts that arbitration is faster and less expensive than resorting to the courts to resolve contractual disputes. Although there are valid reasons to avoid arbitration of public sector labor disputes, the NEA/AFT argument for it underscores the hypocrisy in their war against privatization.

Implications of the War Against Privatization

The NEA and AFT cannot say "We're opposed to contracting out because it's not good for the union" or "not good for the employees." Politically, they must cite public policy, not special interest reasons to justify their opposition. Since the most common feature of contracting out is its reliance on companies for profit, the union attacks on contracting out inevitably degenerate into an attack upon the free enterprise system. The following comment from *The People's Cause* is typical:

> Those who believe the corporate sales pitch that deregulation and skilled private industry management techniques will solve the problems of public education should contemplate the savings and loan debacle, the airline company bankruptcies over the past decade, and the difficulties of airline travel today—all products of deregulation and private industry management techniques. Other notable examples of the genius of the marketplace are the soaring costs of health care in America and the millions of poor people whose primary medical care is in understaffed, overused hospital emergency rooms.[13]

Most economists would be astonished to learn that the savings and loan debacle resulted from "deregulation and private industry management techniques"; some at least were under the impression that ill-advised federal loan guarantees, regardless of risk, plus congressional protection for savings and loan officials who flouted prudent market processes, were the causes.

Be that as it may, the NEA/AFT war on privatization extends far beyond our borders. Former NEA President Mary Hatwood Futrell is the president of Education International (EI), an international confederation of teacher unions that is now the world's largest trade union organization. According to AFT online, at EI's 1994 meeting in Zimbabwe:

> Futrell also criticized the International Monetary Fund, the OECD (Organization for Economic Cooperation and Development) and the World Bank, whose policies have encouraged privatization of schools around the world. . . . Privatization is a cover-up for poor fiscal and management policies in these countries.[14]

Apparently, Futrell was not aware of the fact that fifteen of the twenty poorest economies in the world are one-party African states that replaced their market economies with state controlled ones.

A 1994 AFT resolution also raises serious doubts about union good faith on privatization issues. The resolution calls for "'clear and precise principles of public accountability, independent oversight, and performance evaluation' in service contracts between school systems and private management firms."

The resolution also demanded that all contracts with private for profit providers should limit profits and specify the results promised and the criteria for evaluating them. In a convention news release, AFT president Albert Shanker commented that "Without some strict accountability requirements, these firms will get away with murder." To forestall any such negative outcome, the AFT resolution demands that the "same laws and regulations on open meetings, public disclosure, and conflict of interest that apply to public schools apply to private contractors, and that employees in schools managed by private contractors retain their collective bargaining and other rights."[15]

This is not the AFT's view when it is the government contractor. Since 1983, the AFT has received millions in federal grants to provide education and training services in foreign countries on collective bargaining and democratic government. The arrangements grew out of the 1983 initiative of the Reagan administration creating the National Endowment for Democracy (NED). NED is supposed to strengthen prodemocracy organizations in nations not committed to a democratic system of government. To avoid the appearance that the U.S. government is subsidizing the foreign organizations, NED established four pass-throughs that receive federal funds and allocate them to individuals and organizations in foreign countries. In effect, the Republican Party, the Democratic Party, the U.S. Chamber of Commerce, and the AFL-CIO each control one pass-through. The Free Trade Union Institute (FTUI), the pass-through controlled by the AFL-CIO, was essential to gaining AFL-CIO support for NED. AFL-CIO president Lane Kirkland and AFT president Albert Shanker were on the NED board of directors from 1984 to 1990; in 1990, when Shanker's second term as a board member expired, he was appointed to the FTUI board of directors.

Not surprisingly, the AFT Foundation, of which Shanker was also president, has received millions from NED either directly or through FTUI. For example, in 1993–94 and 1994–95, the AFT Foundation received $551,820 and $622,189 for the Federation's international program.[16] The AFT Foundation has also received funds from the Agency for International Development, the U.S. Department of Education, the Department of Labor, and the Department of Health and Human Services as well as private foundations, but NED/FTUI have been its main source of funds for its international program.

The NED/FTUI grants support AFT activities in dozens of foreign countries. Several are undergoing the transition from government controlled economies to market economies. Ostensibly, the AFT program has two major objectives. First, it is supposed to help teachers in these foreign countries teach about democratic representative government. Second, the program is intended to train teachers and others how to establish and maintain independent trade unions, especially of teachers. Obviously, these objectives raise several public policy issues. The union movement in the U.S. is in a declining mode. Why should tax revenues be used to build or prop it up elsewhere? If such support is a desirable government initiative, is the AFT the best vehicle for this task? To what extent, if any, does the program utilize non-AFT members?

One can easily list dozens of policy and oversight questions that should be raised about the federal funds flowing to the AFT, but they cannot be answered on the basis of the information about the program that is made available. On the contrary, even when information is requested pursuant to the federal Freedom of Information Act (FOIA), one encounters a stone wall in trying to elicit useful information about the program. NED does not even ask for information on who is paid how much to do what, nor does it conduct independent evaluations of its programs. The only evaluations of the program are those conducted by the AFT; it comes as no surprise that all of its programs are very successful and justify additional federal funding. The AFT has one set of principles when for-profit firms receive government funds, but a drastically different set of principles when the AFT is the recipient.

The AFT's resolution opposing contracting out is applicable to for-profit companies, which the AFT and its foundation are not. It would be quite a stretch, however, to say the differences justify the AFT's lack of accountability in spending federal funds. One could hardly argue that for-profit companies but not nonprofit organizations are accountable for their use of government funds. In short, the AFT is not accountable for the millions in federal funds it receives for its international programs. Furthermore, it flouts the proposed regulations that it piously insists be applied to companies paid for services from tax dollars.

Concluding Observations

At its 1994 convention, the NEA voted to lobby the state teacher retirement plans to divest from, and refrain from investing in, for-profit companies that provide services to school districts. The resolution also urged divestment of companies that advertise on Channel One, a commercial news program produced by Whittle Communications. Companies affected by the resolution include McDonald's, Pepsi-Cola, Reebok, Proctor & Gamble, Associated Newspaper Holding, Philips Electronics, and Time Warner.[17] In effect, the NEA proposes to weaken teacher pension funds in order to block contracting out. After all, there is no way to predict how many companies will be interested in providing services to school districts. If implemented, the NEA resolution might require substantial losses in teacher retirement funds.

Anyone who reads NEA/AFT manuals on how to block contracting out must come to this conclusion: The teacher unions are ready, able, and determined to disrupt school district operations to prevent contracting out. Consequently, school board ability to contract out is unlikely to be secure unless and until school boards are better equipped to discipline unions and district employees who engage in such tactics. This reality highlights a weakness in the state tenure laws. When enacted, these laws envisaged disciplinary action against individual teachers. Extensive due process protections were built into the laws for this reason. At the time, large scale insubordination or union disruption of district operations was not recognized as a possibility.

Realistically, school boards cannot conduct individual hearings for thousands or even hundreds of teachers charged with willful failure to report for duty; if private employers had to contend with this problem, they would be utterly helpless to protect their interests. The legislative changes needed to safeguard school board authority include expedited union decertification procedures and school board authority to discipline employees without individual trials in cases of collective refusals to perform fully and competently. Of course, all such measures will be labeled "union-busting" or "punitive," or some other pejorative, but the present framework is clearly inadequate to protect the public interest.

In my opinion, the antimarket attitudes generated by NEA/AFT efforts to block contracting out are a very serious matter. A study of attitudes toward market systems in the United States and the Soviet Union is instructive. The study sought to compare the attitudes of U.S. and Russian citizens toward market oriented practices. For example, the Soviet Union is characterized by shortages of soap, yet there is major bureaucratic and political opposition to establishing companies to manufacture soap. In commenting on this point, the researchers observed that:

> When a country inherits an institutional and political framework that has been anti-market, it serves certain entrenched interests in that country to resist change. Thus, individuals who benefit from the present system may make public appeals to fairness, abhorrence of income inequality, and other attitudes to try to stop change.[18]

The foregoing comment surely applies to U.S. attitudes toward market oriented changes in our educational system; NEA/AFT opposition to such changes is based precisely on the attitudes cited as obstacles to market oriented reforms in the Soviet Union. The NEA and AFT conventions feature attacks on "profits" and "corporate greed" that could easily pass for a series of speeches at a Communist Party convention. Hunger, child labor, inadequate health care, malnutrition—whatever the problem, "corporate profits" and greed are either responsible for it, or stand in the way of ameliorating it. It would be surprising if NEA/AFT rhetoric did not affect attitudes toward market oriented reforms generally, as they are obviously intended to do.

8

EDUCATION'S GRAVY TRAIN

In forty-eight years of experience with NEA/AFT, as a member, delegate to dozens of local, state, and national union conventions, candidate for national AFT president, chief negotiator for or against NEA/AFT affiliates in seven states, and intensive reader of union publications, I have never seen a comprehensive statement of the compensation of individual union officers and staff. By "comprehensive," I mean a statement which includes all the dollar costs of fringe benefits (including payments to pension plans), allowances and expenses paid to each officer or employee.

Why? In my opinion, the number and compensation of NEA/AFT officers and staff is the most important neglected topic in American education. Union candor on the subject would end, once and for all, the credibility of union claims to be "education's defense fund," an army determined to fight for pupil welfare. The NEA/AFT can be considered armies, but plunder for all ranks, especially the officer class, is the driving force.

How large are these armies? The NEA's national office employed 568 employees in 1995–96. A much larger number are employed by the state and local associations. The NEA Staff Organization (NSO) disseminated a statement on merger at the 1996 NEA convention. The statement asserted that NSO "represents over 4,000 professional and associate staff employees of the National Education Association, state education associations, UniServ councils and local education associations throughout the United States."[1] The 4,000 total would not include the elected officers, supervisors and managers, security personnel, and employees, such as NEA's general counsel, carried as independent contractors.

Even if the NSO 4,000 includes the employees working for NEA subsidiaries, such as its foundations and member benefit corporations, total NEA employment would be at least 4,500 employees. The AFT national office employs about 200 staff members; if the AFT, with a budget more than one-third as large as NEA's employs only a third as many employees, the NEA/AFT employ over 6,000 officers and staff. The analysis that follows considers only the compensation of union officers and professional staff, especially the UniServ directors and national representatives in the AFT.

As management, union officials face an internal problem. High salaries for union leaders can lead to rank-and-file resentment that endangers the incumbents' tenure in office. Consequently, union compensation is characterized by generous fringe benefits that are less visible than salaries. They are often less visible because they are purchased with lump sums on a group basis. The rank and file have neither the time nor the information to analyze these lump sums to determine the dollar value per union officer or staff member. In addition, several fringe benefits are scattered throughout union budgets, often under titles that conceal their costs or their beneficiaries. From the documents made available to members and convention delegates, even certified public accountants cannot precisely ascertain the compensation package for NEA officers or employees.

Four sources provide most of the information about union compensation in the following analysis:

- IRS Form 990, Tax Return of Organization Exempt from Income Tax.
- Department of Labor Form LM–2, an annual report filed by labor organizations. Most teacher unions are not required to file an LM–2.
- Collective bargaining contracts between the NEA/AFT and the unions representing their employees.
- Miscellaneous documents such as the NEA budget.

None of the sources provides a comprehensive summary of union compensation. It is not even possible to develop such a summary from all considered jointly. For instance, the LM–2 does not include data on fringe benefits, which frequently are worth one-third or more of salaries.

The Compensation of NEA/AFT Officers

The NEA elects three executive officers. Their budgeted salary and allowances for 1997 were as follows:

	Gross Salary	Allowance and Benefits	Travel Expenses	Total
President, Robert Chase	$182,485[a]	$119,650[b]	$(40,000)[c]	$262,133[d]
Vice-president, Reg Weaver	$160,421[a]	$119,648[b]	$(40,000)[c]	$240,069[d]
Secretary-Treasurer, Marilyn Monahan	$160,421[a]	$119,646[b]	$(40,000)[c]	$240,069[d]

[a]Both the NEA and AFT structure their budgets on a calendar year, September 1 to August 31 of the following year. Since the FY for both unions includes the last four months of any calendar year, and the first eight months of the following calendar year, I treat the compensation rate for the eight month period as the rate for the calendar year; this results in a slight understatement of union compensation for the calendar year.

[b]For 1995–96, the NEA budgeted $358,946 for "Benefits/Living Allowance/Travel" for the three executive officers. The budget does not reveal how much each officer is paid in these categories so I have divided the $358,946 equally among the officers.

[c]Travel is an expense but allowances are paid regardless of whether expenses are incurred; the IRS treats allowances as income to the recipient, and that is the way they are treated here. By subtracting the estimated amount for travel (based on the 1995–96 amount), the figures for salary, benefits and allowances are as shown above.

[d]In February 1997, the NEA increased the benefit package for its three executive officers by $35,000. The NEA has refused to confirm or deny the increase, or to provide the date on which the increase was adopted by the NEA Board of Directors.

Source: Strategic Focus Plan and Budget Fiscal Year: 1996–97 (Washington: National Education Association, 1996), p. 78.

The foregoing data do not include all the fringe benefits for NEA executive officers. Although employed by NEA, its executive officers are not "employees" for accounting purposes. As a result, the executive officers do not participate in all of the employee fringe benefit programs. Instead, the officers receive "allowances" to pay for certain benefits, such as health insurance; however, it is impossible to determine their compensation from documents available to members. One reason is that the officers receive several benefits in addition to their allowances but their costs per officer are not provided.

Even when the additional benefits are mentioned in the NEA budget, it is often impossible to ascertain their dollar cost per officer or employee. In some cases, the figures are so mixed with other costs that it is impossible to determine the benefit cost. For example, "NEA Health Services provides preventive, diagnostic, and treatment procedures and health education and screening programs for NEA employees; administers confidential medical assistance for NEA employees; coordinates the VDT eye care and employee entrance examination programs; oversees the employee wellness program; and maintains the NEA employee fitness center."[2] Some of these services are fringe benefits but not reported as such to the membership. Additional fringe benefits, which are not shown as income to the executive officers, include companion travel and income tax preparation. Furthermore, NEA budget documents do not report the NEA's contribution or the interest rate, if any, on deferred compensation for its officers under the NEA's 401(k) plan. The amount for employees is based on salary, and accumulates at 8.5 percent annually. Presumably, the NEA contribution and rate of return for its officers are at least as high, unless the officers are individually responsible for investing their deferred compensation.

In addition to the three elected executive officers, the NEA's executive committee includes six members elected at large. The NEA pays for a full-time replacement teacher to take over the classroom duties of these executive committee members. The members remain on the school district payrolls, thus building their pensions during their service as NEA officials. In some cases, the school districts continue to pay for their health insurance. With a teacher replacement in the classroom, the members of the NEA's Executive Committee are free to travel on behalf of the association; some run up charges over $50,000 a year in doing so. In addition, members of the Executive Committee receive a taxable stipend, a supplemental fringe package, assistance in tax preparation, an annual physical, and companion travel. The NEA does not provide a breakdown of the amount per member but the 1996–97 budget allocated $160,486 for Executive Committee fringe benefits. For 1996–97, the NEA budgeted the following amounts for the expenses and benefits of six executive committee members who are not executive officers.

Executive Committee Travel	$212,690
Executive Committee Released Time	$270,000
Executive Committee Benefits	$160,486
Executive Committee Support Services	$42,542
Executive Committee Official Meetings	$138,170
Total	$823,888

The main beneficiaries of these arrangements appear to be the headquarters staff, which does not have to be concerned about the presence of the Executive Committee at NEA headquarters.

NEA Employee Compensation

NEA employee compensation requires fitting together the pieces of a complex puzzle. Although the LM–2 lists the salaries of NEA employees, it does not include all of their taxable income from NEA. Payment for unused leave is an example. For FY ending August 31, 1995, the NEA paid 40 employees $278,955 for unused annual leave. Payments ranged from $346 to $33,564, with an average of $6,974.

Severance pay was an even more lucrative fringe benefit. For FY ending August 31, 1995, the NEA paid thirty employees a total of $344,073 in severance pay. Payments ranged from $3,723 to $20,466; the latter amount went to Debra S. DeLee, who resigned from the NEA to accept the position of executive director of the Democratic Party. The average severance payment for 1994–95 was $11,469. Low interest loans are also available to staff. The saving over the commercial rate is a fringe benefit that is not reported as taxable income.

The NEA's retirement plan covers virtually all of its permanent employees in addition to a large number of employees of state and local affiliates. For NEA employees, the plan is funded solely by NEA at 21 percent of salary, and is based upon an 8.5 percent rate of return on pension investments. The insurance benefits include fully paid medical, dental, life, accidental death, and dismemberment. Retirement health benefits, including surviving spousal benefits, are also part of the package. The NEA does not reveal the cost per employee for this extremely generous insurance package. In addition, NEA employees can participate in a 401(k) retirement plan; the employees make voluntary tax deferred contributions and the NEA contributes 50 percent.[3]

The Education Policy Institute (EPI), a nonprofit educational policy organization, employed certified accountants to estimate NEA staff compensation from the LM–2. Recognizing the gray areas mentioned here, the estimate submitted to EPI indicated that 228 of the 568 NEA employees received total compensation exceeding $100,000 in 1994–95. By 1997, the number may have exceeded 300, perhaps by a considerable margin.

In the following discussion, my estimate is that the average NEA fringe benefit package, including retirement benefits, is 40 percent of salary. This estimate is based partly on the fact that the value of insurance and retirement benefits in most states exceeds 30 percent of salary. The 30 percent does not include a host of other fringe benefits to be discussed. NEA refusal to provide the information requested is another factor suggesting that the actual percentages would embarrass the union. The 40 percent estimate is also applicable to AFT compensation and to compensation in the state affiliates of both unions.

State Education Association and UniServ Compensation

The UniServ program is the largest line item in NEA and state association budgets. As previously UniServ directors direct day-to-day union operations in the field. Because they constitute about one-third of all association employees, some idea of how much they are paid is essential to understand NEA operations. Furthermore, their level of compensation affects the talent level attracted to union careers.

Unions are usually generous employers. Union staff contend they lack credibility in negotiating benefits if the union does not provide them. ("How can we credibly ask the school board to provide domestic partner benefits when we don't have it ourselves?") Early on, the UniServ directors emphasized this argument; since they often negotiated against elected association officers without collective bargaining experience, the UniServ unions negotiated very lucrative contracts. Inasmuch as the NEA urges intensive opposition to "give backs" or "takeaways" (that is, reductions in benefits) in teacher contracts, the UniServ directors argue that it would be hypocritical for NEA to reduce staff or staff benefits.[4] In both the NEA and AFT, union staff have occasionally gone on strike, hoping to embarrass their unions into more concessions. UniServ compensation is not the same everywhere. The state associations negotiate contracts with the unions representing UniServ directors. UniServ directors employed directly by local associations negotiate with these local associations. Finally, the NEA negotiates with the Association of Field Staff Employees (AFSE), the union representing UniServ directors in NEA regional offices. Because most UniServ directors are state association employees, I shall focus on this group. The analysis is based mainly on UniServ contracts in Indiana, California, and New Jersey, supplemented by data from other sources.

Compensation in the Indiana State Teachers Association (ISTA)

In Indiana, UniServ compensation is governed by the contract between the Indiana State Teachers Association (ISTA) and the Professional Staff Organization (PSO), the union representing the UniServ directors. The contract also covers some employees who are not UniServ directors. To simplify matters, I shall discuss ISTA compensation from September 1, 1995 to August 31, 1996, the last year of the ISTA/PSO contract.[5] My summary omits some contractual nuances that do not materially affect the analysis.

The 1995–96 salary schedule for Indiana UniServ directors was as follows:

Step (Years of Service)	1995–96
0	$51,849
1	56,072
2	59,242
3	62,397
4	65,564
5	68,720
6	71,870

Step (Years of Service)	1995–96
7	75,037
8	78,744

ISTA employed 39 UniServ directors in 1996. Thirty had eight or more years of service, thus were entitled to the $78,744 salary. No public school teacher in Indiana received half as much after eight years of service. The teachers are required to work about eight weeks less than the UniServ directors, but the latter receive much more time off from work. Let us now summarize the fringe benefits.

1. *Health, visual, and dental insurance.* ISTA paid $9,894 per employee for health, visual, and dental insurance. This was more than the most expensive insurance package available to any teacher in the state.
2. *Retirement.* UniServ directors participated in the ISTA retirement plan, and subject to eligibility, had the option of participating in other retirement plans as well.
   A. *The ISTA retirement plan.* ISTA contributed 15.5 percent of salary to the employees retirement fund; ISTA employees contribute nothing. Retirement benefits under the ISTA plan vest at age forty or after five years of service. Meanwhile, the state of Indiana contributed about 7.5 percent of payroll to teacher pensions under the Indiana Teacher Retirement Fund (TRF).
   B. Nineteen ISTA staff members, including some UniServ directors, were also earning retirement credit under the Indiana TRF. In other words, they were receiving retirement credit from both ISTA and the Indiana TRF for each year employed by ISTA. The state of Indiana paid the state contribution, just as if these nineteen ISTA employees had been teaching in Indiana public schools. This double-dipping was made possible by a provision in the Indiana retirement law that allowed TRF trustees to include other educational employment in the TRF system. Thus in 1992, the ISTA payroll for the nineteen covered employees was $1,321,874, hence the state of Indiana contributed over $99,000 a year (7.5 percent of payroll) for retirement benefits for these 19 ISTA staff members.
   C. *Pension benefits.* ISTA employed thirty-nine "professional staff," mainly if not entirely UniServ directors. For these employees, ISTA contributed 20 percent of salary to a retirement account, while the covered employees contributed nothing. Vesting was 100 percent and immediate. As previously noted, some "professional staff" were also earning state teacher retirement credit at the same time.
   D. *Deferred compensation.* ISTA also sponsored a deferred compensation plan (401-k) for all employees earning over $70,000 annually. Under this plan, el-

igible employees agree to be paid some of their salary at a later date, at which time the deferred amounts are reported to the IRS. ISTA also contributed to the deferred compensation, but the specifics were not available.

3. *Liability insurance.* Liability is covered without an employee contribution.

4. *Long term disability.* Long term disability is covered without any employee contribution. After six months service, disabled employees receive two-thirds of salary; after six months, 90 percent of salary. The cost to ISTA ranged from $93 for clerical to $352 for management employees.

5. *Accidental Death or Dismemberment.* The coverage provided a payout schedule of $95,000 to $150,000. The cost to ISTA ranged from $261 to $522 annually, with no employee contribution. Thus, the coverage for ISTA clerical employees was far superior to this kind of coverage for public school teachers. Management and professional staff were also covered for an additional $110,000 in benefits, at an annual cost of $4,350.72 to ISTA, none to the covered employees.

6. *Severance pay.* A four-year employee receives the unvested retirement amount in a lump sum.

7. *Vacation allowance.* The vacation allowance for "management support" and "associate" staff was as follows:

Years of Service	Number of Vacation Days
Less than 4	13
4–10	19
10–16	24
Over 16	27

The vacation allowance for management and professional staff, which includes the UniServ directors, was more generous:

Years of Service	Number of Vacation Days
4 or less	25
More than 4	30

8. *Holidays.* Fifteen days for all employees, as follows:
Human Relations Day (Martin Luther King's birthday), Washington's Birthday, Good Friday, Memorial Day, Independence Day, Labor Day, Columbus Day, Veteran's Day, Thanksgiving and following Friday, Christmas Eve through January 1.

9. *Sick leave.* Twelve days, all employees.

10. *Personal leave.* Three days, all employees.
Of ISTA's 119 employees, 43 had been ISTA employees 16 years or

more. These employees were entitled to be absent with full pay for sixty working days, almost three full months of service, as follows:

Authorized Absence	*Number of Days*
Vacation	30 (a)
Holidays	15 (b)
Sick leave	12 (b)
Personal leave	3 (b)
	60

(a) More than 4 years service
(b) All employees

11. *Automobiles.* Every ISTA management/professional employee was entitled to the use of a leased automobile at ISTA expense. The president and exec-utive director were entitled to "an automobile of their choice"; the other forty-six received an Oldsmobile Cutlass Supreme or a Buick, Pontiac or Chevrolet equivalent. To eliminate any uncertainty in the matter, it was stipulated that the vehicles include . . . "light group, power brakes, power steering, automatic transmissions, air condition, tinted glass, variable speed delay windshield wipers, cruise control, heavy duty suspension, AM–FM radio, automatic trunk release, clock, steel belted radial white-wall tires, body side moldings, power seat, power door locks, dual mirrors, rear win-dow defogger"—and $750 ($1,500 for managers) for "other options of the employee's choice." Employees received 3,000 free personal miles and paid 10 cents per mile over 3,000, plus the option of buying the vehicle for $200 less than average wholesale cost for used vehicles of its type.

12. *Credit cards.* The forty-eight managerial/professional staff received ISTA credit cards (Amoco, Visa, American Express); ISTA paid for gasoline, oil, and other automobile supplies and services. Of course, teachers do not enjoy this fringe benefit; I doubt whether most school superinten-dents enjoy a comparable automobile allowance.

13. *Companion travel.* Seven management employees were entitled to $1,000 annually for travel expenses of "companions" when attending conferences.

What was the dollar value of the total fringe benefit package? The Indiana Policy Foundation, a public policy organization that investigated the matter, estimated the value of the fringe benefits to be between 54 percent and 78 per-cent of salary. Interestingly enough, the foundation received hundreds of tele-phone calls and letters in response to its analysis of ISTA compensation. Many communications were from teachers requesting permission to disseminate the analysis—an interesting confirmation of the point that teacher union leaders have good reason to avoid candor on the subject.

ISTA compensation appears to be fairly representative of state association compensation. UniServ compensation in California and New Jersey bears this out.

UniServ Compensation in California: The CTA/CSO Contract

The California Teachers Association (CTA) employed over ninety-seven UniServ directors in 1996, more than any other state. This number does not include UniServ directors employed by NEA or by local associations. Compensation for UniServ directors employed by CTA is governed by a three year contract between the CTA and the California Staff Organization (CSO), expiring August 31, 1998.[6] The UniServ salary schedule for 1997 under the CTA/CSO contract is as follows:

Step	Regular schedule	Mandatory CTA contribution to 401-k plan, 2%	Optional CTA contribution to 401-k plan, 3.5%	Total Salary with optional 401-k contribution
	A	B	C	D
1	48,488	969.76	1697.08	51,154.84
2	50,933	1018.66	1782.66	53,734.32
3	53,502	1070.04	1872.57	56,444.61
4	56,200	1124.00	1967.00	59,291.00
5	59,034	1180.68	2066.19	62,280.87
6	62,011	1240.22	2170.39	65,421.61
7	65,138	1302.76	2279.83	68,720.59
8	68,424	1368.48	2394.84	72,187.32
9	71,874	1437.48	2515.59	75,827.07
10	75,498	1509.96	2642.43	79,650.39
11	79,307	1586.14	2775.75	83,668.89
12	83,306	1666.12	2915.71	87,887.83

Column A shows the "regular" salary schedule from January 1, 1997 to March 1, 1998. Columns B and C show the CTA contribution to employee 401-k deferred compensation plans. CTA contributes two percent of salary without matching and up to an additional 3½ percent to match any employee contribution. Data are not available on how many UniServ directors take advantage of the 3½ percent option in column C.

Source: Agreement between the California Teachers Association (CTA) and the California Staff Organization (CSO), September 1, 1995 to August 31, 1998, p. 65.

The CTA contributions to the 401-k plans are only a small portion of the goodies showered on the UniServ directors. The CTA/CSO agreement also includes the following fringe benefits (I have simplified the contract language but retained the contract titles and numbering system).

ARTICLE VIII. *SALARY SCHEDULES REGULATIONS AND FRINGE BENEFITS*

8.2 Provides prior service credit for full-time paid employment with NEA or any affiliate; in addition, new employees must be placed on the UniServ schedule at a figure that is equal or higher than the amount earned by the employee in the 12 months preceding employment.

8.5 *Fringe Benefits: Joint Employer-Employee Trust for Health and Welfare Benefits*

8.501 Fully paid medical and dental benefits for the employees and eligible dependents. The details are not spelled out but are incorporated by reference from other agreements.

8.6 *Physical Examination* An annual physical examination paid for by CTA.

8.7 *Paid FICA* CTA payment of employee social security taxes (FICA) and employee credit for such payments as income applicable to retirement.

8.8 *Disability Insurance* Payments Fully paid disability insurance.

8.9 *Life Insurance* Fully paid life insurance to provide three (3) times the employees salary in effect on the data of death.

ARTICLE XII. *LEAVES*

12.101–12.105 Sick leave credit of one day per month of service with no limit on accumulation; usable for illness of the employee or the employee's spouse, children, dependents, or member of the employee's immediate household. At retirement, employees receives 0.004 years of service credit for each day of accumulated sick leave to which employee was entitled on the last day of service. Such leave need not be accrued prior to taking such leave and may be taken at any time during the year. Credit is given for up to 12 days of sick leave per year accumulated with a prior professional organization provided that the prior organization or employee provide the funds actuarially to support the credit.

12.2 *Child Care Leave* Twelve months of unpaid child care leave which may be extended by mutual agreement. Three days paid leave which may be extended by CTA for birth or adoption of a child.

12.3 *Jury or Witness Duty* Full salary for jury or witness duty leave.

12.4 *Religious Days* Two days religious leave with pay.

12.5 *Bereavement Leave* Five days of bereavement leave with pay.

12.6 *Personal Leave* Four days of personal leave with pay.

12.7 *Industrial Accident or Illness Leave* Industrial accident or illness leave up to 180 days with pay.

12.8 *Political Leave* Unpaid leave to run for office or political campaigning.

12.9 *Other Leaves* "Other" leaves, without pay, not to exceed one year, for up to three unit members.

12.906 Leaves with pay receive all benefits of continued employment.

ARTICLE XIII. *VACATIONS*

13.1 Vacation leave of 23 days per year. Vacation time is earned at the rate of one day per month for the first month of the fiscal year, two days per month thereafter.

13.6 If ill on vacation, employee can convert vacation time to sick leave.

13.762 Employee option to be compensated for all vacation days at current salary rate, in the fiscal year preceding retirement.

13.703 Upon retirement, unit members can convert 5, 10, or 15 days of accumulated vacation to salary with 15–19, 20–24, or 25 or more years of service, respectively.

ARTICLE XIV. *HOLIDAYS*

14.1, 14.2 Sixteen designated holidays, plus December 27–30 for all employees except for 25 who may be required to staff association offices on a "skeleton crew" basis. No employee can be assigned December 27–30 in consecutive years unless no other employee within community distance and less recently assigned is not available. Employees assigned to duty December 27–30 receive days off with pay equal to days served December 27–30.

ARTICLE XV. *BUSINESS EXPENSE*

15.102 Reimbursement of $0.40 per mile for travel on association business.

15.105 Reimbursement for rental and parking charges for private aircraft used on association business.

Reimbursement for private aircraft monthly membership in flying club if membership results in lower rental fee when flying on association business provided that reimbursement does not exceed savings from lower rental rates.

15.301 Lodging at "least expensive" rate available, but class of hotel not spelled out. Meals up to $55 per day.

15.5 *Credit Cards* Employees received car rental card, air travel card, telephone credit card, two or three gasoline cards, all to be used on association business.

15.502 Association pays for annual fee of one general credit card for charges not to be billed to the association.

15.6 *Cash Advances* Cash advances up to $500 for anticipated expenses, $250 more plus cost of air fare if out-of-state travel is involved.

15.7 *Parking Fees,* including fees for space in the near vicinity of the employer's office.

15.8 *Telephone* Charges required on association business, personal calls "necessitated" by association business and "all reasonable expenses related to use of a cellular phone, including monthly access charges."

15.9 *Legal Costs* Costs arising out of any action against the employee in the course of association work, except when employee is grossly culpable.

15.10 *Reimbursement for Membership or License Fees* CTA pays for membership or license fees whenever employee must join any other professional organization, or requires a license by law to carry out official responsibilities. Local, state, and national bar association fees are paid by CTA for its staff attorneys.

ARTICLE XVI. *STAFF AUTOMOBILE POLICY*

16.102–16.107 Automobile cash allowance of $560 monthly for maintaining an automobile for association use at personal cost. In addition to the cash allowance and reimbursement for mileage, the Association pays for insurance, tire replacement, and business use gasoline, oil, lubrication and filter costs. The car may be replaced at any time, but must receive an EPA mileage composite rating of at least 17 miles per gallon. If insurance costs have a negative effect on CTA's insurance costs, the difference is deducted from the employee's automobile allowance.

ARTICLE XVII. *MOVING EXPENSES*

17.1 If change of residence is necessary, Association pays expenses of packing, moving, and unpacking to maximum weight of 9,500 pounds.

17.102 Association pays deposits forfeited by reason of premature termination of employee's lease.

17.103 Association pays telephone and utilities connection and reconnection fees.

17.104 Association pays costs of lodging, travel and meals up to one month if reasonably incurred in connection with a move.

17.2 Time off with no loss of pay or vacation to prepare for and move to new location.

17.3 If employee has children and there are less than four months of school remaining, employer shall waive time lines for moving and provide duplicate housing not to exceed six months.

17.4 Sale of home expenses including the cost of duplicate housing up to six months; realtor services paid by association; reimbursement of differences in interest rates between house to be sold and house to be purchased for up to one year, provided that differences due to upgrading shall not be included in computation of interest; reimbursement up to $1,000 for administrative costs arising out of execution of deeds and mortgages.

ARTICLE XIX. *RETIREMENT*

19.102 CTA's retirement benefits include: a retirement annuity plan; a retirement medical benefit plan; and a 401-k plan. Retirement benefits vest after five years of service.

Employees receive services and benefit credit beyond age 65. Final salary for retirement purposes is based on highest single year of service, including years of service beyond age 65. Leave accumulated after age 65 is added to retirement service credit. In addition, a COLA of 3 percent is added to retirement benefit, full retirement benefits can begin at age 55, retirement benefits apply to non-employee domestic partners and eligible dependents. Benefits continue in effect in the event of any merger or transfer of assets.

Employees receiving a CTA pension are eligible for a post-retirement contract as an independent contractor providing a minimum of 20 percent of a full-time position. In combination with Medicare Parts A and B, CTA expenses to be reimbursed as under the CTA/CSO contract; pays total premium for health, dental, and vision insurance for retirees and their eligible dependents, provided that retirees have served 10 consecutive years before retirement and are at least 50 years of age or are eligible under the Association's disability policy. If retiree pre-deceases spouse, benefits continue for spouse and other eligible dependents.

To fund these lavish retirement and medical benefits, CTA (not the employees) pays a maximum of 21.5 percent of employees taxable wages. If costs exceed 21.5 percent of taxable wages, the CTA and CSO are required to bargain over the actions to be taken to ensure existing benefits.

Finally, the CTA matches on a dollar-for-dollar basis the employee contribution to a 401-k plan up to 3.5 percent of salary. In addition, CTA contributes 2 percent of salary without matching.

To illustrate the CTA compensation package, a UniServ director on the 12th step would receive the following compensation in 1997:

969.76	2 percent of salary to 401(k) plan, matching not required
1,697.08	3 1/2 percent matching contribution to 401-k plan
17,910.79	21.5 percent paid by CTA for employee pension plan
10,000.00	car benefit (estimated)
10,000.00	medical, dental, life, and other insurance benefits for UniServ directors and eligible dependents (estimated)
40,577.63	Benefits (partial list)
83,306.00	Regular salary
$123,883.63	Salary plus benefits (partial list)

Note that the CTA/CSO contract includes several benefits not counted in the above summary. I did not try to cost out the omissions, but they would raise the package to 55 to 60 percent of salary. Note also that the economic benefits are provided in addition to an extremely generous list of employee protections. Furthermore, several benefits that are not regarded as income to employees impose substantial costs on the CTA. For instance, the contract obligates CTA to sponsor a staff training program that employees elsewhere often must purchase from their personal funds.

Another point of interest is Section 6.6, which provides that: "Employees shall be directly responsible to the CTA Executive Director. Employees shall not be directed by any other parties." Thus although the teachers in a UniServ unit can ratify or reject a contract, they cannot direct the UniServ directors to act contrary to the latter's directives from CTA.

Of course, the executive and managerial staff are paid even more than the UniServ directors. A California newsletter reports that "the CTA's 21 board members and three executive officers are entitled to $300 per month for child care. If the member has no children, the money may be used for home, pet, or garden care."[7] To say the least, this is an extraordinary fringe benefit.

UniServ Compensation in New Jersey

UniServ compensation in the New Jersey Education Association (NJEA) appears to be significantly higher than in Indiana and California. The 1994–95 NJEA salary schedule for "field representatives" (that is, UniServ directors) went from $62,794 to $92,790 in twelve steps; however, new hires with appropriate service credit could be employed on the fifth step at $73,702.[8] Probably, most if not all were hired at this level. The $92,790 did not include a percentage increment at the 13th step.

NJEA fringe benefits include the following:
1. NJEA payment of 21 percent (estimated) of salary for employee pensions
2. Twelve holidays plus an extra five (5) at Christmas
3. After one year, 22 vacation days and 15 days sick leave
4. Fully paid life, hospitalization, dental, prescription and optical insurance
5. $1,000 per semester for college courses
6. Interest free car loans up to $3,500
7. Tenure after three years

The above benefits were by no means exhaustive, but they should suffice to convey the picture. Significantly, forty NJEA employees were earning more than $100,000 in salary alone in 1994; eleven were being paid $125,000 or more inclusive of fringe benefits.[9] To repeat, although fringe benefits are common and often taken for granted, I have included them here because they are so extraordinarily generous.

"UniServ" is a term based on the idea of providing NEA members with "Uniform Service." The natural outcome is uniformity in staff compensation, adjusted for cost of living factors. When cost of living adjustments are made, UniServ compensation does not differ so much from state to state.

The state pattern of union compensation reflects the pattern of teacher compensation. Union compensation is highest in the northern states that have enacted bargaining laws, lowest in the southern, right-to-work states that have not enacted them. The longer a state has had a bargaining law, the higher the level of union compensation. Thus, union compensation is highest in California, Connecticut, Illinois, Massachusetts, Michigan, Minnesota, New Jersey, Ohio, and Pennsylvania. These are also the states that employ the largest numbers of union staff. In these states and perhaps eight to ten others, it appears that every UniServ director and managerial/professional employee is paid $100,000 a year in salary and benefits, or is on a salary schedule which leads to this level of compensation within three to five years

On this point, bear in mind that virtually all state associations pay at least 20 percent of salary for retirement benefits; in fact, most pay at least 35 percent just for retirement and insurance benefits. This percentage does not include the costs of automobiles for personal use, vacation pay, holidays, leases, severance pay, credit cards and fees, airline clubs, professional fees, cellular telephones, low cost loans, moving expenses—the list goes on and on. Some of these benefits, such as car allowance, are easily worth $5,000 to $10,000 annually over and above their business use. Inasmuch as most UniServ directors are employed by state associations, most teachers have no idea of how much the directors are being paid.

The AFT as Employer

The AFT has two elected full-time officers, president and secretary-treasurer. Their fringe benefits are not available but probably equal or exceed those available to NEA officers. This conclusion is based partly upon the absence of term limits for AFT officers; officers who are repeatedly reelected will probably be paid more than officers serving a maximum of two three-year terms. Furthermore, the AFT appears to be more generous to its staff below management/supervisory levels. For example, the AFT contributes 23.5 percent of salary to the employees' retirement; the elected full-time officers probably receive at least this much.

According to the AFT's LM–2 for the FY ending June 30, 1995, elected full-time officer compensation was as follows:

Position-Officer	Gross Salary	Allowance	Expenses	Total
President, Albert Shanker	$196,380	$40,800	$35,237	$272,417
Secretary-Treasurer, Edward McElroy	$135,277	$20,400	$31,722	$187,399

Until Shanker's death in 1997, both were entitled to substantial pensions or credit toward their teacher pension while serving as union officials.

Source: U.S. Department of Labor Form LM–2, for American Federation of Teachers, FY ending August 31, 1996.

Until Shanker's death in 1997, both Shanker and McElroy were entitled to substantial pensions from public teacher retirement systems for their service as union officials; undoubtedly, several employees in the NEA/AFT also receive teacher pensions or credit toward teacher pensions while serving as union officials.[10]

Remarkably, the AFT employs five "assistants to the president"; their salaries ranged from $75,723 to $109,693 in fiscal year 1995, the most recent period for which the AFT filed an LM–2. Assuming that fringe benefits are one-third of salary, it appears that the AFT is paying about $650,000 annually for the AFT president's assistants.[11]

The AFT defrays the expenses of its 38 member Executive Council, but spends much less per person on this body than the NEA does. Most council members are full-time AFT officers at the state or local level, hence there is no need to pay for replacement teachers when they travel on union business. Because there are 38 members on the council, the members need not travel as often or as far as the members of the NEA Executive Committee.

Compensation for State Federation Officials

New York is the only state in which the AFT's affiliate is the largest state teacher union. The salaries, expenses, and allowances of the full-time elected officers of the New York State United Teachers (NYSUT) for 1994–95 are as follows:

Position-Officer	Gross Allowances Salary	Reimbursed Expense	Other Disbursements	Total
President, Thomas Hobart	$136,448	$13,020	$18,808	$168,276
1st Vice-president, Antonia Cortese	$123,428	$ 2,597	$ 2,847	$128,872
Secretary-Treasurer, Fred Nauman	$123,428	$ 7,498	$ 1,722	$132,648
2nd Vice-president, Walter Dunn	$ 38,582	$ 2,034	$ 9,464	$ 50,079

Source: Department of Labor Form LM–2, New York State United Teachers, for FY ending August 31, 1995.

The above figures do not include most fringe benefits or increases since 1994–95. Whatever the precise amount, the AFT is a generous employer at the state as well as the national level. One interesting point is that NYSUT pays a stipend for members of its executive committee who are not employed full time by NYSUT. Each such member received $14,400 in 1994–95; thus UFT President Sandra Feldman who was paid $157,719 as UFT president, was paid an additional $14,400 along with seven other members of NYSUT's executive committee.[12] If Feldman's fringe benefits were 30 percent of her UFT salary—a low estimate—she received well over $200,000 in compensation from the UFT for 1994–95.

The practice of paying multiple salaries to union officials for service in different levels of the same union is much more common in the AFL-CIO than in the NEA. As the NEA and its affiliates move away from term limits for executive officers, multiple salaries may become more prevalent in the NEA.

Although all UniServ directors are at least partially funded by the NEA, most are employed by the state associations. In contrast, the AFT is the primary employer of field staff who serve more than one state. The large city affiliates of the AFT (New York, Chicago, Boston, Philadelphia, Miami, New Orleans, Minneapolis, St. Paul, Detroit, Providence, Hartford, Pittsburgh, Cleveland, Cincinnati) elect and employ their own staff. Most AFT employees are in these large locals, not in the national office. Unfortunately, it was not possible to get adequate data on their total compensation. The AFT national representatives perform essentially the same service as UniServ directors; the main difference is that AFT national representatives have a much larger geographical area to cover. Table 8.1 shows the salary schedule for AFT national representatives. Interestingly enough, the AFT has embraced the concept of merit pay, albeit not the phrase. The AFT/AFTSU contract establishes five classifications of national representative (I, II, III, IV and senior national representative). Their work is divided into the following eight categories:

1. Contract negotiations
2. Representation elections
3. Strikes, managing projects and/or political campaigns
4. Organizational campaigns
5. Literature development
6. Professional issues
7. Public outreach programs designed to build public support for the union and its constituencies
8. Leadership training

The contract provides that placement of national representatives into the classifications is based on "proficiency and demonstrated competence" in the categories. For example, "National representative IV shall be self-proficient in all eight (8) categories and competent to direct activities and staff in at least six (6) of the eight categories."[13]

These provisions embody a system of merit pay, that is, a system in which compensation is based, in part at least, on the basis of superior performance on the job. Note that all the national representatives perform the same tasks; the phrase "job descriptions and promotions" is simply a rhetorical device to avoid use of the term "merit pay." In view of the subjective judgments required by Article VI, one has to question the AFT's good faith in objecting to merit pay in school districts as being "too subjective."

Like UniServ directors, AFT national representatives are controlled by the union, not the teachers whom they represent; the AFT/AFTSU contract provides that "the employment and activities of national representatives shall be solely under the direction and control of the AFT."[14] Although terms and con-

TABLE 8.1

Salary Schedule, AFT Field Representatives

EFFECTIVE JANUARY 1, 1995

	Step 1	Step 2	Step 3	Step 4	Step 5
Nat. Rep. I	37,505	38,630	39,789	40,982	42,212
Nat. Rep II	47,506	48,931	50,399	51,911	53,468
Nat. Rep. III	58,757	60,520	62,336	64,206	66,132
Nat. Rep. IV	70,111	71,864	73,661	75,502	77,390
Sen. Nat. Rep.					82,000

EFFECTIVE JANUARY 1, 1996

	Step 1	Step 2	Step 3	Step 4	Step 5
Nat. Rep. I	39,192	40,368	41,579	42,826	44,111
Nat. Rep II	49,644	51,133	52,667	54,247	55,875
Nat. Rep. III	61,401	63,243	65,141	67,095	69,108
Nat. Rep. IV	73,266	75,098	76,975	78,900	80,872
Sen. Nat. Rep.					85,690

EFFECTIVE JANUARY 1, 1997

	Step 1	Step 2	Step 3	Step 4	Step 5
Nat. Rep. I	40,956	42,185	43,450	44,754	46,096
Nat. Rep II	51,878	53,434	55,037	56,688	58,389
Nat. Rep. III	64,164	66,089	68,072	70,114	72,218
Nat. Rep. IV	76,563	78,477	80,439	82,450	84,511
Sen. Nat. Rep.					89,546

Source: Contract between the American Federation of Teachers, AFL-CIO, and the American Federation of Teachers Staff Union (AFTSU), January 1, 1995 to December 31, 1997.

ditions of employment in the NEA and AFT differ to some extent, total compensation in the two unions is substantially similar. The NEA headquarters staff has a higher salary schedule, but it often exercises responsibility for a larger operation even when the job descriptions are essentially similar.

Part-time Compensation at the Local Level

Local affiliates of both NEA and AFT often pay stipends to teachers who serve as union officers. This practice is not so common among large locals which employ full-time staff. UniServ councils sometimes pay stipends to their officers; also, some local associations do so even when they employ a UniServ director.

The stipends appear to range from $1,000 to $3,000 annually—a significant amount to the teachers involved.

Stipends to local union officers for service must be distinguished from payment to part-time negotiators employed in the UniServ program. These negotiators are not officers or even members of the locals for whom they negotiate. They are simply part-time employees of the state association, paid an hourly rate without the fringe benefits of UniServ directors. As pointed out in Chapter 7, these part-time negotiators try to persuade school boards not to employ part-time teachers to avoid paying fringe benefits.

The Policy Implications of NEA/AFT Union Compensation

Altogether, the NEA/AFT employ about 3,000 officers and staff who receive more than $100,000 annually in total compensation. Persistent union refusal to reveal the total compensation of union staff to union members is only one reason to regard my estimate as a very conservative one.

NEA/AFT staff consist mainly of former teachers. When fringe benefits are factored in, their career earnings as union staff are two or three times what their earnings would have been as teachers. These facts go a long way toward explaining the intense NEA/AFT opposition to privatization in any form. The union bureaucracies realize that contracting out is a threat to their economic base. Contracting out does not threaten teachers, any more than contracting out hospital custodial services threatens the welfare of doctors, but the union interest lies in demonizing privatization, even if union members are not affected by it. "Don't even think about it" is the mindset the NEA/AFT seek to establish on privatization.

One might suppose that school districts might pay teachers more if they could pay less for support services. That is, perhaps it is in the interests of teachers to support instead of oppose contracting out support services. The NEA/AFT never raise this possibility because it is in the union interest to organize the support groups.

Recall the question raised in Chapter 1: Why were the NEA/AFT/AFL-CIO willing to accept large scale federal assistance to denominational education in the late 1940s, while being adamantly opposed to it since the advent of teacher bargaining in the 1960s? Presumably, the policy considerations and the impact upon teachers would be the same in both situations. The difference is that in the late 1940s, there was no large full-time NEA/AFT bureaucracy which was threatened by privatization and which exercised the political power to prevent it.

The fact is that intense opposition to privatization did not become a leading NEA/AFT priority until the emergence of a huge affluent teacher union bureaucracy. Ironically, this bureaucracy is shielded from criticism because so many association officers seek union positions. These officers are not likely to challenge union compensation while striving to be employed as union staff themselves. Furthermore, state association managerial staff, not elected association officers, hire UniServ directors. The managerial staff is not likely to hire candidates who contend that union compensation is excessive.

A Teacher Bill of Rights

As a result of Congressional investigations of union corruption in the 1950s, Congress enacted the Labor-Management Reporting and Disclosure Act (LMRDA) of 1959. The LMRDA includes several protections for union members, including but not limited to the following:

- Equal access to union mailing lists in union elections.
- Unions are subject to federal reporting and disclosure requirements, and members must be allowed for just cause to examine union records and accounts to verify the reports.
- Unions must report the salary, allowance, and expense reimbursements of more than $10,000 yearly from the union and its affiliated unions.
- Unions must report direct and indirect loans of more than $250 to any officer, employee, or member, their purpose, security provided and terms of repayment. Also, similar information is required regarding direct and indirect loans to any business enterprise.
- The financial reports must be signed by the union president and treasurer, or other appropriate officials. The officers who sign the report are personally responsible for its accuracy and are subject to criminal penalties for statements known to be false.

As matters stand, union financial reports do not have to show the value of fringe benefits for union officers and employees. This is a major deficiency in the LMRDA. Regrettably, most state and local teacher unions do not have to meet even the weak reporting and disclosure requirements in the LMRDA. This disclosure gap results from the fact that teacher unions are governed by state, not federal statutes. The state statutes on the subject were initially drafted by the public employee unions; naturally, they omitted the safeguards against union abuses included in federal statutes regulating private sector unions. As a result, members of private sector unions enjoy much more protection against union abuses than NEA/AFT members do. In all states, a "Teacher Bill of Rights" vis-a-vis their unions would be a salutary development. Such legislation should require disclosure of all nonsalaried benefits of union officers and staff, and all financial transactions between the unions and the parties they employ.

Unions were established to provide worker protection against unfair and unscrupulous employers; unfortunately, there is also a need for employee protection against unfair or unscrupulous unions. The teacher unions will argue that there is no need for such protection because teachers are content with the representation they are getting. Content they may be, but their contentment may be due more to their lack of information than to the lack of grounds for complaint.

9

PAYING THE BILLS

NEA/AFT Revenues

Including their local, state, and regional affiliates, the NEA/AFT pay for the salaries and benefits of over 6,000 well-paid officers and employees. Substantial revenues are also required to pay for buildings, rent, travel, supplies, equipment, copying, telephones, outside legal and accounting fees, publications, and more. How much is required to pay for it all, and where does the money come from? This chapter and the next provide partial answers.

NEA/AFT revenues are a bewildering morass of union budgets, PAC funds, philanthropic foundations, for-profit companies, member benefit corporations, trust funds, special purpose organizations, title holding companies, capital funds, and credit unions. These entities often participate in complex financial transactions with each other and with local, state, and national affiliates. Another complicating factor is that the NEA and AFT use different accounting systems. In the AFT, local, state, and national dues, as well as dues to local, state, and national AFL-CIO affiliates, are counted as revenues. The locals then categorize the per capita payments to state and national AFT and AFL-CIO affiliates as expenditures. In contrast, the NEA accounting structure often provides a pass-through for state and NEA dues. For this reason, the state and national dues may not show up as revenues to NEA locals. Another consequence is that AFT locals appear to be receiving more of the dues dollar, when in fact this may not be the case. In any event, these complexities rendered it impossible to achieve precise revenue estimates; although I have confidence in the magnitudes, some margin for error should be factored in. Nonetheless, the following analysis reveals the NEA especially to be an enormously wealthy union that conceals critical financial data from its own members.

NEA Revenues

Table 9.1 summarizes NEA revenues for FY 1996–97 at the local, state, and national levels.

TABLE 9.1

NEA Revenues, FY 1996–97

$202,000,000	NEA national office[1]
$600,000,000	State education association revenues[2]
$ 87,650,000	Local and regional association revenues (estimated) 1,643,000 × $50 (teacher) = $82,150,000 + 220,000 × $25 (support personnel) = $5,500,000.[3]
$889,650,000	Total, dues and agency fees

[1]For FY 1996–97, the NEA budgeted $192,767,000 for its national office. This amount does not include $9 million in "external recoveries": sales of publications, advertising in *NEA Today*, recoveries of legal fees, convention income, and other income not from dues and agency fees. Because the NEA retirement plan is so lucrative, NEA officials do not want to terminate their participation in it. When these officials accept a position as executive director of a state association, the latter pays the salary to the NEA, which absorbs the retirement contribution and pays the executive directors as if they were NEA employees. The NEA receives almost $2.7 million from the state associations for these jointly funded positions. When all of these recoveries are factored in, NEA budgeted income was $202 million for FY 1996–97.

[2]Based on state association budgets for 1995–96, adjusted upward 2 percent for anticipated increase in state association membership, dues, and agency fees in 1996–97; less the NEA UniServ grant of $40,516,815 to SEA's in 1996–97.

[3]Based on average local dues of $50 for teachers, $25 for support personnel × number of NEA members in each category. Additional income from agency fees and losses due to nonpayment of dues were assumed to cancel out, although the income was probably higher.

Source: Strategic Focus Plan and Budget Fiscal Year 1997–97 (Washington: National Education Association, 1996), p. iii, 76; state education association budgets for 1995–96.

Table 9.1 does not include the revenues of other union subsidiaries, such as their PAC committees and foundations. Nor does it include the millions in taxpayer subsidies which do not show up as revenues on union financial statements. Even without including the cash value of taxpayer subsidies, NEA revenues are close to one billion annually.

    Estimating NEA/AFT revenues is complicated by transfers between the local, state and national organizations. For instance, in 1996–97 the NEA allocated $40.5 million to its state and local affiliates for the UniServ program. We cannot count the $40.5 million as state and local income in estimating NEA total income. To do so would count the amount twice, perhaps three times. Fund transfers between the state and local associations further complicate the problem of estimating total union revenues. The fact that transfer may be made from the local to the state, or the state to the national, or directly between the national and local unions, adds additional complications.

Dues are the main source of NEA revenue. Nevertheless, the NEA enrolls a substantial number of members who do not pay regular NEA dues. As noted in Chapter 2, NEA/AFT play down the fact that their regular teacher membership has been essentially flat for several years; membership increases have materialized mainly in membership categories that pay much less than regular dues. NEA membership in 1996–97 includes 127,000 retirees who constitute 5.84 percent of NEA members but who pay only 0.8 percent of its income; in addition, about 101,000 life members do not pay any NEA dues. Life membership was abolished in 1973, but individuals who had already purchased life membership retained it by judicial decision. Furthermore, educational support personnel (ESP) pay only half of teacher dues. Overall, about one in four of NEA's 2.2 million members pay less than regular teacher dues, or no dues at all.

From a practical standpoint, we must take into account the off budget revenues of subsidiary organizations that are legally separate but controlled by the NEA. As I use the phrase, "controlled by the NEA" means that the key governance personnel are designated by the NEA. The amount and significance of NEA's off-budget revenues varies widely. At one extreme, NEA-PAC revenues obviously have a direct bearing on the NEA's political power. At the other extreme, some off budget funds do not affect NEA's external influence.

Generally speaking, however, the size and importance of NEA subsidiary organizations are grossly underestimated. These organizations often provide services that tie members more closely to the union. Also, the subsidiary organizations provide opportunities to manipulate the regular budget for various purposes. For example, NEA's for-profit organizations need not report their profits publicly. They can pay NEA generously for services, in effect transferring their profits to NEA, which does not pay income taxes. In this way off-budget revenues can be an important source of NEA support, albeit disguised as payments for services rendered by NEA.

National Foundation for the Improvement of Education (NFIE)

The NEA controls the National Foundation for the Improvement of Education (NFIE), a nonprofit organization devoted to the improvement of instruction. NFIE receives $1 from regular members and agency fee payers, and $.50 from educational support personnel, reserve and staff members. For FY ending August 31, 1995, it showed income of $6,212,731; of this amount, $575,481 was from the NEA itself. Most of the funds were corporate and foundation contributors. NFIE net assets at the end of the fiscal year were $14,145,980.

The roster of contributors to NFIE includes about seventy-five major corporations and corporate foundations. NFIE also receives support from individuals, including several who give through the Combined Federal Campaign. Local and state associations, school faculties, school board associations, PTAs and major philanthropic foundations also contribute to NFIE. In 1994, Microsoft CEO William Gates made a commitment of $3 million to NFIE, to be used to promote educational technology in low income schools.

Health Information Network (HIN)

The Health Information Network (HIN) is another NEA controlled nonprofit organization. Established in 1987, it employs eight professional staff members housed in the NEA building. NEA officers are also officers of HIN. HIN income from the NEA was $472,282 for FY 1995; most of its income, about one million annually, is from the Centers for Disease Control (CDC) and the Environmental Protection Agency (EPA).

HIN publishes and disseminates materials on clean air, breast and prostate cancer, and condom and AIDS education programs. In the NEA Handbook, HIN is described as a "cooperative effort of the NEA, the National Association of School Nurses, the U.S. Public Health Service, the U.S. Centers for Disease Control and Prevention, and the American Academy of Pediatrics"; however, the handbook includes HIN but does not show it as a legally separate organization. By utilizing HIN as the recipient of federal funds, the NEA avoids the adverse publicity that would materialize if the NEA or the NEA Foundation were the legal recipient of them. It comes as no surprise that HIN materials are utilized in health and safety curricula; also local NEA affiliates sometimes propose HIN health and safety guidelines in their contract proposals.

Member Benefit Corporation (MBC)

Through the NEA Member Benefits Corporation (MBC) and the NEA Member Insurance Trust, the NEA sponsors an impressive array of member benefits and services. The programs offered through the Member Benefits Corporation include the following:

Insurance Programs:

NEA DUES-TAB insurance (free life insurance and death benefits)
NEA term life insurance
NEA level premium term life insurance

NEA guaranteed issue life plan
NEA AD&D insurance
NEA MemberCare Medicare supplement program
NEA MemberCare Insurance Programs
NEA MemberCare In-Hospital Plan
NEA MemberCare Excess Major Medical Plan
NEA income protection plans
NEA homeowners insurance
NEA home financing program

Financial Programs:

NEA credit card program
NEA line of credit
NEA credit plan (loan by mail)
NEA higher education loan program

Investment Programs:

NEA Valuebuilder annuity
NEA FDIC-insured money market account
NEA Gold Certificate CD

Legal Services:

Attorney referral program
Educators employment liability program
Kate Frank/DuShane unified legal service program

Special Discount Programs:

NEA magazine service
NEA car rental program

Publishing Programs:

NEA Today (official monthly journal)
ESP (annual edition of *NEA Today* for support staff)
Tomorrow's Teachers (annually, for NEA student members)
Thought and Action (biannual, on postsecondary issues)
NEA Higher Education Adnorate (newsletter for members in higher education)
The Higher Education Almanac (annual reference guide)
NEA Now (monthly newsletter for local/state leaders)
NEA Retired (bimonthly, for retired members)
NEA Online (provides intra-organization online communication)

Customer Guides:

Tax-deferred annuities
Homeowners insurance
Understanding credit
Buying a personal computer

In some cases, the programs are very popular with NEA members: for example, over 700,000 members use the NEA credit card. Nevertheless, the NEA does not operate the benefit and insurance programs. Instead, through the MBC and the MIT, the NEA contracts with companies, sometimes after a competitive bidding process, to provide the benefits.

MBC is a for-profit Delaware corporation that has issued 1,000 shares of common stock, par value one dollar per share. The NEA owns all of the stock, and the NEA and MBC share a common board of directors. MBC has never paid a dividend; its profits can be used to improve the benefits made available to NEA members, or can be siphoned off as expenses paid to the NEA for such services as data processing.

MBC revenues are purchases of services made by NEA members, and the benefits are supposed to go to the individual purchasers, not to the NEA. Very probably, the NEA's byzantine financial arrangements conceal some financial benefits to the NEA, but limited liability and the security of proprietary information are probably the main advantages of funding benefits through the MBC. Directors of a nonprofit organization are personally responsible when the organization cannot meet its obligations, whereas directors of for-profit organizations avoid such liability. Furthermore, for-profit companies are not subject to the public disclosure requirements applicable to nonprofit organizations.

Member benefits raise the question of whether NEA should sponsor benefit programs or simply maximize vendor competition to provide them. The NEA allegedly does both by having vendors compete to be the contractor. Perhaps, but some of these vendors have been NEA contractors for ten years or more. In its fight against contracting out by school boards, NEA contends that contractors engage in "lowball" tactics. That is, they submit unprofitable bids to get the contract. Once awarded contracts, the contractors manage to raise their prices and shut out competition thereafter. Is the NEA able to avoid this danger? If it is, one has to question its good faith in arguing that school boards can't do so. And if the NEA is unable to avoid this evil, one must question how some companies have been NEA contractors for ten years or more.

Much as the unions might object to the terminology, union members are also profit centers. From the NEA's standpoint, the ideal members buy their home mortgage, car insurance, legal services, income and disability protection, computer, college loans, mutual funds, credit cards, travel, books, magazines, and other products and services through companies that provide exclusive benefits for NEA members. Companies selected may not provide similar services to competing unions. This does not mean only to the AFT; the NEA enrolls or seeks to enroll support personnel who are members of, or sought as members by, several other unions such as the American Federation of State, County, and Municipal Employees (AFSCME). Obviously, there is a conflict if the company with the best product or service also provides it to a competing union.

The conflict-of-interest potential is enormous. Although the NEA and its affiliates have taken some steps to guard against conflicts of interest, such as payoffs to union officials for exclusive rights to sell services or products to union members through union publications, the safeguards do not include public disclosure requirements or criminal penalties as they do in the private sector. The situation in Michigan, to be discussed later in this chapter, illustrates the dangers.

NEA Assets

Union assets are an important dimension of their financial status. The union that owns its own building need not rent space, thus making more of its income available for other purposes. Assets also provide financial flexibility. A union that can pledge its assets, such as a building, can borrow at a lower interest rate than if only anticipated dues income is available as collateral.

On its LM–2 for the fiscal year ending August 31, 1995, the NEA showed fixed assets worth approximately $101 million. The NEA's main long term assets are its buildings and land in Washington, D.C., less the mortgage and depreciation thereon. These assets are carried at cost, but their assessed valuation in 1995 was $82.6 million. This is more than the combined assessed valuation of the three highest union-owned buildings in the District of Columbia.

State Association Revenues

Table 9.3 (p. 158) estimates state association revenues to be about $600 million in 1996–97. Based on the fact that their PACs spent over $24 million in the 1993–94 election cycle, they probably spent about $40 million in the 1995–96 election cycle.

Dues and agency fees comprise the main revenue stream for the state associations, but they also sponsor foundations and member-benefit corporations. The latter include some huge conglomerates that enhance union revenues and power. To illustrate, the Michigan Education Association owns and controls three subsidiary corporations: The Michigan Education Special Services Association (MESSA), the Michigan Education Financial Services, and the Michigan Education Data Network Association (MEDNA).[1]

In 1960 MESSA was incorporated by the MEA as a wholly-owned, not-for-profit subsidiary to administer insurance programs for MEA members. The MESSA Board of Trustees includes the president and vice-president of the MEA; and six additional trustees elected from and by the MEA's Board of Directors. The MESSA insurance programs include life, accidental death and dismemberment, disability, health, dental, and vision coverage. Local MEA affiliates are encouraged to include MESSA insurance plans in their labor contracts with school districts. In such cases, the corporation which administers insurance benefits to the school district's employees is affiliated with the organization that represents the school district's employees during contract negotiations. As a result, the MEA has unprecedented leverage in controlling the benefits received by its members. In 1992, MESSA received $360 million from approximately 60 percent of Michigan's school districts for insurance coverage of school district employees including teachers, support staff, and administrators.

In 1973, the MEA created the Michigan Education Financial Services Association. Now known as MEA Financial Services, this subsidiary provides MEA members with numerous investment services, including annuities, investment retirement accounts, credit cards, mutual funds, auto owners insurance, and home owners insurance, much like the NEA Special Services program.

In 1982, the MEA established the Michigan Education Data Network Association (MEDNA) as a wholly-owned, for-profit subsidiary. Unlike the other subsidiaries, MEDNA's purpose is to service the MEA rather than MEA's members. MEDNA provides a wide range of clerical and administrative services to the MEA and its other subsidiaries, including data processing, communications, and accounting. For its services as a resource for the entire MEA conglomerate, MEDNA receives compensation from the MEA and its other subsidiaries.

In regard to the relationships between the MEA and its subsidiaries, a report by the Mackinac Center for Public Policy concluded that "Both the Michigan Education Special Services Association (MESSA) and the Michigan Education Association (MEA) have the necessary resources to fight any attempt at restraining the MESSA operation. The MEA can manipulate many public officials through campaign contributions and political pressure, and MESSA has enough financial reserves to pay for legal services, lobbying staff, and other programs necessary to combat its opposition. Moreover, MESSA can recuperate the costs of self-defense by increasing premium rates, inducing more illegitimate taxpayer support."[2] In other words, if taxpayers try to block contracts that establish MESSA as the insurance carrier, MESSA merely adds the costs of litigation to its premiums, and perpetuates the obvious conflict of interest.

In 1994, Michigan enacted legislation that excluded the identity of insurance carriers as a mandatory subject of bargaining. The legislation resulted partly from the Mackinac Center report detailing the conflicts of interest inherent in the way MEA promotes its own insurance company in collective bargaining with school boards. That is, instead of having insurance companies compete to provide the best insurance coverage at the lowest possible cost, MEA negotiators promoted MEA's subsidiary as the carrier. This conflict of interest arises whenever the unions bargain for insurance benefits sold or administered by a union-controlled insurance company. In at least one state (California), the abuses inherent in this situation led to state action prohibiting the practice. Nevertheless, the MEA is not the only state association in the insurance business. The Wisconsin Education Association Council (WEAC) operates its own insurance conglomerate, the WEA Insurance Group. The latter offers group and individual insurance policies through five nonprofit organizations:

WEA Insurance Trust
WEA Insurance Corporation
WEA Tax Sheltered Annuity Trust
WEA Liability & Casualty Insurance Trust
WEA Property & Casualty Insurance Company

In 1995, an impressive 87 percent of Wisconsin school districts participated in one or more of these plans. At the end of 1995, 165,334 school district employees were insured in one or more plans; in addition, 8,038 employees were covered by new plans not included in the 165,334 covered in the existing plans.[3]

From a public policy perspective, neither the state associations nor their subsidiaries provide adequate information about their relationships. In view of the weak disclosure requirements applicable to state associations, the abuses and conflicts of interest that have emerged in Michigan and California undoubtedly exist in other state associations.

State Association Assets

Although their assets vary widely, the state associations are not asset poor. In many states, their headquarters building is located in prime areas near the state capitol. Furthermore, in some states, the state associations own the buildings that house regional offices or local affiliates. For instance, the Pennsylvania State Education Association (PSEA) owns thirteen properties in various regions of the state. The properties carried a book value of almost $7.8 million in 1994. PSEA rented space in some to for-profit companies. In California, the author has negotiated in CTA owned county offices with ample parking, meeting rooms, kitchen, library, executive offices, and even a few acres of choice farm land.

In data that are available, the state associations did not adopt the same basis (for example, market value or book value) in estimating the value of their real estate. Relying on conservative assumptions, my estimate is that the state associations own about $200 million in real estate. About two-thirds of this amount would be the value of the headquarters buildings in the state capitols.

Although the state associations have financial assets as well, it was not feasible to estimate their values. It appears, however, that their financial assets apart from revenues are not typically a major factor in their financial condition.

Local Association Revenues

Local association revenues including county and regional association revenues are the biggest gap in estimating total association revenues. Approximately 13,000 locals, including about 600 in higher education, are affiliated with the NEA. Although comprehensive data on their revenues is not available, at least to nonunion sources, a few observations may be helpful.

First, "local" does not necessarily mean "small." Several large urban unions, mainly in the AFT, enroll more members than the smaller states do. Membership in NEA's local affiliates ranges from single digits to associations with over 6,500 members. Associations with less than $25,000 in revenues are not required to submit IRS Form 990, and more than half of NEA's local affiliates do not file one. Furthermore, reliable estimates would require clearing up the fund transfers to and from the locals, a complex task that did not appear to justify the resources required to carry it out properly.

For these reasons, I have not tried to estimate local association revenues from local association financial statements. Instead, I have relied upon estimates of local dues, multiplied by the estimated number of members of local associations. In making these estimates, I have tried to take into account inflation, fluctuations in membership, revenues from agency fees, and other factors that would affect the revenues. Accordingly, my estimate is that average local dues in the NEA are $50 per full-time employee. Local dues range from $100 to $250 in districts that employ a full-time UniServ director; in smaller districts that share a UniServ director, local dues are much less, but regional dues kick in. Many small local associations do not employ a UniServ director, either full- or part-time. Although local dues in most districts may be less than $50, dues in the larger local associations tend to be higher. For this reason, $50 should be close to the NEA average for all employed NEA members.

AFT Revenues

Several differences between the NEA and AFT affect the comparability of NEA/AFT revenue data.

- AFT receives and spends a significant portion of its revenues on its 150,000 noneducational employees. Although some expenditures are supposed to benefit both noneducational and educational employees, some clearly would not.
- The AFT enrolls a higher proportion of support personnel who are paid much less than teachers; also, the proportion of retiree members is much higher in the AFT.
- AFT membership is more concentrated in high-salary and high-dues paying states; outside of a few urban school districts, the federation enrolls relatively few members in the southern and the plains states.
- Outside New York, the AFT is primarily a large city organization. Local dues tend to be much higher than local dues in NEA affiliates; state dues tend to be much lower, and national dues ($108.60 in FY 1995–96) are about the same as NEA dues ($107).
- AFT revenues and expenditures at all levels include AFL-CIO affiliation fees, an item not included in NEA revenues or expenditures.
- The NEA and AFT use different accounting systems. In the AFT, local, state, and national dues, as well as dues to local, state, and national AFL-CIO affiliates are counted as revenues. The locals then categorize the per capita payments to state and national AFT and AFL-CIO affiliates as expenditures. In contrast, the NEA accounting structure often provides a pass-through for state and NEA dues. In this way, the state and national dues do not show up as revenues to NEA locals that utilize a pass-through. A consequence is that AFT locals appear to be receiving more of the dues dollar, when in fact this may not be the case.
- The AFT budget combines the regular union budget with special purpose funds that are treated separately in NEA financial statements. About 40 percent of AFT revenues are from New York state; no other state provides as much as 10 percent. Twelve other states and the District of Columbia provide about 50 percent of AFT revenues and the remaining thirty-seven states account for 10 percent. Clearly, the AFT is highly vulnerable to restrictive legislation in New York state.

Rather than try to track separately the financial implications of the foregoing factors, I estimated AFT revenues for FY 1996–97 according to the procedures in Appendix B. Table 9.2 sets forth the estimates:

TABLE 9.2

AFT Revenues, 1996–97

$ 86,000,000	Estimated national office revenues based on revenues of $84.3 million in 1995–96. See 1994–96 *Report of the Officers of the American Federation of Teachers*
$105,000,000	Estimated state federation revenues. See Appendix B for estimation procedures
$159,922,000	Estimated local federation revenues. See Appendix B for estimation procedures
$350,922,000	Total AFT revenues

Table 9.3 summarizes my estimates of 1996–97 NEA and AFT revenues, exclusive of their subsidiary organizations.

TABLE 9.3

Estimates of NEA/AFT 1996–97 Revenues

National:

NEA	202,000,000
AFT	86,000,000

State:

NEA	525,000,000
AFT	105,000,000

Local, including regional:

NEA	131,475,000
AFT	159,922,000
	$1,209,397,000 Total NEA/AFT, exclusive of subsidiary organizations

To reiterate, the above estimates do not include union PAC funds, member benefit corporations, special purpose funds, and foundations. These organizations probably add about $100 million annually to the resources available to the NEA/AFT.

Like the NEA, the AFT has established foundations which receive funds from government agencies, philanthropic foundations, and corporations. Since 1984, the AFT foundation has received millions from the National Endowment for Democracy (NED) and the Agency for International Development (AID) to educate teachers around the world on democracy and the benefits of teacher bargaining, American style. From October 1, 1992, to September 30, 1994, the foundation received almost $1.2 million just from NED for these programs, which are discussed in Chapter 12. The AFT foundation has also been the recipient of various grants from philanthropic foundations and corporations. Similarly, the United Federation of Teachers Foundation in New York City has received Education 2000 funds from the New York state department of education as well as from the New York City board of education and philanthropic foundations. Former AFT President Albert Shanker's praise for the Clinton administration's Goals 2000 program was not as disinterested as unsuspecting readers might assume.

The Chicago Teachers Union, an AFT affiliate, established a center on school restructuring in 1992 with the help of a $1 million grant from the MacArthur Foundation. In 1996, the center received state permission to establish a graduate school expected to enroll about 200 teachers annually.[4] It will be interesting to see how conflict of interest problems are resolved: to whom will Chicago teachers look for support if they have a grievance against the school or one of its instructors? In any event, state and local teacher union foundations are likely to become significant sources of union income where they are not already.

State Teacher Retirement Funds

The foregoing sketch of union revenues has not mentioned the largest source of funds utilized to support union objectives. I refer to the $883 billion in assets of the state retirement funds that included teachers in 1995.[5]

The state teacher unions exercise varying degrees of control over how these assets are invested. Resolution F–51, adopted at the 1996 NEA convention, states that retirement boards should cast their vote as stockholders "by electing to corporate boards members and/or representatives who support public education." The NEA/AFT objective is to have the retirement boards divest or not buy stocks in companies involved in privatization.

Each state has its own laws and regulations relating to control over public employee pension funds. In thirty-three states, the teacher contributions go into a state fund that covers at least some other public employees as well. In seventeen states, the teacher contributions go into a separate state teacher retirement fund, which is managed by designated public officials. Usually the board of directors consists of a combination of elected public officials and teachers elected by the teacher participants in the retirement system. Since no other group has the interest or the access to the membership, the candidates supported by the state association are assured of election. Of course, if the elected public officials are endorsed and supported by the state education association, the latter is likely to be influential regardless of how many teachers are on the board.

The following points summarize the situation:

1. The state education associations are trying to increase their representation on the teacher retirement boards.

2. The rate of return on teacher retirement funds is inversely related to the proportion of elected teacher members.[6]

3. The reason for (1) is that the state education associations elect candidates who follow NEA/AFT policies on social investing. That is, instead of investing to maximize the rate of return on teacher pension funds, the union supported directors promote union objectives when there is a conflict between these objectives and the rate of return. Also, politically dominated investment policies sometimes lead to investments for political reasons, such as efforts to help in-state companies.

4. Although corporate responses to union pressure vary, union economic power includes some degree of control over hundreds of billions in public employee retirement funds.

Regrettably, there is no comprehensive study of the revenues of NEA/AFT subsidiary organizations. Despite nomenclature problems, an informal search by the Education Policy Institute in 1996 identified 152 tax exempt member services corporations (115 AFT, 56 NEA); 39 property title holding companies or corporations (22 AFT, 17 NEA); 1 NEA pension title holding company; 273 retiree organizations (267 chapters, 2 member benefit corporations, 2 housing organizations); and 154 teacher credit unions. Their revenues, and the revenues of state and local teacher union foundations, have not been considered. Unquestionably, these subsidiaries add to NEA/AFT revenues, assets, and political power.

Boycott Issues

While scores of the nation's leading companies are contributing to NEA/AFT foundations, the NEA/AFT and their affiliates are utilizing boycotts to coerce companies and business leaders from supporting policies opposed by the unions. The threatened boycott of Pepsi-Cola products and damage to Pepsi-Cola vending machines in Jersey City schools in 1996 is an egregious example. The company's malfeasance was to provide seventy scholarships to children from low-income Jersey City families to attend private schools.

The Jersey City Education Association threatened a state-wide boycott of Pepsi-Cola. Vending machines carrying Pepsi-Cola were damaged and covered with posters attacking the company. Sad to say, the intimidation induced the company to withdraw the scholarships. Perhaps the NEA's most extensive boycott was against Nestle for promoting infant formula over breastfeeding; allegedly, the use of the formula in Third World countries resulted in "baby bottle disease" affecting 10 million babies annually. In publishing a revised list of Nestle products being boycotted, the NEA reported that its previous list erroneously included several products not marketed by a Nestle company. As *NEA Now* succinctly put it, "We regret the error."[7]

At its 1996 convention, the NEA adopted the following new business item:

> Move that the NEA publish a list of all identified corporations, and their subsidiaries, who subcontract or privatize public school employee positions and/or services in the first issue, the last issue, and one mid-year issue of the *NEA Today.* The NEA shall publish a column in each issue of *NEA Today* highlighting abuses to education which occur through privatization."[8]

It is remarkable that the business community allows NEA's intimidation strategy to continue without a collective business response. In its absence, companies and business leaders are losing the right to act freely as citizens without economic reprisal. As matters stand, boycotts are a risk-free way for the NEA/AFT to intimidate opposition from the business community. The unions launch their missiles from behind an impregnable fortress labeled "pupil welfare." There seems to be no way to fight back, no matter how indefensible the boycott, without hurting the pupils.

This issue should be addressed by the business community. If the NEA/AFT continue to be successful in intimidating companies and business leaders on privatization issues, they will undoubtedly apply the same tactics to other issues, such as economic and tax policies. Companies and business leaders who value their political freedom must be prepared to defend it even when they are not involved individually. At some point, which I regard as having been passed long ago, the NEA/AFT should be confronted by a credible deterrent, not merely withdrawal of corporate support for union foundations. It remains to be seen whether business leaders have the foresight to protect their freedom; in the meantime, the NEA/AFT are likely to expand their resort to boycotts until there is credible risk in doing so.

Taxpayer Subsidies

As incomplete as the data are, the teacher unions are clearly an economic colossus. If appropriate weight is given to the revenues of organizations in which the NEA/AFT play a dominant but not necessarily exclusive role, the NEA/AFT and their subsidiaries control a multibillion dollar cash flow. Nevertheless, we have yet to consider the huge subsidies the teacher unions receive from state and local governments. These subsidies are one of the most important, but are the least recognized (outside the unions), sources of NEA/AFT financial support.

Taxpayer subsidies are defined as costs of union operations that are paid from taxpayer (local, state, or federal) funds. In addition to the union savings involved, taxpayer subsidies have the advantage of not showing up on the union books. If someone buys your lunch, you do not ordinarily count the cost as income, but you have avoided the cost of buying it. This is how taxpayer subsidies function; as we shall see, much more than lunch is involved.

Payroll Deduction of Union Dues, Fees, and PAC Contributions

From the standpoint of frequency and value to the union, the most important taxpayer subsidy is payroll deduction of union dues, fees, and PAC funds (hereinafter, "payroll deduction") at no cost to the union. Payroll deduction of dues is the union's top priority in both the public and private sector. It is virtually always accepted by employers, and a refusal to accept would be regarded as a declaration of war against the union. This is understandable; the cost to the district would be minimal but the benefit to the union is huge, perhaps even survival. Nonetheless, the basic issues should be examined since they affect several subsidies involving considerable costs to school districts.

In the absence of payroll deduction, the unions must collect dues on a person-to-person basis—a very costly, time-consuming procedure. Its disadvantages to the union are as follows:

• Union staff or supporters must get the money from members. This requires considerable time.

• There may not be a sufficient number of members able and willing to persuade teachers to pay union dues, especially if the persuasion must be repeated annually.

• Seeking union dues on a one-shot basis is extremely difficult; teachers are reluctant to write out a check for $200 to $700 to cover the full amount of local, state, and national dues. If, however, the dues are collected face to face in installments, the time and personnel required will be prohibitive.

• The likelihood of disagreement, or of error, or of fraud are much greater under person-to-person collection instead of payroll deduction.

• Teachers may be upset about a union action or action of union officials. It is much more difficult to get teachers to pay dues when this happens.

• Payroll deduction provides an expeditious way for the union to enforce payment of dues when teachers leave district employment or wish to resign from the union.

- The contract can provide a narrow window, or none at all, for the employee to resign from the union during the term of the agreement.

Even without payroll deduction, the employee may sign a payroll form agreeing to be a member for the duration of the contract. In practice, the means available to the union to enforce this obligation are not very effective without payroll deduction. Suing a school district is merely inconvenient whereas suing teachers for nonpayment of dues is a risky course of action. The publicity associated with such lawsuit would probably weaken teacher willingness to be union members. Teachers ordinarily do not think about resignation until they want to resign union membership; only then do they discover this cannot be done until the contract expires. A lawsuit against a teacher for nonpayment of dues would publicize the issue, perhaps in several nearby districts as well. Consequently, the unions try to negotiate language that obviates the need to sue members who resign or try to resign.

In any event, it is hardly possible to overestimate the value of payroll deduction to the unions; without it, their PAC costs would escalate and their PAC revenues would decline drastically. Another bit of evidence comes from comparisons between cash contributions and payroll deductions for PAC funds. As previously noted, when the state of Washington prohibited payroll deduction for teacher union PAC funds in 1995, the number of contributors dropped from 45,000 to 8,000.[9]

School board refusal to collect agency shop fees would also be a major blow to union revenues. Assume that the nonmember teachers face dismissal if they do not pay the fees. In the absence of payroll deduction, each teacher must pay each month, a major bookkeeping operation in itself. If and when teachers fall behind, as is likely some will, the union has to notify the school district: "X, Y, and Z haven't paid their agency fee, so they should be fired unless they pay by December 20." After a few cases like this, the district will want to wash its hands of the entire business.

It is unlikely that school boards will refuse to deduct union dues from payroll; in nine states, the teacher unions have a statutory right to it. Nevertheless, some boards may propose to charge the union for the service. How should we value payroll deduction as a taxpayer subsidy? Should the charge and/or the value of the subsidy be the actual cost to the district or the value to the union? Because this issue arises with respect to several taxpayer subsidies, the issue merits some discussion.

Let us assume that local, state, and national union dues are $500 annually, the actual cost of payroll deduction to the district is $20 per teacher ($2 per month, 10 months) annually, and the value to the union is $200 annually. The $200 figure reflects the additional costs to the union in the absence of payroll deduction, and the loss of revenues due to the collection problems. As a school board negotiator, I never proposed charging the union for payroll deduction, but see no reason not to do so.

Suppose you inherit a corner lot worth $25,000 (fair market value). A developer offers $25,000 for the lot. However, you know that the lot is worth at least $250,000 to the developer because his plans require acquisition of the lot. Do you sell the lot for $25,000? Hardly. Knowing that the lot is worth much more than $25,000 to the developer, you will insist on more. If the developer isn't willing to pay more than $25,000, you are quite willing to forego the sale; you don't need it to get $25,000 for the lot. And nobody would criticize you for such a course of action.

Rhetoric notwithstanding, the school board is in the same position as the lot owner. Both are engaged in adversarial negotiations. The school board can get along without payroll deduction just as the lot owner can live without selling to the developer. The critical difference is that the union, unlike the developer, is demanding other concessions and is usually willing and able to damage the board politically if there is no agreement. This, however, is all the more reason why the board should not simply agree to payroll deduction—not for $20 per teacher annually, certainly not for free as the overwhelming majority of school boards do. And certainly not for an adversary, which the union is, legally, economically, and often politically.

The foregoing comments should not be interpreted as opposition to friendly cooperative relationships between teacher unions and school boards. The question is, however, whether such relationships are fostered by school boards which make extremely valuable concessions without getting anything in return. After negotiating hundreds of school district labor contracts in seven states over a twenty year span, I doubt whether unilateral concessions of this nature facilitate school board/union cooperation. When the unions receive major concessions without making major concessions of their own, both their level of expectation and their demands go up, not down, as a result.

It is difficult to estimate the value of payroll deduction of union dues; my guess is that union revenues would ordinarily drop by one-third or more in its absence. Most emphatically I do not suggest that payroll deduction of union dues should always be made in a hard bargaining mode. The fact remains, however, that school boards unwittingly absorb the costs of several union benefits, thereby contributing substantially to union power as a board adversary.

One fact strongly suggests lack of legislative and public awareness of the importance of payroll deduction. Several states have enacted or considered legislation prohibiting teacher strikes. The typical penalties are a freeze on teacher salaries and loss of two days salary for every day a teacher is on strike. These penalties are often ineffectual because they are directed against teachers instead of the union. A school board faced with a strike for higher wages is not likely to invoke a penalty that would exacerbate teacher opposition. Suppose, however, that the penalty for a strike was decertification of the union and loss of payroll deduction for a few years. The resulting financial losses to the local, state, and national unions would be a more effective deterrent to teacher strikes than the fines, if any, that are imposed on teachers.

Union Participation in State Teacher Retirement Systems

Pension benefits for union officers and staff are a major taxpayer subsidy to teacher unions, especially in large school districts. Most NEA/AFT officers and staff are former teachers. When they accept full-time union employment, they take a leave of absence from their school districts to preserve their pension rights. Typically, the unions reimburse the districts for the appropriate salary, so that the teachers on leave continue to be carried on the school district records as active members of the state teacher retirement system. Invariably, the teachers on leave this way move up on the salary schedule, just as if they were actually teaching. At the same time, the district and/or the states continue to contribute to the teacher retirement system for the teachers on leave this way.

For example, the New York City Board of Education pays the retirement contribution for about thirty teachers on leave as full-time teacher union staff. In some cases, the board's retirement contributions per teacher are $15,000 annually. The total amounts involved are not large in terms of the Board of Education budget, but they are in terms of the union's. Many AFT employees receive a generous pension from the New York City teacher retirement system, even though the union employees involved, such as the late AFT President Albert Shanker, actually served as teachers for a relatively short period of time. This practice is widespread in both the NEA and AFT; in some cases, the school districts even pay for the health insurance for teachers on leave as union employees.

In contrast, private sector companies seldom allow employees to be on leave of absence and retain their pension benefits and full rights to reemployment for five, ten, twenty years or more As Chapter 8 pointed out, most NEA/AFT employees are covered fully by a union retirement plan which is much more generous than the state teacher retirement systems. Inasmuch as most NEA/AFT officers and professional staff are participants in state teacher retirement systems, a substantial number are earning retirement credit from both their state retirement system and from the union for the same years of service.

Released Time with Pay for Union Employees

School boards frequently provide released time with pay to conduct union business. The practice is usually incorporated in collective bargaining contracts under the following headings:

- Released time with pay for union officers.
- Released time with pay for negotiations.
- Released time with pay for processing grievances.
- Released time with pay to attend union conventions or meetings.

Although the taxpayer costs of released time are often substantial, school districts do not track them carefully. School districts budget for substitutes, but many districts do not separate the substitute costs for union business from the costs for other reasons.

Paid leave to conduct union business is not unusual in the private sector, but only on a much smaller scale. As on most issues, public officials are much more generous with public funds than company officials are with company funds. In the latter, competitive and profit factors minimize leave to conduct union business; also, company officials rarely owe their appointment to a union whereas many school board members owe their election to a teacher union.

Quite frequently, subsidies to the teacher unions are characterized contractually as teacher benefits. For example, the collective bargaining contract often provides "personal necessity leave" with pay. The contracts often specify that the teachers need not explain "personal necessity." At the table, the union negotiator explains that teachers should not have to reveal an impending divorce, or that their child was arrested for drunk driving, or some other embarrassing "personal necessity." And so the districts agree, ignoring the maxim that no good deed goes unpunished. Subsequently, the unions urge their members to vote by mail and take "personal necessity leave" on election day in order to staff telephone banks and supply transportation to the polls. The teachers need not give a reason, so the school district cannot prohibit the use of "personal necessity leave" for political purposes while the contract is in effect. Furthermore, having abandoned responsibility for the uses made of "personal necessity leave," the districts are in a weak position to challenge its use. In any case, "personal necessity leave" is frequently a taxpayer subsidy to the union, categorized as teacher welfare.

Union Use of District Facilities

In most school district labor contracts, the union is allowed liberal use of district facilities and equipment, such as copying machines and telephones. As with payroll deduction of dues, the cost to the district may be much less than the value of the benefit to the union; however, not all use of district facilities and/or equipment falls into this category.

Union Access to Faculty Time

Many school district labor contracts explicitly allow the union to place items on the agenda of faculty meetings, also to address teachers at the meeting. Quite often, the cost to the school district far exceeds the value to the union. For instance, assume that the contract allows the union twenty minutes at teacher meetings called by the district. Assume also the following:

250	number of teachers in the district
$45,000	average teacher salary plus benefits
$36	teacher hourly rate
$12	twenty minutes of teacher time per faculty meeting, includes agenda items submitted by the union
$3,000	district cost of time for union business (250 x $12)
10	number of faculty meetings per school year
$30,000	district cost for time on union business at faculty meetings (10 x $3,000)

The above hypothetical omits several costs to the district and savings to the union. Only a case-by-case analysis would show the actual outcomes. Nonetheless, while conceding wide variability in the costs and benefits, the item is a taxpayer subsidy to the union.

Union Sponsored Courses for Salary Credit

In some large districts, the union offers courses for credit on the teacher salary schedule. The courses often are utilized as patronage for leaders of union caucuses: feminist, gay/lesbian/bisexual, ethnic, and other caucus activists, are paid to teach the courses. The largest cost associated with this item consists of the salary and retirement credits that teachers earn this way. The immediate district costs are minuscule compared to the long range costs of the subsidy.

Union Assistance in Health Insurance Administration

In some large districts, the teacher union is paid to administer health insurance benefits paid by the school district. The practice results in major benefits to the union. Teachers often believe they must be union members in order to receive benefits that are contractually available to all teachers. When teachers appear at the union office for assistance, the union utilizes the opportunity to sell union-sponsored benefits to the teachers. This subsidy is discussed in more detail in Chapter 12.

Payment of Union Dues from School District Funds

In a few school districts, the school district pays or has paid the union dues from district, not teacher funds. The dues are not shown as income to teachers. This particular subsidy was in effect in White Bear Lake, Minnesota, from 1990 to 1994; the district paid $337 for local dues for approximately 600 teachers. Payment of teacher dues from district funds, not teacher salaries, is about as close to union heaven as it gets, but the arrangement did not survive criticism in a 1994 school levy. Levy opponents cited the payment repeatedly in the campaign, and the arrangement was discontinued in the 1995–97 contract.

The NEA's Property Tax Exemption

Although most subsidies result from school board action, Congress is responsible for the tax exemption for the NEA buildings in Washington. The exemption was included in the NEA's congressional charter in 1906, when no one envisaged the emergence of the NEA as a labor union. By the terms of the charter, the exemption applies as long as the NEA building is being used for its chartered purposes.

In 1937, the NEA purchased an adjoining building. From 1990 to 1995, the NEA spent $50 million renovating the two buildings—an amount larger than the assessed valuation of any other national union building in Washington. According to district records, the NEA building carries an assessed valuation of $82.6 million. The taxes on commercial property with such an assessment would be almost $1.8 million, about equivalent to NEA dues from 17,000 NEA members. The other six organizations chartered by Congress are the American Legion, the American National Red Cross, American War Mothers, AMVETS, the Boy Scouts of America, and the Disabled American Veterans. The NEA building is the only labor union building enjoying a tax exemption; indeed, former AFT President Albert Shanker tried to eliminate the NEA's exemption, albeit before the merger talks and as long as his role in the effort was not revealed. Ironically, the AFT building in Washington will be tax exempt if an NEA/AFT merger is consummated.

Since 1995, the District of Columbia has faced an enormous budget deficit; the Republican majority in Congress has had every partisan, as well as public policy, reason to eliminate the property tax exemption. Nevertheless, in November 1995, the House of Representative voted 213 to 210 against eliminating it. The NEA argument was that any change should apply to all federally exempted organizations; allegedly, the NEA was being singled out for "punitive" treatment because it was critical of some members of Congress. Of course, the NEA did not mention the fact that unlike the Red Cross or American Legion or other exempt organizations, the NEA had become a labor union after its charter was granted. Not surprisingly, Republicans endorsed by the NEA combined with a strong Democratic vote to defeat the motion to terminate the exemptions; however, in March 1996, the NEA announced that it would pay up to 40 percent of what its taxes would be were it not for the tax exemption. Moreover, while avoiding any mention of its near loss of the tax exemption, the NEA expressed the hope that other tax exempt organizations would follow its lead.

Legally, the District of Columbia could terminate the exemption (as it should) by finding that the NEA is not fulfilling the purpose of its 1906 charter. The NEA has acted astutely to protect itself from such an eventuality. In 1987, the NEA established an "Office of DC Affairs" to establish and pursue relations with DC elected officials at the highest levels of local government. An NEA staff member cochaired the education transition when Sharon Pratt Kelly was elected mayor in 1990. NEA staff members received mayoral appointments to the Commission on Education in Partnership with Technology and the Commission on Human Rights; an NEA staff member chaired the Board of Consumer Claims Arbitration; and the NEA center was utilized for community meetings and other cooperative activities. Needless to say the NEA supports statehood for the District of Columbia.[10]

A remarkable feature of taxpayer subsidies to the NEA/AFT is that many would be illegal under federal labor law. In order to prevent union officials from negotiating "sweetheart contracts" in exchange for personal payoffs under the table. Subsection (9), Section 302 of the Labor Management Relations Act prohibits employers from giving "any money or other thing of value":

(1) to any representative of any of his employees . . . or

(2) to any labor organization, or any officer or employee thereof, which represents, seeks to represent, or would admit to membership, any of the employees of such employer . . . or . . .

(4) to any officer or employee of a labor organization . . . with intent to influence him in respect to any of his actions, decisions, or duties as a representative of employees or as such officer or employee of such labor organization.

(b) (1) It shall be unlawful for any person to request, demand, receive, or accept, or agree to receive or accept, any payment, loan, or delivery of any money or other thing of value prohibited by subsection (a).

Contributions to a union official's retirement fund or subsidies for travel on union business are examples of employer subsidies which are prohibited under Section 302.

Are Teachers Getting Value for Money?

As Chapter 8 pointed out, the NEA/AFT demand that contractors providing services to school districts provide full disclosure of their financial operations. In contrast, the teacher unions do not provide it even for their own members, even though union contracts have a much larger impact on education than the contracts of companies selling services to school districts. Requiring full disclosure from companies in competitive markets, and virtually none from unions operating in monopolistic markets, should be recognized for the inconsistency that it is. Minimally, the states should establish reporting and disclosure requirements comparable to those applicable to private sector unions under the National Labor Relations Act. As illustrated by the omission of fringe benefits, these requirements are inadequate in some respects, hence the states should do more than incorporate the federal requirements in state law.

The magnitude of union revenues raises the issue of whether teachers are getting good value for their investment in representational services. Union communications assert they are, but the issue deserves more than a pro forma response.

Assume that teachers need and should pay for some form of collective representation. Not everyone shares this assumption, but I have no problem with it. It appears, however, that over 2.5 million teachers are paying an average of $500 each for representational services (more in some districts, less in others, but $500 seems to be a defensible average). The total teacher cash outlay is about $1.25 billion. In this context, the NEA/AFT are producers and the teachers are consumers of representational services. The issue is whether the consumers are getting "value for money," to use a British expression.

Large as they are, union revenues do not include the enormous volunteer services devoted to union objectives. Volunteer efforts are not always deemed a "cost" by the volunteers themselves, but they are a cost from an economic perspective. Furthermore, we should not overlook the revenues of other unions, especially unions of state and local public employees. These unions often represent some school district employees and/or support state and local action that is supposed to benefit such employees. NEA/AFT objectives may also be supported by independent unions of support personnel, some of which have large memberships and substantial revenues. As previously noted, the California School Employees Association alone has 170,000 members. All things considered, teachers have reason to question whether their support for NEA/AFT has reached the point of diminishing returns. Assuming that teachers should have and pay for collective representation, how much should they pay for it?

In some respects, the situation is analogous to advertising. Advertising often pays off, but there comes a point at which additional investment in it does not result in commensurate returns on the investment. And just as advertising is sometimes wasteful, so has union representation been from time to time. Clearly, the NEA/AFT have spent substantial amounts on various projects that have changed nothing; their massive effort to enact the Clinton administration's health plan is an example. To cite just one previous example, the NEA spent much of its political capital in the 1970s in establishing a department of education which is on the way down if not out, partly because it cannot demonstrate any constructive impact on American education. Control of union media by the union bureaucracies ensures that the value for money issue is not raised in union media, but it may be raised in others. If that should happen, the NEA/AFT might face a volatile teacher market for representational services.

10

FREE ECONOMIC RIDERS OR FORCED POLITICAL PASSENGERS?

A gency fees are one of the most litigated but least understood topics in U.S. education. The litigants, especially on the union side, understand the issues very well but most citizens, and I would say most teachers, do not. The issues are not all that complex, but the practice of framing them in bargaining terminology has obscured their basic political character. Clarification leads to several disturbing conclusions, by no means limited to teacher unions.

Agency fees are fees that nonmembers of a union must pay to the union as a condition of employment. Refusal to pay requires the employer to fire the employee. Nineteen states either mandate agency fees or allow teacher unions to bargain over the issue. The implications, however, affect education and politics everywhere in the United States.

The NEA/AFT rationale for agency fees can be summarized as follows:

• By law (U.S. Supreme Court decision actually), the union must represent everyone in the bargaining unit regardless of membership or nonmembership in the union. The union cannot negotiate benefits for union members that are not equally available to nonmembers. For example, providing that union members receive more sick leave than nonmembers would violate the union's duty of fair representation.

• Because employees do not have to be union members to receive the benefits of union representation, many choose to be "free riders"; that is, they choose not to join and pay union dues.

• It is unfair for the beneficiaries of the union contract to avoid sharing the cost of negotiating and administering it.

• To solve the free rider problem without compulsory membership, nonmembers should pay their "fair share" of the union's costs for collective bargaining, contract administration, and grievance processing (hereinafter, "collective bargaining"). The fair share is less than the costs of full membership. In many states, the statutes authorizing agency fees are designated "fair share" laws.

Obviously, the rationale has no particular appeal to school boards. Why should they be forced to fire, or unable to hire good teachers who object to agency fees?

The union answer is threefold. If teachers pay an agency fee, they are much less likely to join and support a rival union. A rival union would be a threat to "labor peace." It would try to oust the incumbent union by arguing that it could squeeze more concessions from the school board. This would not be in the board's interest, hence the board should prevent this outcome by agreeing to an agency fee.

Although some courts have embraced "labor peace" as a compelling interest that justifies agency fees, to my knowledge no court has defined it. In practice, "labor peace" is a euphemism for the elimination of challenges to incumbent unions. Incumbent unions, not school boards, appeal to "labor peace" as the rationale for agency fees.

Another appeal to school boards emphasizes the difficult decisions facing many union negotiators. The latter may realize that the union should accept a board proposal that is very unpopular with union members. If the union can be assured that teachers cannot withdraw their financial support, it will be more inclined to accept the unpopular school board proposal.

Like the appeal to labor peace, the argument for agency fees as an aid to union statesmanship is not very persuasive. First, it ignores the possibility that withdrawal of financial support may be the only way to achieve a responsive union. The suggestion that the unions will be led in difficult situations by their least responsible members really undermines the rationale for collective bargaining. Most unions face difficult situations from time to time; if their actions in these situations are guided by their least responsible members, perhaps public policy should not support collective bargaining in the first place. In any event, nonmembers should not have to bear the financial burden of unreasonable union conduct, especially since agency fees will not necessarily solve the problem.

The third union argument for agency fees is not as statesmanlike, but is often more effective. The argument is "Accept agency fees or we'll raise hell until you do."

Because unions, even with employer consent, cannot require membership as a condition of employment, they are constantly faced with free rider problems. The union becomes the exclusive representative by a majority vote in a bar-gaining unit, but the employees need not be union members to vote for union representation. Teachers realize that their individual dues will not affect the outcome of negotiations. At the same time, many teachers prefer to get the benefits of representation without paying for them. (Later in this chapter, I will challenge the view that union representation benefits everyone represented by the union, but let us assume that most teachers would benefit). The upshot is that many teachers refuse to join the union and pay their share of its costs.

The legal status of agency fees in the fifty states and District of Columbia is as follows:

• States that have enacted collective bargaining statutes and require payment of agency fees by state law: Hawaii, Minnesota, New York.

• States that have enacted bargaining statutes that allow teacher unions to negotiate agency fees: Alaska, California, Connecticut, Delaware, Illinois, Maryland (only in Baltimore and four counties), Massachusetts, Michigan, Montana, New Jersey, Ohio, Oregon, Pennsylvania, Rhode Island, Washington, Wisconsin, also the District of Columbia.

• States that have enacted bargaining statutes, but prohibit agency fees, at least in public education: Florida, Idaho, Indiana, Iowa, Kansas, Maine, Nebraska, Nevada, New Hampshire, New Mexico (dues deduction a mandatory subject of bargaining), North Dakota, Oklahoma, South Dakota, Tennessee, and Vermont.

• States that allow collective bargaining as a school board option, but prohibit agency fees: Alabama, Arkansas, Colorado, Kentucky, Louisiana, Missouri, and West Virginia.

• States that prohibit collective bargaining in public education: Arizona, Georgia, Mississippi, North Carolina, South Carolina, Texas, Utah, Virginia, and Wyoming.

Agency Fee Issues

Through a series of cases, the Supreme Court has held that agency fee payers cannot be required to pay for union political activities to which they object. The breakthrough case on the subject was *Ellis* v. *Railway Clerks*.[1] In this case, the contract between Western Airlines and the Brotherhood of Railway, Airline, and Steamship Clerks (BRAC) required nonmembers to pay full union dues. The plaintiffs challenged the chargeability of various expenditures, leading to a mixed bag of rulings on the issues. Union publications and litigation were chargeable only to the extent that they communicated information on chargeable matters, such as grievance procedures or bargaining proposals.

Inexplicably, the Supreme Court held that union conventions were completely chargeable; dissenting Justice Powell noted that at BRAC's 25th quadrennial convention, major addresses were made by Senators Hubert Humphrey, Ted Kennedy, Vance Hartke, and Richard Schweiker; the Mayor of Washington, D.C., and four Congressmen. According to Powell, the union did not show that these politicians "contributed even remotely" to collective bargaining. Obviously, Powell's objections to the full chargeability of union conventions would be applicable to NEA/AFT conventions that have featured President Reagan, President Clinton, Hillary Rodham Clinton, Vice-President Gore, Secretary of Education Richard Riley, and other prominent Democratic leaders.

Although the *Ellis* case was initiated in 1973, the decision in the case actually followed the 1969 Supreme Court decision in *Abood* v. *Detroit Board of Education*.[2] In 1968, the Detroit Federation of Teachers had levied an assessment on all teachers for a political campaign. Some nonmembers objected and their objections ultimately reached the U.S. Supreme Court. The plaintiffs in *Abood* argued that the First and Fourteenth Amendments prohibit government from discriminating against citizens in matters of employment on the basis of their affiliation or nonaffiliation with a private organization, in this case, the Detroit Federation of Teachers. Since Michigan law specifically authorized the use of union dues for political purposes, the plaintiffs, as a condition of public employment, were forced to join an organization that spent their dues for political purposes they opposed.

In its decision, the Supreme Court held that agency fees in the public sector per se did not violate plaintiff's constitutional rights. It also held that agency fees could not be used for political purposes to which the payers objected; the fees could be used only for collective bargaining, processing grievances, and contract administration. All other union expenditures, including but not limited to political expenditures, were not chargeable.

In *Abood,* the Supreme Court did not define "political activities"; instead it assumed that its distinction between public sector bargaining and "political activities" was a practical way to resolve the free rider problem without infringing on constitutional rights. Although *Abood* answered some legal questions, it raised several others, such as:

1. Who has the burden of proof? The union to demonstrate that the expenses are chargeable or the teacher to show that the expenses are not chargeable?
2. Who has custody of disputed funds? Does the union keep the money until the teacher proves it never should have been taken in the first place, or is the union precluded from custody until it proves the fees are chargeable?

3. What should be the procedures to challenge a union determination of the chargeable expenses?
4. For what period of time does a determination govern? If a union negotiates a three year contract, can it base its determination for all three years on the year in which the contract was negotiated?
5. Some activities, such as publications, may be partly chargeable and partly not. How should these expenses be treated?
6. Is the union required to inform teachers of their rights before dues or fees are paid to the union?

Some of these issues were resolved by the Supreme Court in *Chicago Teachers Union* v. *Hudson* (1986).[3] An AFT affiliate, the CTU had offered a 5 percent reduction for teachers who objected to the use of their dues for political purposes; the union had set this reduction from its records without any independent accounting or audit. If a teacher wanted to challenge the 95 percent figure, the teacher nevertheless had to pay it and then submit a letter to the CTU president explaining the reasons for a larger rebate. The union president then referred the claim to the union's executive committee; if the request was not resolved satisfactorily to the teacher, it was referred to the union's executive board. If the latter did not resolve the issue, it was referred to an arbitrator appointed by the union president and paid by the union. Obviously, the CTU version of "due process" depends on whether the union supports a grievance, or is the party against whom the grievance is filed.

Understandably, the plaintiffs in the *Hudson* case objected to the CTU rebate procedure, and the Supreme Court upheld their objections for these reasons:

1. The procedure required only that the union rebate the unjustified charges to the plaintiffs. Thus the procedure would result in an involuntary loan to the union.
2. Although the teacher must object to the union estimate, the union should carry the burden of proof once an objection is raised. The union has the relevant information; teachers should not be required to challenge the union's charges in order to discover the basis for them.
3. The entire process for resolving challenges to agency shop fees paid to the union was union-controlled all the way.

The Supreme Court summarized its decision as follows:

We hold today that the constitutional requirements for the Union's collection of agency fees include an adequate explanation for the basis of the fee, a reasonably prompt opportunity to challenge the amount of the fee before an impartial decision maker, and an escrow for the amounts reasonably in dispute while such challenges are pending.

Hudson also prohibited another union practice in estimating chargeable expenses. The union procedure started with the total amount of dues, subtracted the amounts of nonchargeable costs, and claimed the remaining items were chargeable. *Hudson* reversed the process; the union had to start from zero and justify each cost as chargeable. As the court stated, showing that 5 percent is not chargeable does not constitute proof that the other 95 percent is chargeable. Parenthetically, it is interesting that teacher unions that adamantly oppose school board control over contractual grievance procedures, would litigate, all the way to the U.S. Supreme Court, their right to control member challenges to union actions.

The next major public sector case, *Lehnert* v. *Ferris Faculty Association,* involved challenges to chargeable expenditures by a faculty union.[4] Because the rulings in Lehnert are supposed to govern the chargeability of most NEA/AFT expenditures, I have summarized them in Table 10.1.

NEA/AFT Revenues from Agency Shop Fees

In many school districts, some teachers join the union and pay union dues only because the difference between the agency fee and dues is not worth the hassle associated with nonmembership. For this reason, union financial statements that distinguish dues from agency shop income are highly misleading; a considerable amount of dues income is the result of agency fees.

To what extent are union revenues dependent on agency fees? According to NEA financial statements, 23,000 agency fee payers paid $2.4 million, 1.29 percent of the NEA's $185.7 million budget in 1995–96.[5] These figures refer only to NEA revenues. In right-to-work states, the state and local affiliates receive no income from agency fees; in states which authorize or mandate agency fees, union financial statements show that agency fees are 2 to 4 percent of state and local revenues. To appreciate the misleading nature of these figures, suppose that combined local, state, and national dues in the NEA are $500. Suppose also that the agency fee in district A is 85 percent of dues, but only 50 percent in district B. Keeping the example to the basics, the results are as follows:

	District A	District B
Dues	$500	$500
Agency Fee percent	85	35
Agency Fee dollars	425	175
Teacher Saving	75	325

TABLE 10.1

Supreme Court Decisions on Chargeability in Lehnert v. Ferris Faculty Association

---

Yes: Dissenters can be forced to pay (chargeable).
No: Dissenters cannot be required to pay (nonchargeable).

1. Lobbying, unless necessary to ratify or fund the dissenters' specific bargaining agreement. No: 7–1.

2. Electoral politics, including ballot and bond issues. No: 8–1.

3. Public relations, activities. No: 8–1.

4. Litigation not specifically on behalf of the dissenters' bargaining. No: 7–1.

5. Bargaining and other related activities on behalf of persons in other bargaining units and other states. Yes: 9–0, unless the extra-unit activity is wholly unrelated to the dissenters' bargaining unit and cannot ultimately inure to the benefit of the dissenters' unit.

6. Miscellaneous professional activities, i.e., general teaching and education, professional development, unemployment, job opportunities, award programs, and other miscellaneous matters. Yes: 5–4.

7. Local delegate expenses to attend conventions of the local's state and national affiliates. Yes: 5–4.

8. Threatening and preparing for illegal strikes. Yes: 6–3. Although the issue was not specifically presented, the court also said that a union payment "in the nature of a charitable donation would not be chargeable to dissenters." The Court explicitly did "not determine whether [dissenters] could be commanded to support all the expenses of these conventions." As will be evident, however, union accounting practices render it extremely difficult for nonmembers to challenge union determinations of chargeability.

If there were no agency fees, nonmembers in both A and B would not pay anything to the union. In our hypothetical districts, however, teachers in A might decide that $75 saved by not joining the union isn't worth the criticism and loss of rights to participate in union affairs. It may be that if nonmembers in A were required to pay only $175 in agency fees, they would act like teachers in B, who have concluded that the $325 savings justifies nonmembership. The closer the agency shop fees are to dues, the more teachers will opt for membership and payment of full dues instead of agency fees. When agency fees are successfully negotiated, there is almost invariably an increase in union membership.

Because the point at which teachers will choose union dues over agency fees varies, we cannot say precisely how much dues income is due to the existence of agency fees. Strong evidence on the issue is to be found in state comparisons of "union density," that is, the percent of teachers who are members of the NEA or AFT. Although differences in union density cannot be attributed solely to agency fees, union density goes from high to low in the following pattern:

- States with mandatory agency fees
- States that allow the union to bargain for agency fees
- States that have enacted bargaining laws and are not right-to-work states
- States that allow collective bargaining but have not enacted bargaining laws
- Right-to-work states that have not enacted bargaining laws

Over time, the unions tend to be very successful in negotiating agency fees; for example, it appears that over 95 percent of Michigan teachers are union members, a percentage clearly attributable to agency fee requirements. Within other states that allow unions to negotiate an agency fee, the percentage of teachers who are agency fee payers varies considerably from district to district. Usually, the highest percentages of agency fee payers are in the large urban districts. School boards that employ a small number of teachers, especially in rural areas, are much less likely to agree to an agency fee requirement.

NEA revenues from agency fees are from only twenty-nine states (and territories) which mandate or allow them. In these twenty-nine states, the fee payments may be 4-to-5 percent of NEA revenues from the state. They are also a substantial source of state and local association income.

As of September 30, 1995, the California Teachers Association (CTA) was receiving agency fees from 14,360 agency fee payers. Since some were part-time let us reduce the number by 5 percent to 13,642 fee payers, paying $345 each for local, CTA, and NEA fees.[6] On this basis, NEA, CTA, and California local associations received over $4.7 million from California teachers unwilling to join the NEA. Although this amount does not include agency fees paid to AFT affiliates or other unions, it underscores the state and local importance of agency fees. Although the $2.4 million from agency fees was only 1.29 percent of the NEA budget, agency fees are a much larger percentage of state and local association budgets. The same point applies to agency fees in the AFT.

The fact is, however, that union financial statements grossly understate union revenues from agency shop fees in still another way. Unions are much more likely to raise their dues if employees must pay either dues or agency fees. It is no accident that both the highest union density and the highest dues are in states in which the agency fees are mandatory or negotiable by state law.

In many states, the agency fees are the same as union dues, initiation fees, and general assessments paid by members. How can this be if the agency fee is constitutionally limited to the employees pro rata share of the costs of collective bargaining?

The answer is the same as the answer to this question: Why do teachers frequently strike in states where strikes are illegal? Illegalities are one thing, penalties are another. All the courts have done, even after protracted expensive litigation, is to order the unions to return the nonchargeable amounts with interest. As long as the courts do not penalize illegal takings, the unions have strong incentives to set the fees as the full amount of regular dues and assessment of union members. If teachers do not challenge the assessment, the unions get every penny they could possibly receive. If teachers challenge the assessment, the worst that can happen is that the union will be ordered to return the excess amount with interest.

The asymmetry in costs and incentives is decisive. Individual teachers are not going to spend thousands, perhaps tens or even hundreds of thousands, to recover nonchargeable agency fees amounting to a few hundred dollars or less. Meanwhile, the NEA/AFT have every incentive to litigate agency fee issues to the limit, to discourage any teacher opposition to paying the fees. As will be explained, even class action suits cannot fully redress this imbalance in costs and incentives.

What about school boards? Why do they accept this illegal taking from teachers who do not wish to be union members? Board members often owe their election to the union or fear its opposition if they oppose agency fees. Some board members accept the union argument and others feel that their objections are futile since so many boards have agreed to agency fees. Still others try to get union concessions for an agency fee whose cost comes out of teacher pockets, not school board budgets.

The vast majority of union contracts say nothing about a teacher's right to challenge the amount of the fee. Usually, if mentioned at all, this right is discussed in a letter sent by the local association to new teachers. Frequently, the letter makes a pitch for membership, followed by inaccurate information about the fees and the procedures for challenging them. In any event, the outcome is a huge boost in union revenues. California employed about 225,000 teachers in 1994–95. About 10,000 agency fee payers requested a rebate; of these, less than 3,000 questioned the amount and only about 700 legally challenged it. Inasmuch as the nonmembers were being charged full dues in most districts, the NEA/AFT were (and are) receiving millions every year from teachers unaware of their rights or unwilling to assert them for various reasons.

NEA/AFT Partners in Crime Without Punishment

In Chapter 1, I asserted that the NEA is engaged in questionable accounting practices to maximize its revenues. UniServ directors play a major role in this process. A substantial percentage of union expenses that is charged to nonmembers is based on UniServ time. If UniServ directors devote 85 percent of their time to collective bargaining, 85 percent of their support costs (secretaries, supplies, equipment, etc.) are also allocated to collective bargaining. To support union claims of chargeability, UniServ directors prepare time sheets, usually on a weekly basis. The sheets are used solely for the purpose of supporting union claims of chargeability, if and when such claims are challenged.

How much UniServ time is devoted to chargeable activities? Obviously the answer to this question depends on several factors. If multiyear contracts are negotiated, no time thereafter may be required for two or three years, when it becomes necessary to negotiate a new contract. Poorly drafted contracts may lead to more grievances and more time devoted to contract administration. Personal factors often play a significant role; intransigent local association leaders or school board members may drag out negotiations for several months. The time devoted to impasse procedures is often affected by the availability and attitudes of mediators and fact-finders. In short, we are in the realm of patterns and central tendencies and interpretations and memories—not a very reliable basis for allocating the time between chargeable and nonchargeable activities.

Suppose the UniServ director attends a UniServ council meeting at which the agenda includes:

- Bargaining strategy in the districts;
- Union endorsed candidates for the state legislature;
- Endorsements of candidates in the school board election;
- PAC deductions in the contracts;
- Health insurance in school district contracts compared to benefits in the Clinton health care bill;
- Pending state legislation on state aid to education.

Suppose also the meeting lasts four hours. The UniServ directors are fully aware of the financial implications of their time records. Since they avoid disclosure of nonmember rights if at all possible, we can hardly expect scrupulous allocations of chargeable/nonchargeable time. Legal confusion and faulty memory aside, can there be any doubt of the tilt that is given to chargeable activities? And of the enormous difficulties in impeaching UniServ time sheets years later, if and when the allocations of time are being challenged by nonmembers? All of the participants in the UniServ council meetings will be association leaders and negotiators who have a strong interest in maximizing chargeability.

According to an NEA publication on the subject, the UniServ directors:

- Manage all political activities within their unit;
- Coordinate their activities with local PAC chairs;

- Train union PAC representatives and distribute materials;
- Collect and transmit PAC contributions to the state PAC official within three (3) days.

In conjunction with their other political responsibilities UniServ directors obviously devote considerable time to political activities.[7]

What counts is how UniServ directors categorize their time. How their time is actually divided is practically irrelevant.

Most emphatically, the preceding comments are just as applicable to AFT staff members. In taking credit for the Clinton–Gore victory in 1992, the *American Teacher* pointed out:

> ... AFT staffers were assigned to help coordinate activities in Illinois, Michigan, Ohio, New York, Pennsylvania, Georgia, Missouri, Louisiana, Connecticut, Oregon and Minnesota; others helped write material for distribution to members. The union also boosted its retiree staff to help organize AFT's seniors, and two health care staffers were assigned to work with the Clinton/Gore Healthcare Action Team.[8]

It is unrealistic to assume that agency fees in the AFT were adjusted downward to reflect these nonchargeable activities. One interesting bit of evidence on the issue is how the AFT categorized its expenditures before the Supreme Court decisions on agency fee issues. In 1995–96, AFT dues were $108.40, and the AFT charged 74.82 percent of this amount ($81.25) as the national office share of agency fees. Although less than the 95 percent asserted by the Chicago Teachers Union in the *Hudson* case, 74.82 percent is more than twice as much as the 35.5 percent spent for "collective bargaining and organization" in the 1972 AFT budget, when the revenue implications of this line item were not an issue.[9]

The most persuasive evidence on agency fee issues is the litigation record. According to the National Right to Work Foundation (NRTWF), it has litigated 668 cases against the teacher unions from 1968 to July 1996. Of these, 365 were still open and 303 were closed as of July 1, 1996. Of the closed cases, 270 resulted in a fee reduction.[10] As of April 1996, the National Right to Work Legal Defense Foundation (NRTWLDF) had litigated 587 agency fee cases for public employees who challenged one or more aspects of the fee.[11] The majority of these cases have been against the NEA and its affiliates. NRTWLDF attorneys achieved a reduction of fees in 460 of these cases. Some involved procedures, but procedures are often critical; for example, NRTWLDF attorneys litigated the cases that overturned the union's right to control the rebate procedure from beginning to end, even to selecting the "impartial arbitrator."

The NRTWLDF cases arose in every state that required or allowed agency fees. Perhaps the most compelling fact about the cases is that they were not litigated because they were the most egregious cases of union overreaching. Even if they were, they would constitute a strong argument that the NEA/AFT are engaged in questionable accounting practices in order to maximize revenue streams, but the case for this conclusion is much stronger.

As of March 1996, NRTWLDF had 522 open cases on agency issues; of these, 201 were against the NEA or its affiliates. Bear in mind, however, that NRTWLDF is a charitable foundation with limited resources. Furthermore, NRTWLDF provides legal assistance only if asked to do so. The vast majority of agency fee payers do not ask for legal assistance. In fact, the majority pay full union dues or very close to that amount. Many do not know that help may be available or that their rights are being violated. Many who know that help is available prefer to avoid the publicity and pressure of a lawsuit.

In contrast, the NEA/AFT have strong incentives to fight every effort to reduce the fees. Suppose, for example, that chargeable expenses were only 35 percent instead of 75 percent of dues. The immediate direct loss of revenues from agency fee payers would be only a fraction of the union's losses, and not necessarily the most substantial. More teachers would opt out of the union, and it would be much more risky to raise union dues. As union revenues and membership declined, so would their political clout. The dynamics of the decline could be disastrous. Thus NRTWLDF and nonmembers face strong union resistance to challenges on all agency fee issues; if the union loses any, multiplier effects come into play.

The stakes in the agency fee cases, and the staggering costs involved in litigating them fully, are illustrated by *Belhumeur et al* v. *Massachusetts Teachers Association* (MTA). The case was initiated in 1989 and was still in the Massachusetts courts in 1997. The plaintiffs were over 100 K-12 teachers and university professors; the main issue was whether the MTA had met its burden of proof in setting the agency fee over a five-year period.

After lengthy pretrial discovery, the trial began in February 1993. The trial required fifty-three days, leading to a transcript of 7,920 pages of testimony. Over 11,000 exhibits, many of them long documents, were introduced. The data base eventually included 56,373 records, and required extensive computer services in order to cross index and compare various documents, such as the time sheets of UniServ directors. During the trial, MTA unsuccessfully sought a ruling that the legal expenses of the trial were wholly chargeable to nonmembers. The MTA was also unsuccessful in its effort to retry each item on which it had failed to meet its burden of proof. At one point, the trial days had to be rescheduled because the union's lawyers were on strike against the MTA. In the course of the litigation, NRTWLDF attorneys discovered that the MTA had helped to organize a boycott of Folger's coffee which was contrary to U.S. policy, and opposed by the State Department, the U.S. Catholic Bishops, and labor unions in El Salvador. It was also discovered that the MTA vice-president had met with Cuban trade union officials, traveled to Costa Rica to meet with El Salvadorean unionists, and traveled to Canada to study its "single payer" health care system. The MTA had categorized all of these activities as chargeable to agency fee payers.

The union position is that no illegality is involved even if the contract specifies full payment of union dues and assessments. Under Supreme Court decisions, the nonmembers must object to the fee. If they do not object, they must pay full dues; if they object, they get a refund of the nonchargeable expenses. Illegality would come into play only if a nonmember objected and did not receive due process and/or the appropriate reduction. The NEA/AFT also oppose any legal obligation on their part to inform employees of their rights concerning agency fees. I do not find their argument persuasive on the illegality issue; regardless, deliberately taking advantage of a lack of information about teacher rights is hardly consistent with the ideal of a professional organization devoted to protecting them.

Because of the huge litigation costs involved in agency fee cases, NRTWLDF must take into account the number of plaintiffs, the amounts involved, the record of the judges likely to hear the case, the resources required, and a host of other factors having nothing to do with the merits of the case—but having everything to do with its value as a precedent or showcase example that would have widespread application. The cases that are litigated reflect only a small fraction of the requests for legal assistance, and the requests for legal assistance come from only a small fraction of the districts in which legally excessive fees are collected from nonmembers.

The NEA/AFT contend that the small number of challenges demonstrates widespread teacher acceptance of the deduction of full dues. The insincerity of their position is evident from the fact that the unions seldom notify their members of their agency fee rights—a striking inconsistency in organizations allegedly devoted to protecting teacher rights.

Sometimes NEA/AFT leaders inadvertently invite attention to their lack of candor on agency fee issues. For example, in urging merger with the AFT, NEA president Keith Geiger asserted that "The local affiliates were just tired of spending tons of money fighting each other." . . . They came to the conclusion that spending all that time and money isn't improving education and isn't improving the plight of their members.[12] AFT resolutions and policy statements asserted the same conclusion.[13] Competing for representation rights against a rival union is not a chargeable expense. Inasmuch as the unions now concede that such expenditures aren't helping teachers, it would be interesting to see whether the unions categorized the "tons of money" spent this way as chargeable or nonchargeable to agency fee payers.

NEA/AFT Revenues from Agency Fees

What is the NEA/AFT take from agency fees? My question does not refer to the amounts reported on union financial statements but to the actual difference in union revenues as the result of agency fees. Obviously, the answer is somewhat speculative, but agency fees probably increase union revenues at least 25 percent in the states which authorize or mandate them. Bear in mind that nonmembers must pay the 65-to-90 percent of dues to local, state, and national unions. Agency fees are actually larger in some states than regular dues in others. Second, the fees enable the unions to raise their dues without loss of revenues; the increase in agency fee revenues more than compensates for the small number of members who become fee payers as a result of a dues increase. Understandably, union membership is much higher where teachers are required to pay agency fees.

Note also that agency fees render it extremely difficult to organize a rival organization with adequate resources. Teachers paying $300 to $500 in agency fees are not likely to invest a comparable amount in a rival organization. In the absence of agency fees, the NEA/AFT would have to devote more resources to fighting off rival organizations. Realistic estimates must also consider the issues on a long range basis. If a state abolished agency fees, there might be little change until most of the teacher contracts had expired. The decline in union revenues would not be immediately precipitous, but it would gain as contracts expired.

Elimination of the fee would also conservatize the NEA/AFT politically because more dissatisfied members would or could drop membership. In the final analysis, this could be more important than the revenue implications.

Agency Fees Reconsidered

Despite its acceptance in labor circles, the "free rider" rationale faces increasing criticism on several fronts. First of all, the case for agency fees is based on exclusive representation, but exclusive representation faces an increasingly hostile legal and policy environment. Under exclusive representation, employees in the bargaining unit can no longer contract individually; all lose the right to contract for their own labor. To many observers, this loss of individual rights is not justified by the claim that it is necessary to implement collective bargaining. If unions could represent only their members, there would be no justification for agency fees.

The contention that everyone benefits from union representation is fallacious on its face; some teachers are clearly worse off under union representation. For example, unions negotiate layoff procedures based upon seniority—last hired is first fired. Teachers who are fired under union negotiated procedures, but who would not have been otherwise, hardly "benefit" from union representation. Teachers in difficult-to-staff subjects, such as mathematics and science, would often be paid higher salaries than they receive under union negotiated single salary schedules. Newly employed teachers would often be paid more if the union had not insisted on higher salaries for senior teachers. Single teachers without dependents would often enjoy higher salaries were it not for the fact that the union opted for family health insurance instead of higher salaries. The unions contend that they resolve these conflicts in the interests of the majority of their members; whether or not this claim is valid, it undermines the proposition that "everyone benefits" from union representation.

Are agency fees justified because the union has "the duty of fair representation," that is, because the union must represent nonmembers as well as members without discrimination?

The duty of fair representation was laid on unions in the 1944 *Steele* case involving racial discrimination.[14] Essentially, a union of white railroad employees represented black employees who were not allowed to join the union. When the black employees challenged their exclusion, the Supreme Court came up with "the duty of fair representation" to preserve exclusive representation. Note that internal democracy within the union does not necessarily prevent unfair or discriminatory treatment of either members or nonmembers, or even nonemployees. For instance, in the *Steele* case, the fact that the internal union processes were fair and democratic had no bearing on the injustice against black nonmembers perpetrated by the union. Such cases arise constantly outside of the racial context.

If a teacher union establishes a $25,000 salary for beginning teachers, teachers willing to work for less are deprived of employment. Mathematics and science teachers who could command higher salaries except for union representation may never be able to convince the majority of teachers to accept salary differentials. The rationale for teacher bargaining was that parties affected by a decision should have the right to participate in the decision-making process, but this is not what happens. Parents, prospective employees, taxpayers, and a host of other groups are affected by teacher contracts but are excluded from the bargaining process. The NEA/AFT argument is that the school board should represent these interests; the unions do not explain why school boards should represent these other interests but not the teacher interests.

The unions seek the duty of representing everyone, and would be greatly upset if employees could negotiate their terms and conditions of employment individually. Furthermore, the unions seek exclusive representation even where agency fees are not allowed. And even if agency fees are allowed, it does not follow that nonmembers should pay a pro rata share. For example, suppose that a bargaining unit includes 250 teachers, of whom 249 are union members. The union's costs of representing all 250 may not be a penny more than its costs of representing the 249.

Note also that every agency fee per se results in two losses to the fee payers. They lose the option of contracting on their own and also their leverage in union affairs. In the context of teacher/union relations, the teacher is a consumer of representational services; the union a producer of them. In most situations, withdrawal as a client or customer is the most effective way to influence producers. Taking away the teacher's right not to buy union services is taking away the teacher's ability to influence the union, the only feasible way for most teachers to influence union decisions. Where agency fees are in effect, dissident teachers often have no leverage on the union. Persuading other teachers to take action may require teacher time and resources that are not available. In contrast, if teachers need not pay anything to the union, dissident teachers do not have to be politically active within the union to exert their influence.

Interestingly enough, union security varies in other industrial nations. Only a few require union membership before employment; the most frequent issue is whether it can be required after employment. In some nations, the issue is left to agreements between employers and unions. In a few, employees must join a union, but have the freedom to choose the union. Finally, it is interesting that the European Community Charter on Fundamental Social Rights includes an explicit prohibition of agency fees; the charter language is as follows:

> Employers and employees within the European Community have the right to associate freely for the purpose of forming professional associations or trade unions of their choice, for the defence of their economic and social interests. Every employer and every employee has the right to join these organizations, and is not to be subjected to any personal or work related penalty for doing so.[15]

Union, Political Party, or Both?

The U.S. Supreme Court decisions on agency fee issues in public employment have tried to reconcile agency fees with the First Amendment rights of public employees. The latter include the right not to support political activities and the right not to be a member of an organization against one's wishes. Although Supreme Court decisions have assumed that public sector bargaining can be implemented without violating First Amendment rights, a minority of the court has disagreed with this assumption.

Obviously, much depends on how "collective bargaining" and "political activity" are constitutionally distinguished. Suppose the teacher union is negotiating for payroll deduction of teacher PAC contributions. If this is "collective bargaining," nonmembers can be charged their pro rata share of the costs; if "political activity," nonmembers cannot be charged. Should the union activity be chargeable as "collective bargaining" or nonchargeable as "political activity?"

What is "political activity?" If unions cannot charge nonmembers for "political activity," it must be defined. Some observations by Justice Lewis Powell in *Abood* v. *Detroit Board of Education* are a useful point of departure.

"An individual can no more be required to affiliate with a candidate by making a contribution than he can be prohibited from such affiliation. The only question is whether a union in the public sector is sufficiently distinguishable from a political candidate or committee to remove the withholding of financial contributions from First Amendment protection. In my view no principled distinction exists.

"The ultimate objective of a union in the public sector, like that of a political party, is to influence public decision making in accordance with the views and perceived interests of its membership. Whether a teacher union is concerned with salaries and fringe benefits, teacher qualifications and in-service training, pupil–teacher ratios, length of the school day, student discipline, or the content of the high school curriculum, its objective is to bring school board policy and decisions into harmony with its own views. Similarly, to the extent that school board expenditures and policy are guided by decisions made by the municipal, state, and federal governments the union's objective is to obtain favorable decisions—and to replace persons in positions of power who will be receptive to the union's viewpoint. In these respects, the public-sector union is indistinguishable from the traditional political party in this country.

"What distinguishes the public-sector union from the political party—and the distinction is a limited one—is that most of its members are employees who share similar economic interests and who may have a common professional perspective on some issues of public policy."[16]

By its own admission, the NEA is a "political action organization"; is it also a "political party"? Justice Powell suggested that the difference, if any, between a public-sector union and a political party was in the range of issues on which they try to exert their influence. In view of the NEA's 311 plus policy resolutions, the NEA meets this criterion more comprehensively than either the Democrat or Republican parties. Of course, these parties address issues that the NEA does not and vice versa, but the differences are not important from a constitutional standpoint. After all, many political parties in our history were based upon a much narrower range of issues than is to be found in NEA/AFT resolutions or political objectives.

Ironically, the NEA Series in Practical Politics defines politics as "the art of and the attempt to influence people." Needless to say, this is not the definition used by the NEA in agency fee cases. In an effort to show the importance of politics, an NEA publication lists twenty-two *political* decisions deemed to be critically important to NEA members. At least twelve of them relate to matters, such as salary and fringe benefits, resolved through collective bargaining.[17]

From a political perspective, public-sector bargaining is a form of petition to government. The union is urging public officials to adopt certain policies or take certain actions. Granted, public-sector bargaining involves some procedural differences from conventional ways to petition government, but the differences do not affect the constitutional similarities. The statutes that require payroll deduction of NEA/AFT dues were enacted through political means; the unions persuaded legislators to introduce the bill, hearings were conducted, and votes were taken. The governors signed or vetoed legislation. Why is the bargaining approach to payroll deduction of dues any less "political"? The union is making a proposal to the school board, a legislative body. The bargaining sessions are tantamount to hearings, with the added advantage to the union that no opponents are present. In fact, teacher union bargaining is always "political activity" but may or may not be "collective bargaining." After all, NEA/AFT affiliates in states without bargaining laws often succeed in achieving payroll deduction of dues and PAC funds; the process cannot be regarded as collective bargaining, but it surely is political activity.

The reality is that a union activity can be both "collective bargaining" and "political activity." Suppose an agency fee payer is opposed to government collection of political funds for any private interest group. The objection is not that NEA-PAC or AFT/COPE funds go to candidates opposed by the payer; the objection is to payroll deduction of PAC funds for any candidates, including the payer's. In this situation, the payer is being forced to support union efforts to persuade the school board to adopt public policies opposed by the payer. Surely, the union is engaged in "political activity," whether or not "collective bargaining" is involved.

If union activity is both "collective bargaining" and "political activity," should it be chargeable because it is "collective bargaining"? Or nonchargeable because it is "political activity"? As matters stand, it is chargeable as "collective bargaining." In theory and in practice, this is an absurd result.

Suppose a teacher believes that family health insurance instead of teacheronly health insurance constitutes an indefensible preference favoring teachers with dependents over teachers without them. In the absence of bargaining, this issue would be a political issue to be resolved through the normal political processes. The issue would be placed on the school board agenda, everyone would have notice and an equal opportunity to address the issue, and the school board would act as it deemed appropriate. Under collective bargaining, however, the issue is resolved in bilateral negotiations between the school board and the union. These negotiations, however, are over public policies to be adopted or not by the school board. The fact that negotiations exclude other parties in interest does not transform political activity into nonpolitical activity; it only means that we have a political process from which various parties in interest are excluded.

The exclusions are inherent in the process. To cite one reason, the proposals made in the climactic state of negotiations are often unanticipated by both sides prior to the time the proposals are made. Often, proposals that have been made previously are made in new configurations that have not been discussed with others in the community. Nevertheless, school district negotiators are not going to call community leaders at 6:00 A.M. to elicit their reactions to union proposals offered at 5:00 A.M., to avert a strike scheduled for 7:00 A.M.

In the light of these realities, it makes no sense to say that "collective bargaining" is chargeable but "political activity" is not. Teacher union bargaining, like public-sector bargaining generally, is inherently a political activity. As we have seen, NEA/AFT officials themselves emphasize this point in other contexts. To tell it like it is, the only way to prevent the NEA/AFT from spending nonmember fees for unwanted political activities is to prohibit the fees. The reason is that collective bargaining in public education is inherently and fundamentally a political process.

In retrospect, the Supreme Court decisions that distinguish collective bargaining in public education from political activity have turned out to be a major constitutional blunder with far reaching effects on political and educational affairs. The legal and political erosion of this distinction without a difference is inevitable, with far reaching consequences for the NEA/AFT. The unions can flourish if agency fees are 95 or 75, perhaps even 55 percent of dues; their decline is inevitable if agency fees in public employment are illegal, or limited to their appropriate percentage of dues.

11

AFT PRESIDENT ALBERT SHANKER

Visionary or Union Apologist?

M ost of the matters discussed here are not dependent upon personalities. The events would have happened, or not happened, regardless of the actors. NEA policies would be much the same no matter which candidate served as NEA president for the past twenty years. In contrast, AFT positions and strategies have been dominated by Albert Shanker, AFT president from 1974 to his death on February 22, 1997. It is impossible to understand the AFT's immediate past, present, and future without taking Shanker's role into account; he could not gain acceptance of every policy he supported, but minimally, Shanker could have vetoed any policy to which he was strongly opposed. In my opinion, however, Shanker's influence outside the AFT was much more important than his impact on AFT affairs per se.

Shanker was an AFL-CIO vice-president and member of its Executive Council since 1971; he was the senior vice-president in an organization in which seniority is very important. For decades prior to his death, Shanker was one of the most prestigious figures in American education. He was the subject of laudatory comment in the *New York Times, Wall Street Journal, Los Angeles Times,* and a host of other newspapers and journals; recipient of honorary degrees, the subject of books, and much more. Prominent business and foundation officials accorded the utmost consideration to his views, often through grants that no other teacher union leader could have generated. It would be difficult to find a more impressive résumé in the field of education.

Despite the fact that Shanker was an influential figure in the Democratic

Party, and that the AFT supported Democrats over Republicans about 98 percent of the time, an impressive list of Republicans have praised Shanker for his
educational leadership: President Ronald Reagan, William J. Bennett, and
Lamar Alexander among them. President Reagan appointed Shanker to the
Board of Directors of the National Endowment for Democracy, and President
Bush appointed him to the Council on Competitiveness. It would have been
unthinkable for the Reagan administration to rent office space from the NEA,
but no questions were raised when it rented two floors in the AFT building for
the Office of Educational Research and Improvement (OERI) in the 1980s. At
the time, the director of OERI was Assistant Secretary of Education Chester E.
Finn, Jr., an enthusiastic Shanker supporter among the neoconservatives.
Under Shanker's leadership the AFT has received substantial financial support
from Republican as well as Democratic administrations.

Earlier in this book, we saw that Shanker was a sophisticated, implacable opponent of school choice and contracting out, from the onset of his career as a
union leader. His public statements that he was not opposed to privatization
"in principle" simply masked his long-time all-out opposition to it in practice.
While asserting that privatization doesn't work, Shanker did his utmost to ensure that it doesn't—that it would not be tried, if he had anything to say about
it. Nevertheless, his prestige among conservatives was unparalleled. How did he
maintain it?

My answer draws partly on my personal experiences with Shanker over a
forty-year period. These experiences include, but are not limited to, political
friend and political foe within the AFT; scores of private discussions on a variety of topics, services as a union consultant and columnist at Shanker's invitation; director of foundation-funded projects involving his active cooperation
and support; observations of him at scores of union meetings and conventions;
and countless discussions with his supporters and critics. I certainly agree that
Shanker had many attractive qualities as a person and as a leader. In my forty
years of experience in the NEA and AFT, I have never met an NEA officer who
commanded the respect and loyalty among the staff as Shanker did in the AFT.

At first glance, it seems unlikely that Shanker would have overshadowed
NEA leaders. The NEA enrolls over three times as many teachers as the AFT.
Its revenues are over three times as large, and it is politically active in many
states in which there is no AFT presence or a very weak one. Nevertheless, the
disparity in prestige has existed for over twenty years in which Shanker was the
most prominent figure in the NEA/AFT if not in education generally.

Part of the explanation for this is that the AFT elects full-time officers who
are not subject to term limits; the NEA and the state associations impose term
limits on elected officers. The limits are a major reason why NEA leaders lack

the visibility and prestige associated with leadership of a large powerful national union. After all, if unions generally had adopted term limits, William Green, George Meany, John L. Lewis, and Walter Reuther might never have emerged as prestigious national leaders. To be sure, the NEA is moving away from term limits. Longer terms and the right to run for more than one term are now the trend. Merger between the NEA and AFT would undoubtedly accelerate the process, but the NEA will continue to move away from term limits regardless.

Another reason for Shanker's prominence was institutional. Consider the following constitutional amendments adopted by the AFT at its 1994 convention:

Article V—Officers, Section 2

The president shall be the chief executive officer of the federation and administer all of the affairs of the federation and execute policies of the federation as determined by the convention and the executive council. *The president shall employ, supervise, direct, promote, discipline and discharge staff and retain counsel, accountants and other professional personnel. Initial employment, promotion and compensation of such persons, to the extent that such is not determined pursuant to collective bargaining agreements, shall be subject to the approval of the executive council.*

Article VI-Executive Council, Section 2

Employees not covered by collective bargaining agreements shall be employed by individual contracts with provision for orderly dismissal with the right of hearing and representation by counsel in accordance with a procedure recommended by the president and approved by the executive council. . . .[1]

These constitutional amendments were passed while Shanker was on the convention slate, but too weak from chemotherapy to preside over convention proceedings. There was no explanation of why the amendments were desirable and no one raised a question about them from the convention floor.

To say the least, an amendment giving the NEA president such complete power over the NEA national office staff would not stand the least chance of passage at an NEA convention. It would not even occur to anyone to suggest it, and any NEA officer who proposed it would probably ensure defeat by doing so.

Viewing Shanker's role from the outside, observers were usually impressed by the AFT's unanimity in following his leadership. Their explanations were either that (1) Shanker was such a brilliant, charismatic leader that he persuaded all AFT leaders of the wisdom of his recommendations, or (2) Shanker was a union boss who can retaliate effectively against dissenters.

Both explanations were valid in some respects, not in others. To see why, imagine ten members of a union caucus. Each agrees to support whatever position is adopted by the caucus; also, not to oppose these positions except at meetings of the caucus, which we shall label the "Speak No Evil Caucus." The Speak No Evil Caucus must choose a leader, so delegate X is elected president and chief spokesman. Now whenever X speaks on an issue on which the Speak No Evil Caucus has adopted a position, X will support the caucus position. Likewise, all other members of the caucus will refrain from criticizing caucus positions publicly.

Can we assume that the caucus members support X as president because they are so impressed by X's logic and charisma? No, because the caucus may have adopted a position over X's opposition; X may be a follower, not the all-wise omnipotent leader.

Can we assume that X achieves unanimity because he is a ruthless union boss who can retaliate swiftly and effectively against dissenters? On the facts adduced thus far, we cannot make any such assumption; the caucus agreement, not X's coercive powers, suffices as the explanation for unanimity.

The point here is a narrow but important one. From the fact of unanimity among the AFT's officers and governing body, you cannot logically conclude very much about the explanations. The critical point is that Shanker was the leader of the Progressive Caucus that (1) completely controls the federation and (2) prohibits caucus members from publicly criticizing caucus positions.

As far as being a "union boss" is concerned, Shanker clearly fitted the job description. Inasmuch as one of his political heroes was former Chicago Mayor Richard Daley, I doubt whether Shanker regarded "union boss" as a pejorative. Certainly, AFT employees did not see him as a "boss" in a negative way. Shanker's power was recognized, but there was no widespread feeling that it was exercised arbitrarily. Furthermore, throughout the AFT there is the realization that he brought national recognition and prestige to the AFT as no one else could have—not to mention foundation and government grants due primarily, if not solely, to his influence. Because so many groups in the NEA have veto power over NEA policy, its policies often turn out to be statements that can be interpreted in several ways. Insofar as being a "union boss" means that someone has the ability to commit the union without an interminable and inconclusive policy making process, the NEA could probably benefit from having a "union boss" instead of its diffuse accountability structure.

Shanker's Role in Teacher Bargaining

Shanker was often characterized in the media as the union leader who was primarily responsible for the dramatic growth of teacher unions from 1962 to 1982. He has been characterized as the "father of teacher bargaining"; one prominent columnist has written that Shanker "invented teacher bargaining."[2]

Actually, Shanker was neither the president nor the chief strategist for the United Federation of Teachers (UFT) in 1961, when its victory over the NEA affiliates in New York City triggered a nation-wide upsurge in teacher unionization. Shanker became a nationally prominent union leader in 1968–69 as a result of his leadership of the UFT during the strike that polarized the city along racial lines. New York City had adopted a plan that established thirty-two community school boards with the power to hire staff in their districts. When the Ocean Hill-Brownsville board of education tried to transfer white teachers and principals out of the district, the UFT went on strike to prevent the transfers. The city was polarized along racial lines during and after the strike, but Shanker deserves credit, not criticism, for his resolute leadership against black racism in a highly volatile situation.

The strike, which resulted in a clear victory for the UFT, was followed by an extremely lucrative contract between the UFT and the New York City board of education that solidified Shanker's leadership of the UFT. Ironically, the strike also was a factor in the UFT's successful efforts to organize paraprofessionals in the New York City schools. New York City's black media was extremely critical of Shanker's leadership of the UFT during the strike. This criticism was a factor in the competition between the UFT and the American Federation of State, County, and Municipal Employees (AFSCME) to organize the paraprofessionals working for the city school district. Shanker proposed that the UFT organize school district employees who worked in classrooms, and AFSCME organize support personnel outside the classroom. In view of Shanker's unpopularity in the black community, AFSCME rejected the idea, believing that it could win a majority among the paraprofessionals, who were mainly black.

During the campaign, the UFT initially downplayed Shanker's role in the union. Subsequently, it adopted the opposite tactic, emphasizing that if the paraprofessionals voted for the UFT, Shanker would be their chief negotiator. The idea was to convince the paraprofessionals that they would have strong leadership by voting for the UFT. The UFT won a close election and has represented about 10,000 New York City paraprofessionals since 1970.

Although his leadership was a critical factor in the UFT's successful strike, it emerged years after several large states, such as Connecticut, Massachusetts, Michigan, New York, Oregon, Washington, and Wisconsin had enacted statutes that opened the door to rapid teacher unionization. In Massachusetts, Oregon, and Washington, the AFT had either opposed the legislation or had not adopted a position on it.[3] Indeed, even after Shanker became a nationally prominent union leader, he was much less influential in the growth of collective bargaining in education than a small group of NEA strategists, especially NEA general counsel Robert H. Chanin. Actually, in some states, the AFT surreptitiously blocked bargaining legislation because it feared that NEA affiliates would become entrenched as the bargaining agent. Sometimes, as in Louisiana in the early 1990s, the AFT implemented this strategy by supporting a collective bargaining statute that had no chance of enactment.

Bear in mind also that during the 1960s and 1970s, several unions such as the American Federation of State, County and Municipal Employees (AFSCME) were trying to enact state bargaining laws that applied to state and local public employees generally. Their collective efforts often facilitated unionization in public education more than anything Shanker did. Nonetheless, although Shanker's impact on the growth of teacher bargaining was and is greatly exaggerated, he did more than anyone else to counter the idea that teacher unions are an obstacle to educational reform. His unique role on this critical issue sets him apart from any other NEA/AFT leader, past or present.

As we have seen, the NEA/AFT are the major opponents of education vouchers, tuition tax credits, home schooling, and other reforms receiving substantial conservative support. This being the case, we might expect conservative education analysts to be critical of teacher unionization. Nevertheless, a highly influential group of such analysts has ignored or expressed a benign view of teacher unionization; Shanker was primarily responsible for their views. For instance, former assistant secretary of education (under President Reagan) Chester E. Finn, Jr., wrote in 1991 that: "Unionism per se does not alarm me. Nor do many of the stances and positions that unions take. There aren't a dozen issues, foreign or domestic, on which I have any large quarrel with Albert Shanker, for example. That's why, a couple of years back, I felt comfortable joining his AFT [as an associate member]."[4]

In several articles since then, and despite his support for vouchers, Finn has never suggested weakening the teacher unions in order to enact a voucher plan.[5] Meanwhile, other voucher proponents, such as Milton Friedman, emphasize that unions exist by monopolizing labor markets. In their view, to be opposed to the public school monopoly but not to have any problem with unionism is incomprehensible.

The Heritage Foundation is the largest and probably most influential conservative policy organization in the United States. Like Finn, Denis P. Doyle, its education analyst from 1994 to 1997, does not regard the teacher unions as a problem. On the contrary, Doyle's analysis implies that NEA/AFT opposition to privatization is justified on public-policy grounds. In a book he coauthored with David Kearns, then CEO of Xerox Corporation, Doyle writes:

> When public school teachers don't trust the system enough to use it for their own
> kids, it's no wonder that almost half the public school parents support vouchers or

tax credits for public and private schools. *We are convinced that such an approach is both unnecessary and unwise.* Our public schools are a priceless national resource and we must reinfuse them with their sense of democratic purpose. But to do so, they must change radically, and choice among public schools is the change we need. It would do more to improve the overall quality of public education than any other reform we know of (italics added).[6]

Elsewhere, Doyle asserts: "To many outside the schools, modern teachers unions appear to be part of the problem. We are convinced they are part of the solution." Although the above quotation does not directly refer to Shanker, Doyle quotes Shanker approvingly in the same book: "The poor don't have ready access to all of the available resources, and they often get ripped off in a market system." In view of his high regard for Shanker, it is not surprising that Doyle's solution comes out of the AFT play book: year-around schools and extension of the school day with upward salary adjustments, day care, and lowering the age of initial enrollment "to accommodate children who are now treated as preschoolers."[7]

As others have pointed out, the NEA/AFT are quite comfortable with a school choice strategy limited to public school choice; such strategy poses no threat whatsoever to union membership, revenues, or political and educational influence—in fact, the NEA/AFT support public school choice as a strategy to avoid school choice inclusive of private schools.

Several other analysts widely regarded as "conservative" have also expressed extremely favorable reactions to Shanker personally and his policies.[8] Shanker's success in winning conservative allies was based upon a simple formula: Criticize the NEA on issues that have conservative support but do not affect union powers or privileges. The strategy was evident in President Reagan's address to the 1983 AFT convention. Prior thereto, the NEA had cosponsored a publication urging a ban on nuclear testing. The publication also urged using the savings for education and health care. Shanker labeled the unit "propaganda." Conservatives everywhere lauded Shanker's denunciation of the NEA. Although Shanker had repeatedly denounced President Reagan at the 1982 AFT convention, Reagan accepted an invitation to address the 1983 AFT convention. His address included the following comment:

I also want to commend the AFT for . . . its ringing condemnation of those organizations, one of which I referred to earlier, who would exploit teaching positions and manipulate curriculum for propaganda purposes. [Applause]

On this last issue, you stand in bright contrast to those who have promoted curriculum guides that seem to be more aimed at frightening and brainwashing American school children than at fostering learning and stimulating balanced, intelligent debate. [Applause][9]

Reagan's comment illustrates a common pattern: When Shanker criticized the NEA, the conservatives applauded, but they did not scrutinize AFT practice on the same issue. Were they to have done so, they might have been unpleasantly surprised. For example, Shanker frequently criticized textbooks deemed biased against labor unions.[10] To remedy this bias, the UFT published a teaching unit entitled *Organized Labor.* Shanker, then its president, wrote the preface in which he praised the unit allegedly prepared by experts on the subject. A revised edition was published in 1991 and is still used in the schools.

Under "Why a Worker Joins a Union," *Organized Labor* quotes an "autobiographical sketch" as follows:

"I happened to visit a factory one day when it was practically empty of employees. Noticing my surprise, the employer said, 'Oh, I have plenty of work all right, but I thought it would be good psychology to let the boys walk the streets a few days. It will put the fear of God into their hearts.' Such rule through fear was often practiced. Some employers would affirm that working men were never reasonable except when hungry. . . . I had never studied ethics."[11]

The rest of the unit reflects this blatant effort to indoctrinate a prounion bias; for example, the homework assignments suggest that pupils "write an article convincing people to buy products having union labels." One can only speculate on how President Reagan arrived at the conclusion that unlike the NEA, the AFT does not "exploit teaching positions and manipulate curriculum for propaganda purposes."

Prior to his death, Shanker was regarded as a leader in the standards movement. Its message is plausible enough. Although standards are low, pupils lack strong incentives to meet them; failure does not involve high risks because of multiple opportunities for remedial work throughout our educational system. The upshot is a slackness in effort that retards educational achievement at every level. The solution is "high standards" with negative consequences for failure to meet them.

On several occasions, Shanker criticized the practice of awarding academic credit for "life experiences" or attendance in school. Unfortunately, his actions were not always consistent with his rhetoric. For example, as a director of the George Meany Center for Labor Studies, the educational arm of the AFL-CIO, Shanker approved a cooperative agreement with Antioch University in which substantial amounts of academic credit toward a bachelor's degree are awarded for "knowledge gained through union experience."[12]

Since nobody favors "low standards," the high standards movement seems to evoke widespread support. Nevertheless, the practical issues have yet to be resolved. Who will establish and approve the standards? How will they be implemented? Who will pay for the research and administration required? What subjects will be covered? How will states and school districts relate to the standards? Regardless of when, if ever, these issues are resolved, Shanker's advocacy of "high standards" was a risk-free way of enhancing his and the AFT's reputations. Significantly, none of the prominent conservative analysts who praised Shanker's leadership on standards has contended that teacher unions are a major obstacle to educational reform.

Teacher Training

On several occasions, Shanker has supported testing teachers in their teaching field. As he pointed out, we can test teachers' knowledge of their subject, and those who lack adequate knowledge of their subject should not be teaching it. In practice, however, Shanker's public support for high standards was contradicted by his acquiescence in their demise. In New York City, the UFT was instrumental in eliminating the Board of Examiners, an agency that tested teachers to determine their eligibility to teach in the city's public schools. This happened after Shanker was no longer UFT President but the UFT enrolled one-ninth of the AFT and was the base of Shanker's power in the AFT.

It is doubtful whether Shanker's support for high standards has had any impact on AFT locals. For example, Shanker commentary supporting teacher testing appeared in *United Teacher,* the journal published by the United Teachers of Los Angeles (UTLA). As it had for years, the same issue carried such advertisements as "DOCTORAL DEGREES IN ONE TO TWO YEARS"; requiring "only one-month one-time residency in Nevis, St. Kitts, West Indies," and a "mentor guided dissertation at your home site."[13] UTLA, like some other AFT affiliates, negotiates contracts which allow teachers to get salary credit for courses and degrees that are irrelevant to district needs. Furthermore, some of the larger AFT locals even sponsor such courses for salary credit. These courses are often promoted by caucuses within the union to promote caucus objectives, such as an antihomophobia curriculum advocated by the gay/lesbian/bisexual caucus. The conservatives who applauded Shanker's advertisements in the *New York Times* did not read union newspapers, attend union conventions, or participate in bargaining sessions where AFT locals are involved. If they had done so, the disconnect between Shanker's rhetoric and AFT practice would have been clear.

Of course, Shanker was not omnipotent and should not have been expected to lead every local to the promised land of educational reform. Still, if Shanker, despite his enormous influence within the AFT, could not persuade AFT locals to avoid such academic abominations, there was and is little reason to attach much significance to his rhetoric. When AFT locals bargain, they propose higher wages, shorter hours, more benefits, agency fees, prohibitions against contracting out—in short, their proposals do not differ from those submitted by NEA affiliates. Shanker was much more skillful than NEA leaders in packaging the union interest as the public interest, but despite his lofty pronouncements about standards, there never was any significant difference between AFT and NEA contracts on so-called reform issues.

The AFT program entitled "Responsibility, Respect, Results: Lessons for Life" illustrates Shanker's approach to educational reform. Launched by Shanker at a press conference on September 6, 1995, the program is spelled out in "A Bill of Rights and Responsibilities for Learning"; this ten-point statement includes such "rights" as the following: "1. All students and school staff have a right to schools that are safe, orderly, and drug free. . . . 4. All students and school staff have a right to be treated with courtesy and respect."

Surprising as it may seem, the model for Lessons for Life was the Republican Contract with America, which supposedly led to the sweeping Republican victories in 1994. The Contract with America was based on polls showing that large majorities of the American people supported certain objectives, such as a balanced federal budget. Shanker formulated the AFT program by deliberately adopting a poll-driven approach to reform.[14] Polls showed that most citizens are concerned about certain problems, such as violence in the schools. The AFT program merely adopted the objectives, such as safe schools, that would ameliorate these problems. Unfortunately, adopting an objective is one thing, implementing it is another. The AFT's publicity campaign for the program simply ignored the fact that teacher unions are frequently the obstacle to its objectives. For example, AFT affiliates do not bargain for "clear, rigorous academic standards and grades." Instead, they bargain for exclusive teacher authority to award grades without any right of appeal. Parenthetically, the analogy Shanker draws between "Lessons for Life" and the Contract with America is unfair to the latter in one respect. Contract with America committed its supporters to explicit but controversial action, whereas "Lessons for Life" is largely a commitment to a set of noncontroversial objectives. Almost two years after "Lessons for Life" was launched with national publicity, nothing really has changed. Of course, two years may be insufficient to evaluate the results fairly, but as we have seen in Chapter 7, this was not a consideration when Shanker opposed a program.

Control Over Union Media

Union leadership is political leadership. That is, union leaders achieve and retain their positions by persuading union members to keep them in office. As in contests for political office generally, use of media is an important aspect of holding office. In Shanker's case, since government is the employer of most union members, the role of media is doubly important. In the private sector, some union leaders flourish despite continuing negative media coverage. Their members are satisfied (or helpless) and public opinion does not affect the union's effectiveness. Not so in education; government is the employer and must take public opinion into account in its relationships with unions. Because public opinion is involved, nonunion as well as union media affect member perceptions of union effectiveness. Chapter 5 points out the huge NEA expenditures for influencing public opinion; Shanker has generated much more prounion media treatment for the AFT than the NEA's much larger expenditures for this purpose.

Let me first comment about AFT publications, using "raiding cases" to illustrate a point about Shanker's control of union communications. Raiding cases involve competition between AFL-CIO unions to organize employees. Such competition is governed by Sections XX and XXI of the AFL-CIO constitution, which prohibit competition for representation rights among unions affiliated with the AFL-CIO. No matter how poorly an AFL-CIO union represents employees, and no matter how much the employees wish to be represented by another AFL-CIO affiliate, the employees do not have this option under the AFL-CIO constitution.

Raiding cases sometimes involve large bargaining units. This usually means that a considerable amount of union expenditures and revenues are at stake. For example, Local 99 of the Service Employees International Union (SEIU) filed raiding charges against the AFT in 1988 over AFT efforts to represent 11,000 teaching assistants in the Los Angeles Unified School District. Article XXI, Section 4 of the AFL-CIO constitution provides that an AFL-CIO affiliate may not try to organize employees if another AFL-CIO affiliate has launched "a full fledged organizing drive adequate to organize the employee group in question significantly before any other affiliate and that affiliate has a reasonable chance of successfully organizing the employee group. . . ."

In this case, the arbitrator (Douglas Fraser, former president of the United Auto Workers), found "overwhelming" evidence that SEIU Local 99 had initiated such an organizing drive "for a significant length of time" before UTLA, the AFT local began its campaign in 1989.[15] Fraser's decision meant that the resources that the AFT devoted to organizing the teaching assistants in Los Angeles were a complete waste of AFT dues.

The rank-and-file AFT members, however, were not informed about Fraser's decision, or about other raiding cases involving the AFT. Why is this the case? First, the costs to the AFT should be noted: They include staff time, legal fees, literature, travel, advertising, and communications, to cite some of the obvious ones. Therefore, to spend substantial sums this way, only to be required to withdraw as a violator of the AFL-CIO's constitution, is not something that Shanker wished to publicize. After all, raiding cases are not cases in which unorganized workers would lack representation unless the AFT intervened; the employees would be represented by an AFL-CIO union, even if the AFT made no effort to organize them. Regardless, AFT members cannot object to a practice they know nothing about.

It is a fact of life that the parties who control the flow of information tend to do so in ways that benefit themselves. This is true regardless of the kind of organization (union, church, business, and so forth) involved. I am not criticizing Shanker for doing what everybody else does—only better. Nevertheless, another aspect of his leadership should be noted. The AFT does not accept "political" advertisements. As a result, Shanker's critics within the union have lacked any feasible means of reaching all the members. The prohibition against political advertising is another example of how union actions taken democratically are used to stifle dissent within the AFT.

Where We Stand

A major building block in Shanker's prestige and power was his weekly column, "Where We Stand," carried as a paid advertisement in the Sunday *New York Times*. Through this outlet, Shanker sent a message every week to millions of readers, including a broad range of leaders in education, media, and public affairs. The cost to the AFT and its affiliates was more than $750,000 per year. The columns were included in the *New York Times* index, the only advertisement to be so treated.

"Where We Stand" would articulate an AFL-CIO position, or the position of an AFL-CIO affiliate, thus building Shanker's credits in the AFL-CIO. Academic books and articles that supported Shanker's positions were discussed favorably, thereby building a coterie of academic acolytes whose publications would otherwise have languished in obscurity. The advertisements frequently featured conservative positions that do not pose any threat to the unions. In this way, Shanker appealed to conservatives who have no experience with teacher unions at the school district level. As pointed out in Chapter 7, companies providing services to school districts were frequently attacked with minimal risk: the resources to fight back in the *New York Times* were just not there. With unflappable confidence, Shanker used these advertisements to allege that voucher schools would rely on advertising instead of improved educational achievement to sell their services. That is, Shanker alleged that the companies would do what Shanker had been doing for public schools since 1971.

The Bottom Line

Shanker was personally responsible for two major outcomes. First, he was responsible for the widespread perception that teacher unions are not a major obstacle to educational reform. Although far from unanimous, the perception was sufficiently widespread to divert attention away from measures that would weaken teacher unions per se. The common tendency to identify only the NEA as an obstacle to reform is much more than a public relations coup for the AFT. If the AFT is not an obstacle to reform, then teacher unions per se are not—an implication that is very helpful to the NEA regardless of any adverse comparisons to the AFT.

Shanker's influence is also responsible for the denial of NEA/AFT merger except on the basis of some sort of affiliation with the AFL-CIO. Like them or not, these are significant outcomes; few others are responsible for outcomes of this magnitude.

Shanker is sometimes given credit where none is due; and he is not given credit where it is. For example, he was supposedly a courageous fighter for civil rights. With one-ninth of AFT membership in New York City, and most of the rest in large urban districts—Chicago, Detroit, Philadelphia, Washington, and so on—it would have taken courage on his part not to support "civil rights."

In view of Shanker's strong ties to Jewish organizations and neoconservatives, there is no way Shanker could have accepted ethnic quotas, but he was clearly opposed to them in principle as well as on political grounds. What Shanker did, and what he deserves credit for, is his astuteness in the way he ensured adequate minority participation in the AFT governance structure. The problem was resolved politically, not by quotas, as in the NEA. Because of his control within the UFT and then the AFT, Shanker was able to exclude the "black power" extremists from union governing bodies; at the same time, he exercised his control to ensure substantial minority participation in AFT caucuses and governing bodies. It is regrettable that NEA leadership did not adopt Shanker's approach to the problem.

Shanker is widely credited for his leading the opposition to extremist views on "inclusion," which refers to the practice of placing pupils with special needs or problems in regular classrooms. The pupils involved may be emotionally disturbed, retarded, autistic, whatever. It is likely, as Shanker has argued, that inclusion frequently reduces the learning opportunities for regular pupils. It is difficult to evaluate Shanker's practical impact on the issue, but his position is certainly shared by many AFT members.

Has Shanker otherwise affected what goes on in classrooms? What teachers teach and pupils study? Probably not very much outside of a prounion curriculum in some AFT districts. The editors of our leading textbook publishers have much larger influence on these matters than teacher union leaders. For that matter, even if our attention is confined to union issues, I doubt whether Shanker has had the most influence on the course of events.

The Shanker Impact: A Comparison

Previously, I opined that since the mid-1960s, NEA general counsel Robert H. Chanin has had a larger impact on American education than any other individual. In conjunction with Donald H. Wollett, a fellow member of the law firm employed by NEA in the 1960s, Chanin was the key adviser to NEA leaders on strategy and tactics in its competition with the AFT. Chanin drafted the state bargaining statutes which the NEA's state affiliates sought and sometimes succeeded in enacting. He frequently testified on proposed legislation before state legislative committees on behalf of the state associations; once legislation was enacted, he often negotiated the first contracts to demonstrate that the NEA was an effective union. In addition to his work on bargaining, Chanin played a key role in the development of NEA-PAC and the state association PACs.

Probably Chanin's most influential role has been his service as NEA's legal counsel in critical Supreme Court cases. In the *Lehnert* case, Chanin successfully argued that the NEA and its state affiliates as well as the local union were entitled to agency fees. A contrary ruling would have reduced union revenues minimally by tens of millions annually. Chanin also argued the *Perry* case, in which the Supreme Court upheld the constitutionality of contractual provisions that allowed incumbent unions exclusive access to school district facilities. In effect, the decision rendered it extremely difficult to decertify incumbent unions, an outcome that was very valuable to the NEA because its affiliates are the exclusive representative in most school districts.

I mention Chanin's role simply to underscore media inadequacy as it relates to public education. The media do not identify the key players, because media personnel do not understand who they are. It was in Shanker's interest to generate favorable publicity; in Chanin's, to avoid publicity. The fact that both Shanker and Chanin were extremely successful in their media objectives reveals more about the media than about the actual role played by either individual.

The foregoing comments are not allegations of pro-Shanker bias in the media. Individual reporters and editors have biases, but that is not the crux of the problem. It is the fact that the structure and dynamics of media militate against a well-informed public on teacher union issues. This point can be illustrated by the lack of attention to Shanker's role in the AFL-CIO.

For thirty-five years, Shanker was a maker and undeviating supporter of AFL-CIO policy. A remarkable aspect of Shanker's prestige among conservatives was and is their inattention to this fact. What does the AFL-CIO stand for that explains Shanker's insistence on affiliation with it as a condition of merger?

A recent history of the AFL-CIO by Max Green sets forth a disconcerting answer to this question. Green begins his book by stating that ". . . no institution in America has changed more since the late 1960's than the American labor movement." He then describes the changes as follows:

> By the early 1980's, labor had changed sides. Increasingly disaffected from American capitalism, it relinquished any serious claim to a distinctive character and for the first time became an integral part of the American Left. Organized labor came to

mirror the Left in its criticism of capitalism; in its commitment to statist economic policies; in its abandonment of the traditional American value of individualism in favor of the race-and-gender-based policies of the civil rights, feminist, and gay rights movements; and in its strong penchant for challenging the pursuit of U.S. interests abroad, particularly but not exclusively its opposition to the new bipartisan policy of promoting free market economies through free trade and other means.[16]

Green's analysis is especially interesting because of his explicit references to Shanker, whom he greatly admires. Starting as a dedicated democratic socialist, Green worked for the United Federation of Teachers under Shanker from 1973 to 1983. His book, which tracks AFL-CIO policy to 1996, utterly demolishes the idea that Shanker demonstrates the compatibility of conservatism and union imperatives—on a few issues, perhaps, but not on most that underlie either conservatism or unionization. In his undeviating support for AFL-CIO policies, Shanker favored expanding the role of government, higher taxes, no limits on government spending, avoidance of competition in union labor markets, prohibitions against privatization, and several other objectives commonly regarded as contrary to conservative principles.

In this context, Shanker is an anomaly—a public sector union leader with tremendous prestige among conservatives. Clearly, the anomaly cannot be explained by convergence between AFL-CIO and conservative policies. Instead, it highlights the troublesome question about Shanker's ability or willingness to distinguish union from public policy interests. In "Where We Stand," Shanker conceded "that competition would force schools to be sensitive to what customers (parents and students) want." He went on to say there is "precious little evidence that what they want is a rigorous education." From this premise, Shanker drew the conclusion that competition in education would be on the basis of such criteria as free trips to Disneyland or the size of school swimming pools.[17]

As Green points out, Shanker's argument would justify government operation of every industry in which consumers do not always choose wisely—just about the entire private sector. It also overlooks the fact that discriminating consumers typically are responsible for improvements that benefit all consumers. Unfortunately, it is only one of many in which his protection of union interests relies upon extremely weak factual and public interest arguments.[18]

To cite perhaps the most egregious example, Shanker's last column in the *New York Times* asserted that public schools were "the glue that has held this country together" since it was founded. Factually, his argument is an embarrassment. For more than half a century after our nation was founded, private schools widely predominated and every state provided assistance to denominational schooling. Until the early years of the twentieth century, much less than

10 percent of the school age population graduated from a public high school. Even in contemporary terms, Shanker's argument is more than a factual error. Today, the effort to impose majoritarian solutions on our highly diverse society is one of the major causes of conflict within it. As early as 1962, Milton Friedman pointed out that the controversies over what public schools should teach were generating more social conflict than our political system can safely absorb. Shanker never confronted this possibility in a straightforward way. Partly for this reason, he may go down in history as the Mikhail Gorbachev of American education. Just as Gorbachev tried to save communism by reforming it, Shanker tried to do the same for public education. If its deficiencies are inherent in the system, the analogy is a valid one.

Predictably, the AFT Executive Council elected UFT president Sandra Feldman to be the interim AFT president until the 1997 convention. Ideologically, Feldman is a Shanker clone with excellent political skills. The process by which she became AFT president illustrates the tight top–down control of the AFT. Feldman did not conduct an overt campaign for the presidency. With about one-third of the AFT in New York State, the only question was whether she wanted the job. The fact that Feldman retained the presidency of the UFT demonstrates how the first consideration was maintaining her control over the UFT, hence over the AFT. The upshot is that one person again holds the two biggest jobs in the AFT. What about the New York City teachers, who reelected Feldman as UFT president on April 2, 1997 (35,684 to 13,119 over her opponent), without any inkling that she was about to assume the presidency of the AFT? When you control union communications completely, you can ignore member interests in the intentions of union leadership.

Between Shanker's death and the election of Sandra Feldman as interim president on May 6, AFT affiliates won the right to represent over 6,000 Maryland state employees. These victories, in conjunction with the absence of any significant gains in teacher representation, underscore the AFT's transition from a teacher union to a union that enrolls a wide variety of government and health care employees as well. The implications of this change will be discussed in Chapter 13.

12

TAKEOFF PROMISES, LANDING REALITIES

The NEA and AFT have been major players in public education as unions since the 1960s. They have a track record that was not available during their takeoff period. In this chapter, I assess that track record in light of the rationale that persuaded teachers and then legislators that unionization was desirable.

Legally and practically, unions are supposed to act on behalf of the employees they represent. How effective have the NEA/AFT been in this regard? The answer to this question is highly complex and controversial. Although salary data are usually available, data on many other kinds of compensation are not. For instance, school districts ordinarily do not show the vested retirement benefits of their teachers, yet retirement benefits are an important component of compensation. The states frequently contribute to the teachers retirement systems, but their contributions are not usually included in estimates of teacher compensation.

In addition to the uncertainties about actual teacher compensation, the union role in achieving it is a conundrum. And even if we know the union impact on compensation, interpreting the results would often be problematic. For example, suppose the union negotiates a salary increase but the district increases class size to pay for it. In some situations, teachers have preferred smaller classes to salary increases. Thus the fact that unions have increased salaries does not necessarily demonstrate their beneficial impact on teacher welfare. By the same token, unions may not be responsible for salary increases, but may have achieved reductions in class size, increased job security, and other benefits. Wage increases so not unequivocally demonstrate union success; the absence of wage increases does not necessarily demonstrate union failure.

207

Teacher unions must sometimes decide whether to accept higher salaries with some layoffs, or lower salaries with no layoffs. Usually, the union prefers the first option; better to have most members satisfied with a raise and larger classes than all members dissatisfied with no raise. When the unions point to the higher salaries, they do not say anything about the teachers who have lost their jobs as a result. Should the job losses count in assessing the union impact on teacher welfare?

On additional complication. Suppose we know that teacher compensation is higher as a result of union activity. Does it matter whether the funds to pay for the increase were from affluent taxpayers, low-income payers of sales taxes, or unorganized support personnel in school districts, to cite a few of the possibilities? I mention them only to illustrate the complexity of teacher welfare issues; unless the complexity is recognized, conclusions on the subject can be true but very misleading.

The Union Impact on Teacher Salaries

Let me begin with an implausible proposition: Teachers' salaries are lower than they would be in the absence of teacher unions. Although the proposition may seem absurd, several leading economist, liberal and conservative, agreed in the past that labor unions have a negative impact on wages.[1] I do not agree with the proposition insofar as teachers are concerned, but it is a useful caveat in our analysis.

First of all, the issue is not whether union wages are higher than nonunion wages. The teachers in highly unionized states like Connecticut were paid more than teachers in nonunion states like Mississippi before the advent of unionization, and they would be paid more if teacher unions were completely abolished in Connecticut. The issue that matters is whether the teacher wage level less the costs of unionization (for example) would be even higher in the absence of unionization.

We start with an assumption that the NEA/AFT universally accept. Benefits granted to employees are much more difficult to reduce if the employees are represented by a union. In the private sector, employers act upon this assumption by withholding or delaying benefits. They do so because it will be extremely difficult if not impossible to reduce the benefits if there is a downturn in the company's business.

Unquestionably, the underlying principle often applies in public education. Every experienced school board negotiator has held back benefits to have concessions available in future negotiations, or because it is so difficult to take benefits away if the need arises.

Generally speaking, collective bargaining exaggerates the union's role in achieving benefits. In the absence of bargaining, employers tend to increase benefits incrementally. Because there is no union present to take credit for the improvement, there is no publicity. Under unionization, however, changes are made every two or three years. The union publicizes the improvements, giving the impression they are due solely to the union's efforts. The fact, or at least the possibility, that the improvements would have materialized anyway, perhaps even sooner, is overlooked. Employers would antagonize their employees and the union by pointing this out. Reporters have never thought about it and even if they did, the possibility would receive little attention compared to the daily stream of contractual improvements allegedly achieved by the unions.

The number of teachers suggests an additional reason why the NEA/AFT impact on teacher compensation tends to be minimal. Unions are most successful when they represent essential employees who (1) cannot be easily replaced; and (2) constitute a small proportion of the employer's total costs. Suppose that in company X, union A represents 50 workers, union B, 500 different workers at the same wage level. It is much easier for union A to negotiate a 10 percent wage increase because the total cost to the company will be much less. In education, however, teachers are by far the largest group of employees; substantial increases in their wages would create severe pressures on school district budgets and levels of taxation. From this perspective, notwithstanding possible exceptions in some districts, it is extremely unlikely that the NEA/AFT have achieved a substantial increase in the compensation of three million public school teachers.

Research on the NEA/AFT impact on teacher salaries differs with respect to the research procedures, the time covered, the treatment of inflation, the area covered, and in other ways. The resulting conclusions range from a negative impact to a significant positive one. One study compared the changes in teacher salaries between states with bargaining laws and states without them. Over the ten-year period 1969–70 to 1979–80, thirty states had bargaining laws, twenty states did not. The national average classroom teacher salary increased 89 percent during this ten-year period. Whereas only 50 percent of the bargaining law states experienced increases over 89 percent, 65 percent of the nonbargaining law states experienced salary increases higher than the national average. The average increase in the nonbargaining law states was 92.3 percent; in the bargaining law states, the average was 87.2 percent.

The study found a similar pattern for the two year period 1977–78 to 1979–80, albeit with a different set of states. The study also pointed out that the states that paid the highest salaries after unionization were usually the states that had paid higher salaries before unionization. Thus the union/nonunion salary differential was not due to unionization.[2]

How persuasive is this evidence? About as persuasive as the evidence that unionization has brought about substantial improvements in teacher compensation—which is to say, not very. First, the comparisons left out fringe benefits, a major component of teacher compensation. Second, it did not consider the possibility that it might be more difficult to increase compensation in the bargaining law states due to nonbargaining factors. Also, the comparison did not consider the possibility that the nonbargaining states raised salaries to head off unionization.

To further illustrate the conflicts in the research, consider the following quotations from the book reporting these studies:

> Studies of teacher unions show that collective bargaining increases teacher salaries an average of 15 percent.

> At the state and local government level, both the longitudinal and cross-sectional analyses suggest that the differential in earnings between public and private sector workers was small and positive in the 1970s, but became negative by the mid-1980s. Furthermore, the empirical analysis finds no evidence of a difference in pay between union and nonunion members in the public sector.

> The major finding is that union membership does not have a statistically or economically significant effect on the wages of state and local employees. . . .

> It should be stressed that our inability to find a statistically significant difference in pay between union members and nonmembers does not necessarily imply that unions have no effect on public sector compensation. It is possible that unions raise wages for all public sector workers (i.e., through lobbying). Furthermore, unions may have a substantial effect on fringe benefits and working conditions.[3]

As these quotations demonstrate, even in a single review there is no consensus on the impact of the teacher unions on teacher compensation. A fact of the utmost importance is that teacher bargaining emerged on a large scale from 1965 to 1980, a period characterized by high inflation. Because of this, NEA/AFT affiliates were able to negotiate unusually large salary increases compared to the preceding nonunion years. Many economists believe that inflation enables unions to maintain an aura of success in negotiating wage increases.[4] Be that as it may, the NEA/AFT were unquestionably the beneficiaries of inflation during unionization's takeoff years. Conversely, the absence of inflation weakens union ability to take credit for higher teacher salaries. This problem will be especially acute if the antitax, antibig government forces prevail politically; unions are much more attractive in distributing benefits than equalizing sacrifices.

Fringe Benefits

The teacher unions have probably increased fringe benefits more than salaries. This outcome might be anticipated for several reasons. Fringe benefits are ordinarily not taxable to employees. Instead of receiving higher salaries and buying their health insurance with after-tax dollars, teachers prefer to avoid the taxes by having school districts buy their health insurance. The unions, paradoxically, also *gain* from the appearance of lower salaries. Because of the visibility of salaries, there is a tendency to increase fringe benefits so as to avoid taxpayer resistance. A personal experience when I was negotiating for teachers illustrates this point. The school board was willing to provide a salary increase, but feared political reprisal for adopting the highest salary schedule in the state. The solution was to have the board pay into a tax deferred annuity which teachers could withdraw after one year. To taxpayers, the salary schedule was not higher than in neighboring districts. In the real world, the teachers were the highest paid in the state.

Fringe benefits, especially teacher pensions, often conceal the real costs and benefits of teacher compensation. For instance, New Jersey law provides that retiring teachers shall be paid their unused sick leave at their final salary rate. When enacted, the immediate cost was minimal; since the benefit had not been anticipated, payment for unused sick leave was not a major problem. Over time, however, teachers accumulated sick leave, knowing they would eventually be paid much more than their current daily rate of pay for it. Suppose a school district employee who started at $15,000 a year, retired twenty years later at $50,000, and averaged five unused sick leave days annually—not at all unusual with annual allowances of ten days or more each year. The teacher at retirement was now entitled to a $27,800 payment for 100 days of unused sick leave at $278 per day. As thousands of teachers take advantage of the benefit, the actuarial foundations of the New Jersey retirement system are weakening under the escalating costs. Needless to say, with so many teachers (and other public employees) benefitting from the legislation, eliminating or reducing the benefit is very difficult politically.

The NEA/AFT role in teacher pensions also illustrates the difficulty of estimating their overall impact on teacher welfare. The teacher unions have lobbied successfully to protect or enhance pension benefits in many states. Sometimes cooperation with other public employee unions was essential, but NEA/AFT support has been a major factor when teacher pensions are involved.

At the same time, however, the unions have had a negative impact on teacher pensions in other ways. Both the NEA and AFT have supported "social investing," that is, investment policies intended to promote a political agenda instead of maximizing returns to retired teachers. As we have seen, the 1994 NEA convention adopted a resolution that encouraged the state teacher retirement systems to divest and/or refrain from buying stock in companies that supported privatization or television commercials in the classroom.[5]

Unquestionably, social investing results in a lower rate of return on investments, since the pension fund is forced to restrict its options.[6] The problem here is that it is impossible to quantify the teacher losses due to social investing. Theoretically, there may be no loss to teachers if the taxpayers make up the difference between what the retirement funds earned and what they would have earned without social investing. In view of the widespread underfunding of teacher retirement systems and the questionable nature of the social policies involved, retirees and potential retirees might prefer to avoid social investing, but the NEA/AFT are moving in the opposite direction. They are trying to increase teacher representation on the state retirement boards, even though there is a negative correlation between the proportion of union representatives on the boards and the returns on retirement fund investments.[7]

Teacher Unions and Teacher Compensation: Concluding Observations

In a private sector monopoly, a union may be able to raise wages without raising prices. This is possible when the employer is earning a large profit from the monopoly; the union may be able to shift some of the monopoly profits to the employees. The employer would not raise prices if the prices already maximize profits.[8]

The educational monopoly differs from private sector monopolies. First, school boards cannot pass on increased costs as readily as companies. To pay for wage increases, school boards may need increased state aid, or higher property taxes or some other legislative action not controlled by the school boards. Unlike companies, school boards cannot add the cost of wage increases to meet their budget needs. The additional revenues needed to pay for wage increases must be in hand or committed before teacher compensation can be increased.

Another point of difference relates to bargaining power. In the private sector, union bargaining power depends on union ability to inflict economic losses on employers by strikes. In most states, however, teacher strikes are illegal. Although teacher unions have often conducted successful strikes, even in states where strikes are illegal, the power to strike is not as useful to teacher unions as it is to private sector unions.

Notwithstanding their disadvantages, the teacher unions have advantages over private sector unions that often more than compensate for their disadvantages. One advantage is their ability to participate in the election of public officials who decide teacher compensation issues. Union participation in the election of school managers and policymakers has no counterpart in the private sector, and it is highly conducive to management concessions.[9]

What, then, is the answer to our question about the impact of the NEA/AFT on teacher welfare? The answer is that there is no answer that takes into account all the categories of teacher compensation and all the costs of getting it. Indeed, it is questionable whether such an answer is feasible.[10] The present value of some future benefits cannot be assessed, even on a collective basis. What can be said without fear of contradiction is that there is no clear and convincing evidence that unionization per se has resulted in significant improvements in teacher welfare. Improvements there have been, but they have materialized in nonunion as well as unionized districts, and in other occupations as well.

Although this conclusion appears neutral on its face, it is anything but neutral in its implications. The burden of proof here is on the unions. With billions in revenues, they do not lack the resources to demonstrate their value in ways that will withstand critical scrutiny. Perhaps they can, but the fact remains they have not.

Single Salary Schedules

Regardless of whether the NEA/AFT have increased teacher salaries generally, some subgroups of teachers are paid less as a result of unionization. This is evident if we consider the implications of single salary schedules.

Single salary schedules are a high NEA/AFT priority. Under such schedules, teachers are paid solely on the basis of their years of teaching experience and academic credit. The subjects taught, grade level, of teaching effectiveness play no role in salary determination in the overwhelming majority of school districts.

In bargaining, the teacher unions do not cite the shortages of mathematics and science teachers to raise the salaries of mathematics and science teachers; instead, they cite the shortages to raise the salaries of all teachers. The result is that to recruit an adequate number of mathematics teachers, school districts must pay all teachers higher salaries.

Assume that a school district that employs 1,000 teachers needs ten mathematics teachers. Average teacher salary plus fringe benefits amounts to $40,000 per teacher. Because mathematics teachers can earn more outside of teaching, assume that it will take $10,000 more to recruit the needed supply of mathematics teachers. If the school district paid the $10,000 differential only to mathematics teachers, it could meet its needs by paying ten mathematics teachers $50,000 each, a total of $500,000. Under single salary schedules, however, the district must pay 1,000 teachers $10,000 more, a total of $10,000,000.

In practice, school districts overpay many teachers but not enough to attract all the mathematics teachers they need. Potential mathematics teachers are not going to teach for a few thousand dollars annually over the average for all teachers; an increase this small would still be far short of their anticipated earnings in nonteaching jobs. Of course, some mathematics teachers in the public schools are competent and willing to teach for less than they could earn in other work. Nevertheless, the pool of such teachers is much smaller because the NEA/AFT oppose salary differentials, based on the subjects taught.

At one time, it was common practice to pay secondary teachers more than elementary teachers. Since there are twice as many elementary as secondary teachers in teacher unions, it is impossible to become a union leader while advocating higher salaries for secondary teachers. To justify single salary schedules, the teacher unions rely on various rationalizations that are deemed self-evident truths. One is that elementary teachers should be paid at least as much as others because the elementary years are supposed the most critical. Of course, nobody pushes this to the point of advocating equal salaries for day-care teachers and professors of physics.

True, single-salary schedules were prevalent before unionization. The issue, however, is not how or when they emerged, but what can be done now to mitigate their harmful effects; on this issue, the NEA/AFT presence is the overriding obstacle. It is overriding not only because departures from single-salary schedules meet adamant union opposition, but because the union rationale on the issue permeates the culture of public education.

We cannot estimate precisely the harm that results from single-salary schedules, but it must be severe indeed. To see why, imagine the problems of operating a university if professors of medicine were paid the same as professors of English. If the salaries were based on what is required to attract competent professors of English, they would be far too low to attract competent professors of medicine. This explains why universities with professional schools reject unionization. The academics whose talents command high salaries outside the universities are well aware of their fate under unionization.

Unions are political organizations devoted to economic ends. Conceptually at least, control is based upon one person, one vote, not on shares of stock or economic power. Union leadership must satisfy a majority and avoid internal conflict that weakens group solidarity. This is why single-salary schedules are an NEA/AFT imperative. The teacher unions oppose higher salaries for mathematics teachers, even when there are severe shortages of mathematics teachers and large pools of qualified candidates in other subjects. To allow differentials based on subjects taught would lead to internal divisions over which group should be paid more. The teachers who would be paid more will always be in a minority in the union, hence their salaries will never reach the levels that would emerge if market forces prevailed.

Opposition to salary differentials by subject is not the only way the NEA/AFT have limited salaries for some teachers. The unions adamantly oppose merit pay as a sham to avoid paying higher salaries to most teachers. The reality is that the absence, not the presence, of high salaries for the few depresses teacher salaries. Because teaching offers so few opportunities for risk takers and entrepreneurs, individuals who can raise the productivity level of the education industry enter other occupations. The harm that results is not subject to precise measurement, but the same is true for most of the alleged benefits of union representation.

The Union Impact on Teacher Quality[11]

For the sake of discussion, assume that the teacher unions are responsible for significant increases in teacher compensation. Aside from increasing teacher income at the expense of others, what are the public policy implications of such an outcome? Virtually every educational reform report has recommended higher salaries to attract a higher talent level into teaching. The union view is that by increasing teacher salaries and improving conditions of employment, the unions make teaching a more attractive career to talented individuals. Supposedly, this is a contribution to a public policy objective.

The reality is that higher teacher salaries have not led to any improvement in the talent level of public school teachers. When teacher salaries are raised, all teachers are paid more. The increases are not based on subject, grade level, or merit. As a result, teachers considering retirement often decide to continue to teach instead of retire. The reason is that teacher pensions are based upon a percentage of teacher salaries in the last one to three years of service. When salaries go up, teachers considering retirement often continue to teach in order to raise their pensions. To this extent, there are fewer vacancies, and fewer vacancies have a depressing effect on the number of talented individuals who could become teachers.

Paradoxically, higher teacher salaries has a much broader negative effect on the career decisions of highly talented individuals considering a teaching career.

Highly talented individuals in college must decide on their career objectives. In areas with high teacher salaries, they are readily aware of the fact that there are literally hundreds of applications for most vacancies. For this reason, the individuals making career choices are naturally discouraged about their job prospects as teachers. Furthermore, the courses required for teacher certification do not enhance their job prospects outside of education, but the individuals can enter other attractive occupations—the more talented they are, the more options they have. Inasmuch as the cost associated with fulfilling certification requirements are substantial and they have other attractive options, the highly talented individuals choose not to go into teaching.

Before relating the problem to union policies, let me point out an interesting anomaly. Although private schools pay much less than public schools, they attract as high or even a higher level of teacher talent. Several factors contribute to this state of affairs, but the most important is that private schools are usually not required to employ certified teachers. This fact provides the private schools with a larger talent pool—more than enough, it appears, to overcome their much lower levels of teacher compensation. This fact helps to explain how and why teacher union policies on teacher certification have a negative effect on teacher quality. The unions are constantly trying to increase certification requirements, allegedly "to raise standards." The actual outcome is to discourage more talented individuals to turn away from teaching as a career. These individuals are not concerned about their ability to meet higher standards. They are concerned about whether jobs will be available.

Note that training in most professions is valuable regardless of the particular jobs taken by the trainees. The student who goes to law school may go to work for a large law firm, start a small office, work for the government, or be employed in many capacities that utilize his training. This is not the case with programs of teacher education. If you do not become a teacher, teacher training is largely a waste. In view of their other options, the highly talented students are more influenced by the large number of applicants for teaching positions than by the increases in teacher compensation. Counterintuitive as it seems, eliminating certification requirements instead of increasing them might raise the talent level in education. It would make available an extremely large talent pool that avoids training for positions that appear unlikely to materialize. The more standards for teaching are raised, the more we exclude individuals who have other options and decline to undertake teacher training that has little value outside of teaching.

The Costs of Teacher Unionization

For present purposes we can treat the costs of collective bargaining as the costs of teacher unionization. My reference here is to the costs of the process, not to the costs of the negotiated contracts.

The costs of collective bargaining fall into three categories: costs to the teachers; costs to the school boards; and costs to the taxpayers other than those incurred by school boards. In toto, public school teachers are paying about $1.3 billion a year for representational services. In addition, they are devoting huge amounts of unpaid time to union activities. This huge teacher investment supports an immense union bureaucracy whose value to the rank and file is highly dubious. In addition, its accountability is suspect. The NEA spent huge amounts of member dues to establish the U.S. Department of Education. It is impossible to discern any benefit from the department except to the bureaucrats employed there. The department does not even claim that it has brought about a significant change in American education. Nevertheless, no NEA officer or staff member has experienced any negative consequences over the waste of NEA resources devoted to creating the department, an agency likely to be eviscerated by a Republican Congress.

Chapter 9 questioned whether teachers were receiving an adequate return on their investment in the teacher unions. The issue was discussed there in terms of union effectiveness in achieving broad policy goals. To most teachers, the issue should be resolved primarily in terms of teacher welfare, so let us consider it from that standpoint.

In the early years of bargaining, a small investment in unionization may have paid substantial dividends. As teacher compensation rises, however, it becomes increasingly expensive to raise their compensation to even higher levels. Quite possibly, teachers are spending more and more to achieve less and less. Whereas a company can relate increased sales to increased advertising, teachers cannot so easily relate increased dues to increased benefits. The complexities enable the union bureaucracies to argue that teachers should invest more in representational services; their control over union communications ensures that teachers will not be exposed to contrary views.

School district costs include negotiators, lawyers, secretaries, and management and staff time. School board time is also a cost even though it may not be reimbursed. In addition, school district costs include travel, conferences, released time, publications, training, and copying, to mention only the most common. Other taxpayer costs include state labor boards, mediators, factfinders, and judicial proceedings. Many of these taxpayer costs are scattered through local, state, and federal budgets. For instance, mediators employed by the Federal Mediation and Conciliation Service (FMCS) sometimes serve in school district negotiations. Some of the costs of litigating constitutional issues are absorbed by the federal judiciary, and so forth.

Of course, any procedure to resolve terms and conditions of employment has costs, and costs are not the only aspect to be considered. Still, they should not be ignored, as has been the case thus far.[12] The total costs of teacher bargaining (management time, legal and consulting fees, state labor relations agencies, arbitrators and mediators, teacher dues and agency fees, judicial procedures) undoubtedly amounts to several billion annually. This estimate does not include the costs (and benefits) that cannot be quantified, such as the impact upon school district morale. Whatever the actual figure, the amount justifies serious consideration of alternatives, a topic to be considered in Chapter 14.

The Union Impact on Student Achievement

The union impact on productivity is a highly controversial topic. All too often, the research conclusions appear to depend more on who sponsors the research than on its quality. For example, research sponsored by the Economic Policy

Institute, a policy organization supported mainly by unions, draws the following conclusions:

- Unions do not impair U.S. competitiveness.
- Unions increase or do not lower productivity.
- The higher prices and lower employment rates associated with unions are offset by higher union productivity and lower rates of profit.
- How management deals with unions, not unionization per se, determines the effects of unions on productivity.[13]

Not surprisingly, these conclusions conflict with research conducted by others. Furthermore any conclusions based on private sector experience do not necessarily apply to education. Various biases appear in educational research on productivity, but one difference works to the advantage of the teacher unions. Educational research tends to focus on student achievement as the sole criterion of educational productivity. This focus overlooks the possibility that excessive resources are being utilized to achieve a given level of achievement. Productivity is a relationship between resources and outcomes, hence the teacher unions benefit if costs are neglected and attention is focused only on the outcomes.

Nonetheless, what is the union impact on student achievement? Allegations that teacher unions are responsible for declines in educational achievement are made frequently; so are NEA rebuttals asserting there is no decline or if there is, teachers are not responsible for it. In the NEA's view, allegations of decline are attributed to right wing extremists determined to weaken public education for various purposes, all nefarious. The AFT line is to concede the fact of decline while denying that union activity is a causal factor.

Although a thorough analysis of educational achievement issues is beyond the scope of this book, the union role in the matter merits discussion. Theoretically, student achievement may have declined through no fault of teacher unions, or of public education generally. Likewise, it might have improved because of nonschool factors. Changes in the absolute levels of educational achievement cannot fairly be characterized as "failure" or "success" of public education apart from an understanding of why the changes took place.

In the propaganda wars over the issues, it is easy to show either "decline" or "improvement"; one need only choose a particular criterion and a particular year as the starting point. These "proofs" of "decline" or "improvement" may be important politically, but they are irrelevant to the union effects on educational achievement.

Unquestionably, academic standards in public education have declined. In 1900, only 3 percent of the teenage population graduated from high school, which was largely a college preparatory institution. Academic standards for high school graduation were indisputably higher than they are today. Nevertheless, few of us would welcome a world in which only 3 percent of our teenagers are high school graduates. Some critics of unions assert that "All children can learn" to give the impression that unions and public education are responsible for all educational deficiencies. Meanwhile, union supporters assert "All children can learn" as the rationale for more funding to educate children who are not learning, for whatever reason. Partisans on both sides seem to believe that reiterating this shibboleth demonstrates their devotion to democracy or to the ability of all children to benefit from a high level curriculum.

Animals, birds, and insects can learn. Our concerns should be what can children learn, with what resources and to what ends. The reality is that the resources devoted to some educational objectives are often far out of proportion to the benefits, either to the individuals or to society. Unfortunately, the unions cannot accept this reality because to do so would antagonize its members who benefit from the excessive expenditures. More funding for the status quo is an inherent tendency in unionization.

Efforts to estimate the union impact on student achievement encounter a plethora of research problems. Researchers disagree on the following:

1. Whether student achievement improved, deteriorated, or remained stable during the bargaining era.
2. The extent to which nonschool factors, such as immigration, the drug culture, family breakdown, and television affect student achievement.
3. Whether student cohorts in the bargaining years were equally talented and/or motivated as those in the prebargaining era.
4. The criteria for assessing educational achievement. Test scores have been the most commonly used criterion for assessing pupil achievement. The two tests most frequently cited for this purpose are the Scholastic Aptitude Test (SAT) and the American College Tests (ACT). Intense controversy rages over the use of these test scores, or any others, to measure student achievement.

Critics of unions have emphasized that the decline in student test scores on the Scholastic Aptitude Test coincided substantially with the period of time in which teacher bargaining became widespread. Union supporters counter that lower average SAT scores should be attributed to a larger proportion of less talented students taking the tests. The unions also argue that social conditions, such as increased immigration of students who do not speak English, the decline in stable two-parent families, the rise of the drug culture, and the advent of television confront teachers with major obstacles that were not present on such a large scale in earlier times.

These issues are highly technical and the positions adopted by most parties relate more to their interests than to objective assessment of the evidence. Obviously, the issues are politically important; if the public schools are "failing," there will be more receptivity to basic change. If the number of low achieving students is due to conditions over which teachers have no control, there is less reason to change our educational system.

One of the most sophisticated efforts to assess the union impact on educational achievement was research conducted by Sam Peltzman of the University of Chicago. Peltzman concluded that academic achievement declined from 1960 to 1980, then leveled off from 1980 to 1992. Using various statistical techniques, he tried to identify the educational developments that would be consistent with this pattern. Two were identified: the growth of teacher unions and the shift from local to state revenues as the main source of school district financial support. While conceding that his research could not provide a full explanation, Peltzman nevertheless concluded that teacher unionization was a significant causal factor in the decline.[14]

Caroline Minter Hoxby conducted a more recent review of the studies of the union impact on educational achievement. Her analysis showed that increasing expenditures for education was associated with gain in achievement prior to 1960, but not afterwards. This is consistent with the argument that the unions are a major obstacle to educational improvement. As Hoxby pointed out, the increases in school expenditures since 1962 have been allocated mainly to teacher salaries and reducing class size. Theoretically, these objectives might have led to increased student achievement, but student achievement has not improved during this period. As evidence on this point, Hoxby pointed out that unionization is associated with a higher dropout rate despite the fact that the unions generate larger appropriations for education. As Hoxby concludes, "Although unions increase inputs, their direct effect on students plus the fact that input productivity falls means that their overall effect on student achievement is negative."[15]

Eric A. Hanushek has estimated that the productivity of U.S. schools has declined 2½ to 3 percent a year from 1967 to 1991. Although Hanushek's explanation does not explicitly attribute the decline to teacher unions, it supports this conclusion. For example, Hanushek shows that major union objectives, such as lower teacher/pupil ratios, accounted for a significant portion of the increased costs without any corresponding increase in pupil achievement.[16]

A study by economist Richard Vedder of Ohio University also concluded that educational productivity has declined in the United States in recent decades. Thus even if educational achievement has increased under unionization, which is very doubtful, it would still be true that productivity has declined.

Any increases in student achievement were made possible by huge increases in spending for education, far out of proportion to the results obtained.[16]

One union response to criticisms of their impact on education is simple enough. Unions don't train teachers, hire or fire them, or reward teachers. Unions do not establish the curriculum, pass/fail standards, or graduation requirements. Furthermore, in countries where students appear to achieve more than U.S. students, teachers are allegedly heavily unionized. Whatever the problems, collective bargaining and unions are not responsible for them.

The foregoing response is just plausible enough to conceal its basic superficiality. True, legally, the unions are not responsible for hiring and firing teachers, or for evaluating them. Yet, they do share responsibility for the procedures that govern the ability of school officials to carry out these responsibilities effectively. Similarly, on the other issues which the unions deny legal responsibility, they completely ignore their influence on the legally responsible parties.

For the unions to assert that they bear no responsibility in these matters is simply false. School officials naive enough to assert that tenure is solely a school management responsibility would immediately face a barrage of union attacks for denial of the union role in this matter.

More frequently, the NEA/AFT assert that collective bargaining is beneficial to pupils. Their assessments cite less turnover as a result of good contracts; more preparation time, so teachers are better prepared; lower class size, so teachers are better able to individualize instruction. For instance, a 1991 study found that black students in unionized schools achieved higher SAT scores than black students in nonunion environments. Conceding that its results were counter to other studies, the authors theorized that "union work rules may reduce the possibility of discrimination by the school staff, or that unionized districts mix capital and labor inputs differently than do nonunion districts and that these mixes are more suited to the learning styles of minority students."[17] In fact, the teacher unions have emphasized that seniority should govern transfers and assignments in inner city schools. Since most teachers prefer safer outlying schools, the inner city schools employ a higher percentage of new and inexperienced teachers. When large urban school districts tried to assign more experienced teachers to inner city schools, their efforts were rejected by AFT locals, sometimes to the point of strikes over the issue. Needless to say, the AFT locals involved have never claimed that new and substitute teachers were better for inner city students.

Another study concluded that unionization improved average pupil performance (but had a negative effect on students significantly above or below average). The explanation suggested, which the researchers conceded was speculation on their part,[18] was that unions increase the use of standardized instructional techniques. Obviously, the explanation contradicts the union argument that collective bargaining protects teachers' freedom to adopt whatever techniques they wish to use.

An even weaker prounion argument is that "students have higher test scores in unionized states"—as if unionization is the reason why student test scores are higher in Connecticut than Mississippi.[19] Still, candor requires conceding the fact that some of the research critical of the union impact is of no higher quality.

Although no systematic data supports union claims, they have a certain plausibility. Theoretically, the unions may have a beneficial effect upon student achievement even if it has declined under unionization; the decline might have been greater were it not for union activities. In view of this possibility, we need to examine more closely how unionization impacts educational achievement. The best way to do this is to scrutinize what the unions try to negotiate.

Union contract proposals include scores of proposals that could affect educational achievement in some way. Of course, many union proposals are rejected by school boards, or amended before their inclusion in a contract. Nevertheless, as someone who has bargained with NEA/AFT locals in six states, the controversies over their educational impact seems highly unrealistic, almost ludicrous.

In several states, the state education association disseminates a model contract to its local affiliates. The model includes proposals on every conceivable subject of bargaining. The local unions simply fill in their name and duration of the contract, and submit the model contract as their own proposal. The following list is fairly representative of their contents:

1. Teachers should be entitled to generous vacations and leave allowance for:
    illness or accident
    personal necessity
    pregnancy
    service as union officer
    service on union business
    military service
    adoption
    child care
    study
    candidacy for political office
    service as public official
    religious observances
    court appearances
    bereavement

2. Teachers cannot be required to report for duty more than fifteen minutes before the regular pupil day, or remain in school more than fifteen minutes after the regular pupil day.
3. The number of teacher duty days shall be reduced one to three days.
4. All teachers, regardless of grade level or subject, must be paid solely on the basis of their academic credits and years of experience.
5. Teacher attendance at evening meetings, including PTA meetings, and "open houses," to be voluntary on the teacher's part.
6. Assignments, including extracurricular assignments, to be made on the basis of seniority among all qualified.
7. Adverse material in teacher files must be removed after a specific period of time, usually two years.
8. Transfer and assignment shall be based on seniority.
9. Promotions must be filled by appointments from the bargaining unit.
10. Teacher evaluations shall be limited to two annually for probationary teachers and once annually for tenured teachers—sometimes not at all for teachers nearing retirement. Also, no adverse action against a teacher can be taken unless the evaluation procedures are followed in great detail.
11. In order to keep their jobs, teachers must join the union or pay agency fees to the union.
12. Teachers should receive salary credit for any courses or advanced degrees chosen by the teacher. The union argument is that the teachers know better than any bureaucrat or administrator what they need to improve their instruction. Unfortunately, woe to the school district that accepts this plausible argument, as many have. Teachers often take the easiest or least expensive courses for salary credit, regardless of course relevance to their teaching assignments. Many take courses to prepare for an administrative position or for careers outside of education.

To understand the impact of the unions, it is essential to understand their dynamics. If the union does not demonstrate "gains," members will question its nature. The upshot is constant pressure on school districts to provide more benefits, regardless of their implications for educational achievement.

Negotiations on sick leave illustrate the dynamics. The union seeks to expand eligibility for sick leave, the purposes for which leave is granted, and the number of sick leave days. Sick leave expands from coverage of the teacher to coverage of the immediate household to coverage of anyone in the immediate household (that is, domestic partners) and from actual illness to medical and dental appointments. Similarly, personal necessity leave goes from leave for an accident requiring immediate attention to leave for meetings with lawyers to discuss a divorce or property settlement or for whatever teachers claim to be "personal necessity." As a few teachers stretch the definitions and limits, others feel like chumps for not doing the same, hence resort to leave increases. If leave does not accumulate, there is no incentive not to use it, hence use becomes rampant. If payment for unused leave is introduced, use goes down, but costs go up. The union negotiates a sick leave bank, so that teachers can draw upon a sick leave bank established from contributions of sick leave from all teachers. This eliminates concern that sick leave will be exhausted, which in turn reduces incentives to save sick leave days for future emergencies.[20] Research is hardly needed to conclude that these dynamics have a negative impact on pupil achievement.

In practice, it is impossible to track the precise educational impact of scores of such union proposals in thousands of school districts. Still, it would be astonishing if their cumulative effect did not weaken educational achievement. Furthermore, union proposals which allegedly would foster achievement often have the opposite effect. For instance, the unions invariably propose reducing class size to facilitate higher levels of educational achievement. Although the positive effects of smaller classes are highly controversial, let us assume that a higher level of achievement would result. Even so, the costs of reducing class size must be considered. The practical question is not whether reducing class size leads to higher levels of educational achievement; it is whether reducing class size is the most effective use of the funds available. Whenever it is not, as often happens, the unions are blocking instead of facilitating increased educational achievement by insisting upon smaller classes.

We should not criticize the teacher unions merely because they negotiate teacher benefits that conflict with student achievement. The teacher unions represent teachers, not students. At some point, it becomes unreasonable to ask teachers to subordinate their interests to pupil interests; If teacher and pupil interests coincide, the NEA/AFT negotiate policies that benefit pupils. When teacher union interests conflict with pupil interests, the pupil interest loses out; if it does not, the reason is usually management's opposition to union demands, not union concern about pupil welfare. Research techniques may be necessary to assess the union's educational impact precisely, but it is not credible to regard its overall thrust as in doubt.

NEA/AFT efforts to advance teacher welfare are a daily occurrence in every state. It is impossible to track the effects of each effort. Realistically, it would be the coincidence of all time if the pursuit of teacher welfare turned out to be the way to foster educational achievement. If it is, school management should be encouraging teacher unionization for productivity reasons. Although school management's capacity for error is not to be underestimated, its failure to promote teacher unionization as a way to raise educational achievement is hardly grounds for criticism.

The strongest argument for the teacher unions is that their pursuit of teacher interests is no different in principle from the pursuit of self interest by other interest groups. Most individuals and companies that praise competitive markets do so only pro forma; it is difficult to identify a large company that has not tried to use tariffs, quotas, tax breaks, regulations, and subsidies to avoid or minimize market competition. In a culture that praises competitive markets while most try to subvert them, there is no point to moralizing about teacher union efforts to promote teacher and union welfare. The teacher unions invest more in government largesse because government is their employer, not because they are more self-serving than corporations.

The Impact of Teacher Unionization on the PTA

A profound but widely overlooked outcome of teacher unionization is that the National Congress of Parents and Teachers, widely known as "the PTA," has become a tool of the NEA. The PTA is the sixth largest voluntary organization in the United States. It was founded in 1897 as the National Congress of Mothers, and did not have teacher membership as such until 1924, when the title was changed to the National Congress of Parents and Teachers. As an organization purporting to represent parents, the PTA might be expected to challenge teacher unions who represent the educational producers. In practice, the PTA never does.

Three kinds of evidence confirm PTA's total subordination to NEA policies. First, in response to my written inquiry in 1992, the PTA's legislative representative in Washington, D.C., could not cite a single instance of PTA disagreement with the NEA. After this response was published, the PTA never challenged it in any way.[21] It should be noted that until 1993, NEA subsidized PTA space in the NEA building in Washington.

Second, attendance by me and others at ten national and state PTA conventions from 1994 to 1996 failed to turn up a single instance of such opposition; one would not know teacher unions existed from attendance at these conventions.[22] The most decisive evidence, however, is PTA policy relating to teacher negotiations. Some excerpts from these guidelines are as follows:

National PTA Position Statement (Reaffirmed 1987)

The PTA, because of its strategic position, has become involved in activities related to negotiations and may find itself on the horns of several dilemmas.

1. If the PTA provides volunteers to man the classrooms during a work stoppage, in the interest of protecting the immediate safety and welfare of children, it is branded as a strike breaker.
2. If the PTA does not take sides in issue[s] being negotiated, it is accused of not being interested.

3. If it supports the positions of the board of education, which is the representative of the public in negotiations, *the teacher members of the PTA have threatened to withdraw membership and boycott the local PTA activities.* (Italics added)

To resolve these dilemmas, the PTA guidelines cover the pre-strike period, the period during the strike, and the aftermath of the strike. Typical guidelines are as follows:

Pre-strike period

1. Continue to work for quality education. Efforts in this regard reassure teachers that parents are helping to achieve their goals of greater job satisfactions and improvement of substandard salaries.
2. Be alert to early symptoms of teacher dissatisfaction:
   a. Abnormal turnover in teaching staff and administrators.
   b. Teacher-supported legislation defeated by state legislature.
   c. Growing dissatisfaction of teachers as evidenced by complaints.
3. Seek action that corrects the basic causes of dissatisfaction—student conduct, teaching conditions, lack of participation in decision-making. . . .
5. Urge school boards and local teachers' organizations to consider the advisability of developing written agreements on negotiating procedures including grievance procedures . . .
8. Teachers as well as parents should join and participate by individual choice. The teacher continues as a willing partner in the PTA when participation is free of unwarranted expectations.

During the Strike

. . .

2. Through informed public opinion see that the negotiated agreements which settled the strike are faithfully implemented."[23] (Note that in the overwhelming majority of cases, it is the union, not the school board, which alleges violations of the contract.)

The guidelines include eighteen recommendations that either imply or suggest that strikes are justified or ensure PTA support of typical union positions during a strike. There is not the slightest hint that a teacher strike might be due to school board refusal to accept unreasonable union demands. On the contrary, by urging PTAs to "seek action that corrects the basic causes of dissatisfaction," the resolution is clearly biased in favor of the union. The repeated support for "negotiations" implies the school boards have not fully met their obligations to bargain in good faith before the strike.

Note also that PTA policy does not address parental concerns that are mandatory subjects of bargaining. Several, such as the following, should be high priority issues in the PTA:

1. What are teacher responsibilities to help pupils outside of regular class hours?
2. How long do teachers remain in school after class to assist pupils and/or confer with parents?
3. Are there adequate student/parent grievance procedures?
4. Is there any appeal from teacher grades, or negative recommendations to employers and institutions of higher education?
5. Do teacher contracts provide adequate opportunities for parents to confer with teachers? For example, if parents work during regular school hours, are there opportunities to meet with parents at some other time during the day?

Surely, an organization that represents parents should have positions on these issues, and strive to have them adopted. Nevertheless, the PTA does not address them, or any others that might lead to conflict with the teacher unions. In contrast, the teacher unions aggressively bargain for their positions on all such issues. For instance, the teacher unions typically propose the following:

1. Teachers cannot be required to return in the evening or on weekends for parent conferences; if they do return voluntarily, they must be paid generously.
2. Parent complaints cannot be considered as a basis for disciplinary action unless the complaint is in writing and the teacher has had time off with pay to prepare a response.
3. If a parent has a complaint, the teacher has the right to have a union representative present when the complainant faces the teacher.

The PTA's avoidance of important parental issues inevitably leads to its preoccupation with trivial ones. The California PTA is the nation's largest state PTA; at its 1994 convention, the main item of business was a resolution on the effects of electromagnetic fields on school children. At this same convention, the PTA took credit for defeating Proposition 174, an initiative that would have provided parents with vouchers to implement school choice. PTA leaders proudly asserted that the teacher unions provided the dollars, but the PTA provided the bodies that defeated the initiative.

How did the PTA, supposedly an organization devoted to parental interests, emerge as a compliant tool of the NEA? During the years when teacher collective bargaining was spreading rapidly, PTAs often disagreed with teacher union positions, especially on strike issues. As the PTA's 1987 resolution points out, PTA opposition to teacher demands and teacher strikes resulted in teacher and union threats to withdraw and to urge parents to withdraw from the PTA. Faced with this ultimatum, the full-time PTA bureaucracy opted for neutrality over the PTA's role as the advocate for parents.

Prior to teacher unionization, the PTA dilemma did not exist. School boards elicited advice on parental issues from teachers and parents, and then adopted whatever policies on these issues they deemed appropriate. If teachers threatened to boycott the PTA, the school district could take disciplinary action, which is why such threats were not made.

Teacher collective bargaining transformed this power structure. Parental issues were negotiated by school board and union representatives in a process that excluded PTA representation. Given the weakness of local PTA's, without staff or substantial resources, school board negotiators did not oppose union proposals that disadvantaged parents. In addition, school boards lost the right to discipline teachers for refusing to participate in the PTA. The balance of power on parental issues shifted from the school administration to the teacher unions, and the latter promptly exercised their power to promote their producer interests, regardless of the detrimental effects on parental interests.

The PTA celebrated its 100th anniversary in 1997. Today, its activities consist largely of fundraising for school activities and support for NEA/AFT legislative positions. Because the PTA retains the aura of dedication to children, its support (even its neutrality) is often very helpful to the NEA/AFT. After all, car manufacturers would have been spared several headaches if Ralph Nader had been neutral on safety issues.

In several ways, the NEA's influence over the PTA is a remarkable but widely overlooked fact. NEA success in neutralizing, nay mobilizing, a national organization of almost 7,000,000 members, whose interests conflict with union interests on several critical issues, deserves much more attention than it has received in the media or professional publications.

Finally, it should be emphasized that the unions may be an obstacle to reform even if they are not responsible for low levels of educational achievement. Suppose that market-oriented reforms, such as educational vouchers, tuition tax credits and/or competitive contracting would lead to quantum improvement. The teacher unions themselves agree they are the major obstacles to these changes. Whether market-oriented reforms would be helpful is, of course, a highly controversial issue. If they would be helpful, the NEA/AFT are obstacles to reform regardless of their responsibility, if any, for low levels of educational achievement.

The Erosion of School Board Authority

The erosion of school board authority is one of the most important consequences of teacher unionization. This erosion of school board authority has not consisted solely of a transfer of power from school boards to teacher unions.

Unionization has also resulted in a transfer of power from school boards to school administrators. Prior to unionization, school boards considered teacher terms, and conditions of employment on their own schedules. If health insurance was the topic, boards could place it on their agendas as they deemed appropriate. If a blizzard disrupted the schedule, the board rescheduled the topic at its convenience.

Teacher bargaining ended board freedom to function this way. Under collective bargaining, terms and conditions of teacher employment must be resolved as a package by a certain date, usually the expiration date of the existing contract. Somebody at the bargaining table must have the authority to accept, or to reject, or to trade off, or to amend union proposals. Prior consultation with the school board notwithstanding, the board's negotiator must have the authority to bargain, that is, a measure of discretion over the issues being negotiated. Thus the inherent tendency of bargaining is to concentrate authority in the hands of the negotiators.

Most school district revenues are spent on teachers. The policies governing their employment are established through collective bargaining. With multiyear contracts, a shrinking portion of district revenues is available for discretionary spending by school boards. To the extent that increased teacher compensation requires reductions in other line items, such as textbooks, transportation, and support personnel, school board discretion is also reduced accordingly.

As previously noted, state aid is now the major source of school district funds. We have also seen the enormous political clout of the state teacher unions. Understandably, state aid is accompanied by rules and regulations oriented to union objectives. The upshot is that although formally responsible for managing public schools, school boards exercise authority only at the margins. Not surprisingly, the NEA/AFT like it this way. They can more easily dominate school boards, elected in nonpartisan elections without powerful constituencies, than full-time mayors who direct all public services and who have significant nonteacher sources of political support.

The Impact of Teacher Unions on Social and Political Issues

Most of the attention devoted to the NEA/AFT relates to their role in education. In my opinion, however, another very important outcome of NEA/AFT activity has been the advancement of a liberal social agenda. In this context, "liberal social agenda" is a descriptive term, including but not limited to affirmative action; abortion rights; inclusion of gays, lesbians, and bisexuals under civil rights coverage; comparable worth; avoidance of restrictions on taxation; prohibitions against delivery of services financed by government and by religious organizations; sex education; and a high level of government intervention in the economy. This has happened even though most NEA/AFT members probably oppose at least some elements of this agenda, and most union leaders may be indifferent to it except as a means of promoting core NEA/AFT issues.

Public officials elected to state and federal office vote on a broad range of topics: the economy, taxation, foreign policy, ethnic and gender quotas, abortion rights, immigration and so forth. Although allegedly based on education issues, NEA/AFT endorsements do not reflect a random distribution of support on noneducational issues. On the contrary, there is a high correlation between support for NEA/AFT positions on educational issues and support for a liberal social agenda. For this reason, the noneducational outcomes that can be attributed to the NEA/AFT may be as important as the educational ones.

A recent study of NEA-PAC illustrates this point. The study shows that through the end of April 1996, NEA-PAC had contributed $643,030 to congressional candidates. On the average, NEA-supported candidates for the U.S. Senate voted for $30.4 billion more in government spending in the first session of the 104th Congress. NEA-opposed candidates voted to reduce federal spending by an average of $31.8 billion. The results were very similar in races for the House of Representatives. NEA-supported candidates voted for an average increase of $28.9 billion; NEA-opposed candidates voted to reduce federal spending by an average $32.4 billion.[24] The public officials elected with NEA/AFT support vote on all legislative issues. Their positions on noneducational issues are heavily tilted toward liberal positions on virtually every major public policy issue. For this reason, it is quite possible that the NEA's impact on noneducational issues may overshadow its impact on educational policy.

The Political Impact of Teacher Unions:
Democratic Representative Government

The NEA/AFT have played a pivotal role in diminishing representative democratic government in the United States. This conclusion is certain to evoke the strongest possible challenge from the teacher unions; nonetheless, I regard it as the most defensible as well as most important conclusion about their impact.

To appreciate the argument, it is essential to understand how collective bargaining relates to school board authority to manage public schools. Under collective bargaining, terms and conditions of employment are negotiated by school boards and teacher unions. Once an agreement is reached, the school board cannot change the terms and conditions of employment unless the union agrees to the change or until the parties have bargained to impasse and exhausted the impasse procedures. Only in the latter situation can the school board act unilaterally.

Now let us consider a run-of-the-mill example of how collective bargaining plays out in public education. My example is a three-year contract that provides salary credit for up to "five years of teaching experience." Prior to the contract, the school board allowed five years of credit for prior public school teaching experience, and this is the board's contractual intent. Nevertheless, due to the negligence of its negotiator or for some other reason, the board has contractually agreed to award salary credit for "five years of teaching experience." Shortly after the contract is ratified, however, the union files a grievance over district refusal to grant credit for five years of private school teaching experience. The grievance eventually is submitted to binding arbitration, and the arbitrator rules in favor of the union. The basis for the arbitrator's decision is that the contract does not specify "public school experience," and the arbitrator refuses to write that interpretation into the contract.

In political terms, the district is now required to implement a public policy on salary credit for three years—a policy that no member of the school board or administration supported at any time. In the absence of a collective bargaining contract, the issue would have been resolved as the school board deemed appropriate. If board policy was improperly drafted, it could be corrected because it was not part of a contractual agreement. Under bargaining, however, the policy differences are resolved by an arbitrator, responsible to no one in the school district.

The NEA/AFT see nothing wrong with a system of public employment relations that leads to such outcomes; in fact, they are doing their utmost to expand the system to states which have not adopted it. This is not the place to rehash the arguments for and against public sector bargaining, but as a prounion activist in the 1970s, I can safely assert that the conflict between democratic representative government and teacher bargaining was not articulated in the takeoff period.

The conflict is not widely recognized because teacher bargaining is discussed in labor relations instead of political terms. In political terms, teacher bargaining is the negotiation of public policies by legislative bodies with one special interest in a process from which other parties in interest are excluded. If discussed in this way, collective bargaining in public education would be unacceptable to most citizens. Because an NEA/AFT merger will lead to greater public awareness of this basic issue, I turn next to merger issues and their implications for education.

13

NEA/AFT MERGER

Teachers in the AFL-CIO

This chapter is devoted to the possibility of an NEA/AFT merger. Although the merger is not a certainty, it is highly probable and imminent. The unions have officially expressed their interest in merger (see Appendix C) and have set the summer of 1998 for reaching a decision. Unquestionably, the merger will require or lead to several changes in the policies, leadership, and governance structure of both unions. And even if the merger does not materialize, the issues it raises will be on union and public policy agendas for years to come. Let us see what is at stake.

Merger of the NEA/AFT is not a new issue. In 1959, the author published a book advocating it.[1] At the time, the NEA allowed unrestricted administrator membership; although only a small proportion of NEA members, school superintendents controlled the NEA. The author proposed the merger on the basis of exclusion of school administrators and disaffiliation from the AFL-CIO.

My support for disaffiliation was based on the perception that many teachers were willing to accept unionization but not affiliation with the AFL-CIO. Three years later, as a candidate for president of the AFT, I received about one-third of the convention votes, despite my published support for disaffiliation. Although other factors played a role in my defeat, the convention vote indicated that a significant proportion of AFT members were willing to accept disaffiliation.

Merger issues surfaced again in the early 1970s but the intensive competition between the NEA and AFT had antagonized most members in both unions. Irreconcilable differences, especially over affiliation with the AFL-CIO, quickly rendered merger talks futile.[2]

Merger talks were initiated in 1993 and culminated in the jurisdictional agreement in Appendix C. The merger is not likely to be consummated in less than one year; probably at least two years will be required to effectuate it. In any case, the jurisdictional agreement reflects a serious effort to merge that has excellent prospects to succeed.

Despite the breakdown of previous merger talks at the national level, NEA/AFT mergers have taken place at the state and local levels. For a brief time, the New York State United Teachers (NYSUT) was affiliated with both the NEA and AFT, but the merger broke down over several issues. Several locals around the country are currently affiliated with both national unions; the teachers pay the same local dues and choose to pay either NEA or AFT state and national dues.

The existence of two unions competing for the right to represent the same industry-wide group of employees is unusual, albeit for reasons to be questioned shortly. In education, one of the major issues dividing the unions was affiliation with the AFL-CIO. The AFT would not consider merger without affiliation with the AFL-CIO; at the same time, the NEA would not try to force unwilling state and local associations to affiliate with the AFL-CIO. Theoretically, there could be an agreement to merge without affiliation; as pointed out in Chapter 11, there was no such option as long as Albert Shanker was AFT president. Shanker's death renders it more likely that affiliation with the AFL-CIO will be resolved more on NEA terms. Be that as it may, I shall discuss merger on the basis of affiliation at the national level, with an option to affiliate at the state and local levels; this will probably be the short-range resolution of the issue. The merger agreement will have to specify whether the state and local associations must act to affiliate, or must act to disaffiliate; regardless of how this issue is resolved, an NEA/AFT merger requires some attention to the AFL-CIO.

The American Federation of Labor-Congress of Industrial Organizations (AFL-CIO)

The American Federation of Labor-Congress of Industrial Organizations (AFL-CIO) is the largest labor organization in the United States. Unions—not individuals—are members. The AFL-CIO is a confederation of 78 national and international unions. In 1995, AFL-CIO paid membership was 13 million.

The highest level of governance is the National Convention, which is held in the fall of every odd-numbered year. Between conventions, the AFL-CIO is governed by its Executive Council, which includes the president, secretary-treasurer, and fifty-one vice-presidents, all of whom are elected at the national convention. The Executive Council also includes an executive director (since

1995), and nine departments, consisting of unions that share common interests. The departments are autonomous bodies that have their own governing bodies, conventions, and dues within the parameters of the AFL-CIO constitution. The departments also function at the state and local levels through over 600 local councils. The AFT is a member of the Public Employee Department (PED), which includes thirty-five AFL-CIO unions that enroll some public employees. Regional activities are carried on by fifty-one state and 625 local AFL-CIO councils, and 45,000 local unions.

AFL-CIO operations are financed by dues, or "per capita taxes" in union terminology. Each AFL-CIO affiliate pays the per capita tax based upon its membership. In 1995, the per capita tax for the AFL-CIO was $.35 per member per month, or $4.20 per year. Dues for the unions are much higher.

The AFL-CIO claims to be the collective voice of U.S. workers. The claim is an exaggeration, since only one of every six workers belongs to a union affiliated with the AFL-CIO. The claim that the AFL-CIO represents "organized labor" is closer to the facts, but still misleading. Although most unions are AFL-CIO affiliates, some large ones, especially of public employees are not. Although the NEA is the largest union not affiliated with the AFL-CIO, many state and local unions of school district support personnel are not affiliated with any other labor organization. For instance, the California School Employees Association (CSEA), which enrolls about 170,000 members, is not affiliated with the AFL-CIO.

For most practical purposes, the AFL-CIO's constituent unions are autonomous. For example, each union can endorse whomever it wishes for public office. The result is an organization that acts only when there is a high level of internal agreement; there is much more veto power than the power to act in the AFL-CIO. The officers of AFL-CIO unions often exercise strong control over their unions, but AFL-CIO action usually requires a high level of agreement among its constituent unions.

The underlying rationale for the AFL-CIO is that the benefits of mutual support outweigh the costs of mutual aid and assistance. Thus the AFL-CIO supports restrictions on foreign cars that raise the price of cars to everyone, including all members of the AFL-CIO. The quid pro quo is that the United Auto Workers will help each of the other unions achieve their particular objectives. Thus the AFL-CIO seeks protection for a host of unionized industries: automobile, steel, machine tool, telecommunications, electronics, shipping, defense, textiles, apparel, shoe, and "office and other service sector jobs." Unorganized consumers and nonunion workers are the net losers in this arrangement, since they do not receive any quid pro quo to offset the higher prices they pay for union-made goods and services. In fact, union solidarity is more of a threat to unorganized workers and to consumers than to employers who can pass along the costs of union demands to consumers. How many employers can do this is debatable, but the number is undoubtedly much lower than the unions assume.

Patterns of Union Membership

In 1953, the peak year in terms of percentage, 36 percent of the private sector labor force was unionized; in 1994, only 11.2 percent and will likely drop to single digits by the year 2000. The unionized percentage of the labor force in 1994 fell even below the 1929 predepression level of 12.4 percent. In terms of the number rather than the percentage of union members, 1979 was the peak year, with over twenty million enrolled in labor unions; membership has declined steadily since.

Why the decline? The union answer is intransigent employer opposition, that is, "union-busting." This answer has led to union legislative proposals to thwart employer opposition to unionization. The proposals include:

1. Certifying unions on the basis of authorization cards instead of representation elections. This would minimize employer campaigns against union representation.

2. Decreasing the time between notice of a representation election and the actual election. Since the unions are ordinarily the moving party in representation elections, they could initiate the request for an election at the most opportune time, leaving employers little time to mount an opposition campaign.

3. Compulsory arbitration of first contracts. The union argument is that employers try to avoid any contract that would enhance union credibility after winning a representation election.

In view of the Republican majorities in Congress after the 1996 elections, these changes will not be enacted for several years to come, if enacted at all. It appears, however, that the union diagnosis is essentially fallacious. Private sector union membership has been declining in virtually all Western industrial democracies, and for much the same reasons that underlie its decline in the United States. Although their relevance to teachers and teacher unions is debatable, let me review these reasons briefly.

The most important factor conducive to union decline appears to be the increase in competitive labor markets. Union viability depends upon union power to monopolize labor markets. The union monopoly need not be perfect or complete, but it must protect union members from major competitive threats.

Generally speaking, unions try to minimize competition in their labor markets. One way is to create obstacles to goods and services produced by competing labor forces. Thus tariffs and quotas on automobiles and clothing are intended to protect U.S. workers in these industries by excluding or raising the prices of products made by foreign labor. Generally speaking, unions oppose enlarging labor markets if to do so leads to competition from workers previously excluded by protective measures. The decline of private sector unions in Europe was partly due to the fact that the European Common Market enlarged the area of competitive labor markets. The member nations could no longer protect their workers and their unions by tariffs, quotas, and other measures that excluded products from other common market nations. Similarly, prior to the adoption of the U.S. Constitution, each state tried to protect its workers from competition by imposing tariffs on goods imported from other states. After the adoption of the Constitution, the states could no longer protect their monopolies this way, although the United States as a whole can do so.

Public sector unionization in the United States has followed a much different pattern than unionization in the private sector. In the latter, the unions organized workers who were not members of any employee organization. In the public sector, however, most employees were members of associations of public employees. Unionization was a process of transforming existing public employee organizations into unions. The NEA is the leading example of this process.[3]

NEA and AFL-CIO Policy Convergence

The NEA/AFT and organized labor share a common interest in keeping children in school. Organized labor's interest is in keeping children out of labor markets. The NEA/AFT interest is to maintain or expand the market for teacher services. This mutuality of interest has played an important role in education. In the early 1900s labor unions were successful in enacting federal legislation prohibiting interstate commerce in products made with child labor. This legislation was held unconstitutional by the Supreme Court in 1918; thereafter, although organized labor had always been supportive of public education, the unions turned to compulsory education as the way to protect workers from competition with child labor. Although child labor was declining for economic reasons, organized labor and the growing public school lobby certainly accelerated the decline.[4] Of course, all such efforts are portrayed as union solicitude for children, not as efforts to expand teacher markets or protect union members from competition.

As a practical matter, it is open to question whether the alleged beneficiaries of union action always benefit from it. For instance, we could equalize life-time incomes much more if young people not interested or able to stay in school could go to work sooner. Furthermore, if formal schooling had to compete sooner against the work option, the pressure on the former to demonstrate positive results would be much greater—a positive outcome for consumers. Whether or not child labor laws benefit children, union support for these laws pays little heed to their actual impact on their ostensible beneficiaries.

Organized labor also played an important role in vocational education. The unions feared that if business controlled vocational education, students would be indoctrinated with antiunion curricula. To forestall any such outcome, the unions insisted that vocational education be provided by public schools. The unions were also concerned that vocational education would be inferior if provided through a separate system of vocational schools. On both issues, the unions found allies in the growing public school establishment. The latter were concerned that a system of separate vocational schools would be a competitor for financial resources; also that it would lead to a classical education for the elite and a vocational education for everyone else.

AFL-CIO policies have always been supportive of public education, but one earlier position presents a remarkable contrast with current policy. As mentioned in Chapter 1, in 1947, the NEA sponsored a federal aid to education bill. One of the issues was whether federal aid to education should be available for denominational schools. The AFL and NEA supported legislation that would allow the states to resolve this issue. Under such legislation, denominational schools in many states would receive federal aid; the Catholic Church supported the bill for this reason. The NEA supported it as the price that had to be paid to enact federal aid for public schools.[5]

Although the AFT also supported the legislation, the federation initially opposed it. Eventually, the AFT adopted the AFL position under pressure from the latter. Today, the NEA and AFT are adamantly opposed to education vouchers that parents could use to defray the costs of private schooling; their reason is that parents would be an "inconsequential conduit" to denominational schools. This is deemed to be a violation of the First Amendment prohibition against federal aid to religious institutions. Neither the NEA, the AFT, nor the AFL-CIO has explained how federal aid to denominational schools, which was constitutional and acceptable in 1947, has become unconstitutional and unacceptable in 1997. Whatever the explanation, contemporary AFL-CIO positions on education merely adopt the AFT position on the issues. The 1947 scenario in which the AFL-CIO pressured the AFT to support federal aid to denominational schools is no longer a realistic possibility.

If one considers NEA and AFL-CIO policies and political alignments in their entirety, there are no differences that should preclude merger. Under a merger, the AFL-CIO would undoubtedly adopt the educational policies of the teacher union, which would be the largest in the federation. Clearly the NEA has adopted most AFL-CIO positions on noneducational issues as well, NEA publications invariably praise the AFL-CIO, and the two organizations rarely find themselves in conflict over noneducational issues. In view of the fact that thirty-five AFL-CIO unions enroll some public employees, we should expect considerable convergence between NEA and AFL-CIO legislative and political agendas, and with few exceptions, convergence is what we see.

In fact, merger is encouraging as well as reflecting NEA/AFT political convergence. The two unions have established the AFT-NEA Joint Council, consisting of fifteen members of each union. The purpose of the council is to develop common positions on issues of common interest; merger issues continue to be the responsibility of the teams negotiating the merger.[6]

In the past, the political differences between the unions have often been due to competition between the unions. Inasmuch as it would not be prudent to acknowledge the fact, the NEA and AFT cite other reasons. The result is that most NEA/AFT members are not aware of the extent to which union political positions are based upon competition with the rival union. For example, in 1980, the AFT supported Senator Ted Kennedy for president in the Democratic primaries; the NEA supported President Jimmy Carter's bid for reelection. The split was due primarily to Carter's close relationships with the NEA and to the fact that the AFT had opposed the establishment of the U.S. Department of Education during Carter's presidency. Under a merger, all such differences would be resolved within the merged organization. Because the competition between the unions is often disguised as a policy dispute, fewer policy differences would arise under merger even though internal conflict would not disappear.

Race Relations

On the whole, teacher union and AFL-CIO social agendas are remarkably similar. Race relations are the major area of disagreement, but union policies on the subject are also moving toward convergence.

The AFL-CIO, NEA, and AFT faced a common problem during the 1950s and 1960s. All were national organizations which (1) depended on state and local affiliates for revenues; (2) included state and local affiliates adamantly opposed to racial equality and racial integration; and (3) risked membership and revenue losses if they took strong action against affiliates or leaders who supported discriminatory policies.

The AFL-CIO and NEA especially faced painful dilemmas over discrimination issues. The AFL-CIO nationally opposed racial discrimination even though union officials and members in the South were frequently leaders of organizations supporting racial segregation. The AFL-CIO's problems were exacerbated by the fact that its Southern strategy called for empowerment of Southern black voters. Time after time, the AFL-CIO supported legislation that was blocked in Congress by southern Democrats allied with northern Republicans. AFL-CIO leadership concluded that the only way to overcome this alliance was to elect pro-labor Democrats over conservative ones. The Southern black vote was essential for this purpose, thus the AFL-CIO dilemma. Whenever it supported legislation to empower black voters, or tried to remedy discriminatory practices in AFL-CIO affiliates, it risked a loss of support, especially from its southern affiliates.

Whatever criticism can be made of AFL-CIO efforts to resolve the dilemmas, its national leadership was much more active than the NEA's in opposing racial discrimination. After the 1954 U.S. Supreme Court decision holding government-imposed racial segregation in public education to be unconstitutional, NEA leadership sought to avoid the problem. The NEA's annual convention avoided adopting a position on the issue until 1961, when it adopted a resolution supporting the Supreme Court decision. Nevertheless, merger of the NEA's separate black and white state affiliates was not completed until 1977. To the surprise of the naysayers, by 1979, membership in the merged state organizations increased an average of 87 percent over the combined membership of the separate associations.[7] Meanwhile, the AFT had expelled its Atlanta locals in 1957 for failure to end racial segregation; however, because the AFT had few southern affiliates, it had much less to lose than the AFL-CIO or NEA by expelling segregated locals. Arguably, the expulsion of the Atlanta local resulted in membership gains for the AFT, as it did for the NEA several years later.

In recent years, all three organizations have become very dependent on black support, both politically and in terms of union membership. The NEA's support for policies espoused by its black caucus is especially remarkable; no other major organization in the United States has embraced racial quotas as explicitly and as pervasively as the NEA. The NEA constitution and bylaws provide that:

- A minimum of 20 percent ethnic minority representation on each appointive committee.
- Ethnic minorities shall comprise at least 20 percent of the Board of Directors.
- Ethnic minorities shall comprise at least 20 percent of the Executive Committee.
- NEA affiliates "shall take all reasonable and legally permissible steps" to achieve "ethnic-minority representation that is at least proportional to the ethnic-minority membership of the affiliate . . ."
- As vacancies arise, the NEA shall employ ethnic minorities "at all levels of service" in the same ratio as the minorities or to the total U.S. population.
- Ethnic minority "shall specifically include Black, Mexican-American (Chicano), other Spanish-speaking groups, Asian-American, and Indian."[8]

As the AFL-CIO becomes a predominantly public sector union, its constituencies will be more likely to support an NEA type approach to race relations. This outcome will be especially evident where AFL-CIO unions represent employees in lower socioeconomic levels. Although the AFT is opposed to the NEA's support for racial preferences, the AFL-CIO is more likely to do so under the merger.

NEA and AFL-CIO Political Convergence

As the NEA/AFT emphasize repeatedly, political action is essential to achieve union objectives. This imperative raises a critical issue. Should the union be aligned with one particular party on a long-range basis? Or should the union treat each issue independently, using its political resources on an issue by issue basis as the occasion demands? Like the NEA/AFT, the AFL-CIO has opted for a de facto alliance with the Democratic party after initially adopting an issue by issue approach.

Until the 1940s, the AFL followed an issue-by-issue approach to political action. A shift away from this approach emerged in the 1940s and became institutionalized in the 1960s. Part of the explanation is the change in union composition. In the early years of the AFL, its membership was predominantly in craft unions serving local markets. These unions could effectively implement an issue-by-issue approach to politics. The emergence of large industrial unions employed in national markets required or was deemed to require a national approach. Federal policy was much more important to the industrial than to the craft unions.

Few if any issues are more important to the NEA/AFT than their choice of political strategy. In their situation, government does not merely establish the ground rules for bargaining with employers; government is the employer. Consequently, the teacher unions have even stronger reasons to elect supportive public officials. Of course, the NEA will be more concerned than the AFL-CIO about state and local elections, but the different union priorities on this issue should be easily managed.

Merger Perspectives

There is some opposition to merger and/or affiliation in the NEA. First, there is the concern that the AFL-CIO will try to dictate NEA policies. This concern is groundless, and would be even if the merged organization did not become the largest union in the AFL-CIO, as is likely if the merger takes place.

Objection to being identified as a "union" instead of a "professional organization" is also a factor but a declining one as the NEA enrolls more support personnel. Although the debate over professionalism may continue, it is becoming irrelevant as the NEA devotes more resources to organizing and serving support personnel. Of course, aspirants for union positions or offices will evaluate merger in terms of its impact on their careers. Since it would not be prudent to say this, they will cite other reasons for their positions. Nevertheless, I do not anticipate much opposition from parties disadvantaged by merger.

The AFT is essentially an urban union. Although it has hundreds of affiliates, over one-third of its membership is drawn from New York state; one-ninth is from the United Federation of Teachers, its New York City local. Most of the remaining AFT teacher membership is from its large urban affiliates in Chicago, Philadelphia, Boston, Detroit, Miami, Minneapolis, St. Paul, Cleveland, Cincinnati, Pittsburgh, Hartford, and Providence. Most full-time AFT personnel are employed by these urban locals and their employment situation would not be adversely affected by the merger. Outside of New York, the AFT employs minimal staff who can be easily absorbed by the state education associations. The problem of excess personnel, if any, would exist mainly at the national level; however, the tremendous resources that will be available to the merged organization should preclude any sacrifice by the vast majority of union employees.

Inasmuch as the most severe educational deficiencies are in the large urban districts, some NEA leaders are privately concerned about the advisability of representing teachers in such districts, but their reluctance does not appear to be a major factor.

Representation issues may be more difficult to resolve. The AFT structure allows one individual to cast all the votes for his/her local; the NEA structure requires an individual delegate for each vote. From the standpoint of convention efficiency, some movement toward the AFT structure is imperative, but the NEA takes great pride in the broad delegate base at its national conventions. Another complication is that state federations are represented on a more liberal basis than state associations are represented at the NEA conventions. Because agreement on these issues could affect the distribution of power in the merged union, they may be difficult to resolve.

Member benefits may also be a merger issue. Both unions may be reluctant to abandon companies that have provided services for their members for a long time. Allowing companies to compete under the merger umbrella might violate the existing contracts that provide exclusive access to the union market. Another consideration is that AFT members have access to AFL-CIO member benefits, such as the AFL-CIO credit card. In such cases, the AFL-CIO and its service providers might have to agree on NEA/AFT member benefit issues. To outsiders, the issues may not seem to be especially important, but union staff members and several large companies have a stake in the outcome. Furthermore, substantial union revenues are involved, even if they do not show up this way on union balance sheets.

The Case For and Against Merger

The most commonly cited argument for merger is that it would avoid duplication and inefficient use of resources. Instead of two union representatives testifying at a legislative hearing, one would be sufficient. Instead of two union conventions or two union newspapers, one would suffice. Interestingly enough, however, NEA/AFT leaders do not emphasize efficiency gains as the main rationale for the merger. Instead, their statements supporting the merger emphasize the union resources that have been wasted in NEA/AFT competition to represent teachers.[9] These arguments bear a striking resemblance to the arguments made by competing businesses that merger would save the "unnecessary" costs of competition. Not surprisingly, the arguments are just as weak as they are in the private sector.

Teachers are consumers of representational services; unions are the producers of them. Ordinarily, teachers are better off as consumers when their vendors have to compete for their business—a point that should hardly require elaboration. Why would teachers be better off without an option to change, and without any competition from their vendors to provide better service at a lower cost? Every bit of evidence indicates that if there is only one union, its tendency will be to charge more for less, as is the case generally with monopolies.

Until the NEA/AFT jurisdictional agreement, the unions monitored each other; with the merger, this possibility disappears. Note that the jurisdictional agreement requires the parties not to lower their dues in efforts to attract union members away from the other union. Would teachers be better off if automotive companies or grocery stores or doctors also agreed to avoid price competition? It is difficult to see how or why, but the argument against a merger for this reason is not being made. The reason is that the teacher unions are busily demonizing competition in order to protect teachers and the unions from it. The teacher union that opposes competition to provide instruction naturally opposes competition to provide representation.

NEA/AFT leaders justify merger on the grounds that the competition between the two unions was and is a huge waste of resources. Their premise is valid, but the solution is not to have teachers give up their opportunity to choose another union. It is to get rid of the leadership responsible for the waste of resources. After all, it was not necessary for the NEA/AFT to waste hundreds of millions of dollars in futile efforts to oust each other as the bargaining agent.

In this connection, note the anticompetitive implications of Article XX of the AFL-CIO constitution.[10] No matter how badly an AFL-CIO union represents employees, and no matter how much the employees themselves want to be represented by a different union, no other AFL-CIO union is allowed to replace the incumbent union. This is a monopolist's dream, and it is precisely what merger and affiliation are all about. The union bureaucracies naturally support merger, but why should teachers? The savings from a merger will not be used to reduce union dues while the disappearance of competing unions will weaken union incentives to improve services or lower costs.

Perhaps the strongest argument for merger is one not made by either union—to wit, that it would reduce staff control of the NEA. Chapter 11 pointed out that AFT president Albert Shanker exercised complete control over AFT headquarters staff. In contrast, the NEA elects three executive officers to run an organization with 568 headquarters staff. With the possible exception of a few secretaries and assistants, the NEA's elected executive officers exercise weak line control over NEA staff. Despite the public position that the staff carries out policies adopted by elected officials, Don Cameron, the NEA's executive director, may be the most powerful official in the NEA.

The NEA's modus operandi also fosters staff control. Members of the NEA's Executive Committee travel constantly at NEA expense, representing NEA at hundreds of functions throughout the country. Meanwhile, except for the three executive officers, who are themselves away from Washington for considerable periods of time, the staff operates without supervision by elected officers or their appointees. One can be critical of the AFT structure, but at least it provides a level of accountability that is virtually absent in the NEA. Merger would provide a window of opportunity to create a much more responsive and accountable organizational structure than currently exists in the NEA.

The Union Perspective

Most union mergers materialize among declining unions; on the surface at least, an NEA/AFT merger would be an exception. Nevertheless, a merger does pose some risks for the NEA. From the NEA's perspective, the basic issue is whether the baggage that the merger would bring is worth the anticipated benefits. The baggage includes the AFL-CIO's low standing in worker and public opinion.

Perhaps the best evidence on this issue is to be found in a poll commissioned by the AFL-CIO itself. The poll revealed that:

1. Almost 90 percent of nonunion workers were satisfied with their job; 51 percent were "very satisfied."

2. Almost 60 percent of nonunion workers indicate that unions stifle individual initiative.

3. About 78 percent of nonunion workers believed that their employers were sincerely concerned about the welfare of their employees.

4. About 57 percent of nonunion employees agreed that unions were not es-

sential to getting fair treatment. Another 57 percent also agreed that their employers were paying their employees all they reasonably could.

5. A substantial majority of nonunion workers are opposed to union negotiations and would vote against it in a representative election. Of course, this does not negate the fact that majorities of workers in specific companies or government agencies may support unionization.[11] The NEA must also factor in the opposition to affiliation from a sizable number of NEA members. These members may or may not be guided by good reasons, but NEA leaders cannot ignore a sizable body of opinion in their ranks on such an important issue.

For the AFT, on the other hand, merger does not appear to have any major downside. It has been clear for over twenty-five years that it has no chance of becoming the dominant teacher union. The AFT's frantic efforts to organize noneducational and nongovernmental employees obviously reflect recognition of its limited growth possibilities in education. The merger agreement could take good care of the AFT headquarters staff, and the rest of the AFT staff could work for the NEA as easily as it does for the AFT.

An NEA/AFT merger is highly probable because their leaders support the merger. The leadership controls the union publications, the programs at union conventions, and the information and arguments made available to members and the media. In politics, incumbents are often opposed by interest groups with ample resources not controlled by the incumbents. Such opposition is much less likely in union affairs. After years of controlling the flow of information about the issues, the unions will give equal time to "both sides" in a union convention, and the process will reach its preordained conclusion amidst high praise for the union's democratic procedures. There will be pockets of resistance to the merger in the NEA, probably none of any significance in the AFT. Actually, since the anti-incumbent faction in the AFT regards merger as its only hope of achieving a leadership role, there will be little opposition to the merger in the AFT.

14

WHAT IS TO BE DONE?

Generally speaking, there are three attitudes toward teacher unions in American education:

- The positive effects outweigh the negative ones. On this view, corrective action, if any, tends to be minimal.
- The unions are an obstacle to reform; the task is to persuade them to change their antireform policies.
- The unions are an obstacle to reform because their obstruction is inherent in the nature of public sector unionization; the task is to weaken their power to block reforms.

The latter position is not confined to supporters of market-oriented reforms; many critics of such reforms nevertheless agree that the NEA/AFT are blocking reforms, such as changes in teacher tenure, that are intended to improve public education. In the following discussion, my emphasis is on curbing excessive union power while maintaining a viable system of teacher representation.

First, a word of caution. The teacher unions are likely to be affected by a host of unpredictable, noneducational factors. The appointment of a Supreme Court justice, enactment or repeal of right-to-work laws, new restriction on taxes, or legislation on PAC contributions—such broad developments could strengthen or weaken the teacher unions, as the case might be. In the 1960s, the NEA supported teacher-only bargaining laws. In the 1970s, the NEA found that its interests were better served by bargaining laws applicable to state and local employees generally. By the same token, the most feasible way to affect teacher union power may be through legislation or programs applicable to all public employees, or all unions, or all public employee unions. It is not feasible to analyze these possibilities here, but they have as much potential as actions affecting only teacher unions.

Restructuring

The NEA/AFT are well aware of the criticisms directed at them. In response, the teacher unions are eager to demonstrate their commitment to educational improvement, as long as union prerogatives are not jeopardized.

A 1997 study commissioned by the NEA emphasized that "public education, and the NEA, are in a state of crisis. And only a focused, crisis-oriented mode of operations will suffice." The study, conducted by a public relations firm with close ties to the Democratic party was based upon forty-two interviews with state and national NEA officials, including all members of the NEA executive committee; analyses of thousands of articles, press releases, television interviews, NEA print materials, and NEA focus group and polling data.[1]

The report's major recommendation was that NEA "establish itself as *the* champion of public education through a new initiative to produce *better teachers, better students, better public schools,* and a call for all Americans to join in the challenge." (Italics in original.) Inasmuch as the report was based partly on interviews with NEA officers, its findings and recommendations simply reflect the crisis mentality that has shaped NEA strategy in recent years. Upon his election in 1996, NEA president Robert Chase announced that the NEA was in the process of "reinventing" itself to facilitate a change in emphasis from teacher welfare to educational achievement.[2] In an astonishing reversal of its position in the 1960s, the NEA has embraced a private sector approach to labor/management relations as a model for public education. In the 1960s, the NEA had argued that the approach to collective bargaining in the private sector was not appropriate in public education. In 1997, however, the NEA was urging its affiliates and school management to adopt the labor/management arrangements at the General Motors Saturn plant in Spring Hill, Tennessee. The NEA sponsors visits to the Saturn plant and even subsidizes visits by school district negotiators.

What is so desirable about the labor/management relations at the Saturn plant? The United Auto Workers (UAW) represents the unionized employees there. According to UAW officials, there are very few contractual restrictions on the utilization of plant personnel. The conventional hierarchical structure of management has been replaced by the devolution of decision making to teams of workers on the shop floor. As a result, the creativity of the workforce has been supposedly unleashed to an unprecedented degree. A plethora of facts and figures are cited to demonstrate the superior productivity of the plant, both in terms of car quality and costs.

It all seems to be too good to be true, and it is, at least insofar as public education is concerned. According to UAW representatives at the Saturn plant, the union is an equal partner in operating the plant, with the power to veto most management decisions. When I asked a UAW representative what decisions would be made jointly if the Saturn model were adopted in public education, he answered without a moment's hesitation: "The curriculum." Further discussion revealed that he had not the slightest reservation about school boards sharing their legal responsibilities with the union, a private organization. What if the teacher union and the school board agreed on a curriculum that turned out to be a dismal failure? The public could remove the school board, but it could not dismiss the union leaders or the teachers who were jointly responsible for the disaster. In public education, the Saturn model is a prescription for more union power along with the complete absence of any teacher or union accountability for results.

Furthermore, even the union officials at the Saturn plant concede that in the absence of competition from other carmakers, the innovative relationships at the Saturn plant would not have emerged. This point is critical. In the private sector, the major threat to unions and employers is competing companies, not management. Employers can point to competing services or products, and credibly assert, "Unless our company can do better, we'll be out of business." As we have seen, however, the NEA is determined to prevent any competition with public education. To the extent that its efforts are successful, they will also eliminate the employee and union incentives that undergird successful restructuring in the private sector.

Although the details differ, the AFT is pursuing the same strategy. The federation does not concede that teacher salaries are adequate. Instead, it contends that the union has won the battle against top down management that treated teachers like assembly line workers, and students like standardized products. Having established a strong union that has ended this management style, teachers "are free to speak out for higher educational standards, better learning conditions, safer schools, adequate funding and more effective teaching methods."[3] Clearly, by 1996, NEA/AFT were embarked upon a huge public relations campaign to persuade the public that the unions' highest priority is student achievement.

A realistic way to evaluate the NEA's claim to be "reinventing" itself is to examine the resources devoted to its allegedly new role. In 1997, the NEA's legal position was that 71 percent of its resources were devoted to collective bargaining, grievance processing, and contract administration. Bear in mind that this is the

NEA's position. Everything else—organizing, political action, public relations, outreach, entertainment—allegedly absorbs only 29 percent of the NEA's budget.

Presumably, a new emphasis on student achievement would require a change in the allocation of NEA resources. There is no indication of any such change in NEA budgets; in fact, the NEA is legally opposed to claims that it is spending less on collective bargaining than it has in the past. If such claims were valid, the NEA would be required to reduce its agency fee revenues, something the NEA strenuously opposes.

Regardless of the specifics, "restructuring" will not change the union role in education. The reason is that the conditions that generate pressure to restructure in the private sector do not exist in public education. In the private sector, both management and the employees face productivity and efficiency imperatives. It is in their mutual interest to maximize productivity to ward off competition or to share in the gains. This is not the case in public education. Teachers do not share in productivity gains. If teachers educate more pupils at a lower cost, and no loss in achievement, the teachers would not benefit.

In the private sector, restructuring is based on bottom lines such as profits. Profits do not exist in education and public schools are not set up to return productivity gains to the various factors of production; on the contrary, the union culture, like the culture of public education generally, is adamantly opposed to any such approach to compensation. Absent the incentives and imperatives that drive restructuring in the private sector, "restructuring" is just another buzzword in public education.

In fact, many teachers believe that the concept of productivity has no applicability to education. "Efficiency" and "productivity" are evils to be avoided; in the teacher culture, they are synonymous with sweatshops, corporate greed, lower wages, reduced benefits, and other union no-no's.

On productivity issues, it will be very difficult for the NEA/AFT to change entrenched habits and attitudes. Like other unions, the NEA/AFT were established to resolve distributional problems, especially the amount of school revenues and the share going to teachers. Efforts to increase appropriations for education and the teacher share thereof are based entirely on political/legislative means. Improving service efficiency and quality plays no role in NEA/AFT approaches to teacher compensation. In the private sector, however, loss of job is more of a threat than low pay. For example, airline employees tend to view other airlines instead of management as the major threat to their welfare. Under these circumstances, it is easier to persuade unions to "restructure" in order to increase productivity. Of course, distributional problems cannot be ignored, but they become secondary in a competitive industry.

The NEA/AFT are doing their utmost to prevent K–12 education from becoming a competitive industry. By doing so, they hope to avoid productivity issues. If K–12 education becomes a competitive industry, the NEA/AFT emphasis will have to shift from redistribution to increasing productivity. Any such shift would be extremely difficult to implement successfully; it will require basic changes in the union culture as well as in its theory and practice.

To be candid about it, confusion on educational productivity issues characterizes both union critics as well as supporters. Conservatives often criticize the NEA/AFT because their contracts emphasize teacher welfare, not student achievement. In response, the NEA/AFT proclaim their intent to utilize collective bargaining to facilitate education reform. Outgoing NEA president Keith Geiger emphasized this shift in union priorities at the 1996 NEA convention. Unfortunately, bargaining on educational reform proposals is a disaster waiting to happen, with a very brief waiting period. School management should be trying to limit the scope of bargaining, not expand it to include "reform" issues. It is safe to predict that whatever policy is placed on bargaining tables, the union position will be based on what is good for the teachers and/or the union. I do not say this because teachers and their unions are more self-serving than other interest groups. My reason is that despite having convinced themselves to the contrary, the teachers and their unions are no less self-serving than the interest groups they routinely revile as greed-oriented exploiters.

Of course, if teachers have a stake in increased productivity, they might be more receptive to a system that fostered it. It is doubtful, however, whether the NEA and AFT, which are geared to political action as the route to higher compensation, would or could accept any such change. In my opinion, the NEA and AFT will accept productivity responsibilities only if they must in order to survive; the question is whether they will be in an adapt or perish mode in the next decade.

Charter Schools

Currently, charter schools are the reform *du jour.* The phrase "charter schools" refers to a wide variety of arrangements that make it possible to establish new schools. The arrangements differ on virtually every conceivable issue: Who can charter a school? How many schools can be chartered? What are the conditions of eligibility for charters? What is the role of teacher unions in charter schools? What about the state-aid formula? The list of issues that distinguishes some charter schools from others is endless.

Conceptually, charter schools are supposed to be public schools free of stifling state regulations. The extent of such freedom varies, but the NEA/AFT have set forth their own criteria for approval of charter schools. Not surprisingly, these criteria are usually a wish list of union demands, including that teachers be covered by an existing union contract or one to be negotiated by a union representing teachers in charter schools.

I see no reason to oppose charter schools—but much reason to doubt their potential for improving American education. The restrictions on them, their small scale and the lack of incentives to expand them are major weaknesses. Parents don't want to start schools; they want their children educated in the schools they attend. It is wishful thinking to assume that hordes of teachers chafing under bureaucratic restrictions are eager to teach in charter schools, or that large numbers of entrepreneurial teachers are eagerly awaiting opportunities to demonstrate how schools should be run. The charter school movement could be useful if it enables schools for profit to enter the education industry. Unfortunately, most charter school legislation does not allow this. In this eagerness to show progress, proponents of charter schools typically accept restrictions that impair their usefulness as models for a different approach to education.

Regional Bargaining

In most states, teacher union power follows a pattern that is evident in the private sector. When a national union faces a multiplicity of small employers, the union enjoys an overwhelming balance of power. No one employer has the resources to hold out against excessive union demands. The private sector solution is to have the various employers bargain jointly, with severe penalties for employers who break ranks and settle on their own with the union. In the Nevada casinos, employers who do this are subject to liquidated damages of $500,000 per day to the employer association—a penalty severe enough to discourage casino owners from going it alone.

In education, state-wide bargaining is occasionally advocated to counter the teacher union strategic advantage; however, except in Hawaii, which already has state-wide bargaining in public education, there is no movement in this direction. There is much more interest in regional bargaining—that is, bargaining by clusters of school districts in contiguous areas as an employer association.

For various reasons, this strategy is not readily available to school districts. One is that it would be an unlawful delegation of school board authority to delegate the power to reach agreement to a consortium of school districts. Changes in state law would be required to legalize this strategy, but the unions would probably oppose such changes. Although some school boards that despair over their inability to counter union pressures are willing to accept regional bargaining, it may not be feasible for confidentiality reasons. Under regional bargaining, it will be virtually impossible to maintain essential confidentiality about management's bottom line. If several school boards combine for bargaining purposes, one union supporter among the school boards may be enough to destroy the viability of such collaboration.

School Choice and the Teacher Unions

Unquestionably, school choice legislation that strengthened opportunities for private schooling would have a negative effect upon the NEA/AFT. The practical issue, however, is what has to be done about the teacher unions to enact vouchers, not what would happen to them if vouchers were enacted. Although the NEA/AFT assert that vouchers would endanger public education, their underlying concern is that vouchers would weaken the unions. It is much more difficult for the NEA/AFT to organize teachers in private schools; it would be even more difficult if education were a competitive industry.

Up to this time, strategic errors have clearly weakened the voucher movement. One such error has been to overemphasize parental support, such as by using "Parent" in the title of voucher initiatives. Parents with children in school are a shrinking proportion of the voting population. More importantly, most parents are satisfied with their schools. This is especially true in affluent suburban areas. On this issue, polls of voter attitudes toward Congress are suggestive. Most voters are critical of Congress collectively but approve and vote for their incumbent congressman. Similarly, most parents express dissatisfaction with schools but not the school their children attend. And the more the proponents assert that the vouchers will enable inner city pupils to attend affluent suburban schools, the more they weaken suburban support for vouchers.

Up to the present time, the provoucher forces have never adopted a strategy that would split teachers from their unions. Here, the strategy followed by the British government under Prime Minister Thatcher is instructive. In privatizing nationalized industries, the government offered stock at a deep discount to employees in the industries to be privatized. This strategy weakened union ability to persuade employees to oppose the privatization measures. It also provided a safeguard against renationalization. The employees who had purchased stock did not want to lose their gains because of renationalization.

Although the provoucher forces in the United States have never adopted such a strategy, they are likely to do so in the future. Of course, they cannot offer stock in private schools at a deep discount, but voucher initiatives could offer teacher incentives, such as early retirement credit, to support vouchers. As this happens, the NEA/AFT will find it increasingly difficult to maintain unified teacher opposition to vouchers.

Back to the Future

Notwithstanding their current opposition to government assistance for private schooling, the NEA/AFT and AFL-CIO may eventually support such assistance as they did in the 1940s. NEA/AFT support was reluctant, but support it was—and may materialize again, unlikely as that seems now. My thought rests upon the logic of the situation, not upon any evidence that the NEA/AFT are moving in this direction.

Competition often leads to monopolies, and monopolies often lead to competition. At some point, the public and private school lobbies will conclude they can do better by cooperating than by fighting each other; the private school lobby will support increased funding for education because private schooling will get a share of the appropriations. Public and private schools have joined forces in the past to lobby for a larger education pie from which each takes a larger slice than could have been achieved from solo efforts. I see no reason why it can't happen again, and much reason to believe it will.

In the 1960s, government and nonprofit schools worked together to prevent competition from schools for profit.[4] Indeed, from a public policy perspective, public/private nonprofit school collusion is much more to be feared than government regulation of private education. It is a shibboleth that excessive government regulation inevitably accompanies government dollars. To cite just one example, the public payrolls include hundreds of thousands of professors who are largely free of regulation or supervision. Certainly they are much less subject to government regulation than businesses coping with OSHA, EPA, IRS and a host of other government rules and regulations. Chapter 7 pointed out that the AFT has received millions in federal funds without any requirement to show who is paid how much under its contracts with the National Endowment for Democracy, and there are countless other examples.

Despite the prevailing cliches, government financial support for private schooling will not necessarily lead to excessive regulation of private schools; in some situations, the political coalition that achieves government support for private schooling will also prevent the imposition of burdensome government regulations. The fact that over half of private schools are denominational will also weaken efforts to regulate them.

The NEA/AFT will accept a rapprochement with private education only when they have lost ground politically. Supporting government assistance to private schooling, after decades of proclaiming it to be a threat to democracy, will be a problem, but a manageable one. From the union perspective, the main problems will be the legal obstacles and the difficulty of organizing teachers in private, especially denominational schools. If denominational schools are unionized, government agencies will be forced to resolve conflicts between labor law and religious doctrine. Teachers in denominational schools may assert that they were fired for protected union activities; archbishops, rabbis, and ministers, prospective defendants in unfair labor practice charges, will assert the teachers were fired for violating religious doctrines. Faced with the prospect of having to resolve such conflicts, the U.S. Supreme Court has held that the National Labor Relations Act is not applicable to religious institutions.[5] The applicability of its decisions to state bargaining statutes is still in doubt. On the practical side, it is more difficult to organize small numbers of teachers in a large number of schools than a large number of teachers employed by a single school district. Nonetheless, as government appropriations for education become more difficult to come by, the NEA/AFT may be forced again to make a deal with private school forces. The rationale will be the same as underlies labor unity in the AFL-CIO—the parties can get more by working together for larger appropriations than by going it alone. Of course, the issues are more complex than I have shown, but the logic of the situation points in this direction.

Local Only Teacher Unions (LOTUs)

The foregoing analysis appears to present a hopeless prospect for teachers opposed to inclusion in a huge industrial type union with an extremely liberal political and social agenda. In my opinion, this conclusion would be highly erroneous. Although several statutory changes are highly desirable, I believe that major union reforms are possible within a few years even in their absence.

First, it is essential to recognize the strategic importance of the state bargaining laws. In states that have not enacted them, nonunion teacher organizations can and sometimes do enroll a substantial number of members. In Missouri and Texas, the nonunion teacher organizations enroll more members than either the NEA or AFT affiliate. In a few other states (notably, South Carolina and Georgia) the nonunion teacher organizations enroll a significant proportion of teachers in the state.

In the thirty-four bargaining law states, however, nonunion teacher organizations are not a significant factor. The record is clear: In states that have enacted bargaining laws, teacher organizations will not be a significant presence unless they embrace collective bargaining or unless the teacher bargaining laws are repealed or amended. To resolve this dilemma, my suggestion is that teachers join local only teacher unions (LOTUs). LOTUs would provide low cost union representation, but without several features of NEA/AFT representation that teachers find objectionable. Local only unions would not require repeal or amendment of the state bargaining laws, a critical strategic advantage over any reforms that require legislation.

The most important difference between the NEA/AFT and LOTUs is that the teachers who join the latter would not be members of a national union; they might or might not be members of a state union. Inasmuch as the revenues from the state governments comprise almost half the revenues available to local school districts, most teachers accept the need for a state organization. In the bargaining law states, however, the union alternative to the NEA/AFT will be local only teacher unions at the outset. Since most teachers are in the bargaining law states, I suggest that "local only teacher unions" are a viable alternative to the NEA/AFT, bearing in mind that the eventual pattern would probably be membership in state as well as local unions. This is the pattern in the states that have not enacted bargaining laws, and it appears to function fairly well. If participation in national affairs is desirable, it can be arranged through a confederation of state organizations instead of rank-and-file membership in a national organization. National membership may be essential to compete effectively against the NEA/AFT on member benefits, but national membership for this purpose would not undermine the rationale for local only teacher unions. This approach would not preclude teachers from political activity on noneducational issues. It would, however, minimize union power to promote social and political positions that should not be on union agendas.

If a local union needed outside services, the services would be purchased by contract, not acquired through membership in state and national unions. For example, if a local needed assistance in fact-finding, it could purchase such services from a state or national organization or from private parties who provide them for the local only union market.

To understand the rationale for LOTUs, it is essential to understand why nonunion teacher organizations do not survive in the bargaining law states.

1. The nonunion teacher organizations are opposed to collective bargaining. Where a bargaining law is in effect, organizations opposed to bargaining are seldom able to decertify unions that support it. There is a wealth of experience on this point. It is simply unrealistic for an organization to say: "We are opposed to collective bargaining but please vote for us as your bargaining agent."

2. Organizations that are chosen as the bargaining agent can render it extremely difficult for any other organization to decertify or compete with them. As we have seen, NEA/AFT affiliates typically negotiate exclusive rights to dues deductions, use of the district mail system, access to bulletin boards, and other provisions that stifle challenges.

3. Teachers will seldom pay substantial dues to two organizations. To protect their interests, they must join the incumbent union; otherwise, their interests may be ignored in collective bargaining. But if teachers join the incumbent

union, they have little time or resources to support an alternative organization. In every state, once a bargaining law was enacted, union membership has increased, membership in other teacher organizations has decreased, usually to the point of extinction. In fact, membership in the NEA or AFT usually disappears when the other union is the bargaining agent. The upshot is that nonunion organizations in the bargaining law states enroll only isolated individuals on a scale insufficient to decertify incumbent unions. Nonunion teacher organizations have never weakened the NEA/AFT in a bargaining law state, and there is no reason to believe that they will in the future.

In the absence of national dues, there would be no national staff, hence no national union political or social agenda. Depending on the number of teachers in the bargaining unit, a LOTU could employ a negotiator for less than $50 per teacher. For example, a district with 1,000 teachers would have $50,000 to employ a negotiator and pay for backup services. This amount would be more than ample. A bargaining unit with 100 teachers could raise $10,000 at $100 per teacher—probably more than enough to pay for negotiating services, including representation in grievance arbitration. Inasmuch as most unions are pattern followers, not pattern setters, most local unions would not be disadvantaged by the lack of national support in setting terms and conditions of employment.

Where LOTUs are the bargaining agents, teachers would still be free to pursue their political and social agendas through other organizations. Local only unions would not restrict teacher political activity; they would restrict only the practice of using the teacher union for this purpose. This minimizes the possibility that dues will be used for candidates and/or causes opposed by some teachers in the union.

The mere existence of an alternative union with a low dues structure would conservatize the NEA/AFT. Teachers unhappy about union policies and programs would have an alternative; "no representation" would no longer be the only alternative to the NEA/AFT.

LOTUs would be an effective strategy in the bargaining law states. In some of the others, teachers belong to a local and state, but not a national association. The state association policies on education are similar to the policies advocated by state NEA/AFT affiliates, but they have not adopted the broad NEA/AFT political and social agendas; also their dues are much lower than NEA/AFT dues. Inasmuch as these states have not enacted a bargaining law, opposition to bargaining is not a major deterrent to membership in nonunion organizations. NEA/AFT affiliates are trying to persuade teachers that a bargaining law is essential. The critical fact is that teachers will join a nonunion organization in the absence of a bargaining law; they are much less likely to do so if the state has enacted such a law. In its absence, the survival of nonunion teacher organizations depends largely on their ability to prevent enactment of a bargaining statute.

The Feasibility of Local Only Teacher Unions

Considerable evidence suggests a fairly substantial teacher market for LOTUs.

1. Since 1972, teachers who join the NEA must do so at the local, state, and national levels. Prior to 1972, it was possible to join only one level (local, state, or national). NEA membership was much lower than state membership, and state membership was much lower than local membership. In short, when options are available, many teachers prefer the local only option.

2. As previously noted, nonunion organizations enroll a substantial number of members in states without a bargaining law. If LOTUs enrolled the same percentage of teachers in the bargaining law states, the result would be a severe weakening of the NEA/AFT. This is precisely why the NEA/AFT are making a strenuous effort to enact bargaining laws in the states that have not enacted them.

3. The NEA's own polls show that teachers tend to regard the NEA as a remote organization. This is a common phenomenon in national unions. The national office is perceived as a remote entity, and information received from it is considered less reliable than information from the state or local.

4. In a few states, local NEA affiliates have severed their state and national ties and employ their own negotiator from local dues. This phenomenon has also emerged among other public sector unions. The fact that local only unions have emerged in the absence of any systematic effort to encourage them suggests major growth potential.

5. Dues in the NEA/AFT average about $500 a year. In the NEA, national NEA and some state and local dues increase automatically with increases in average teacher salaries. Regardless of how adopted, as NEA/AFT dues rise, so will the number of teachers interested in a low-cost union alternative. The fact that teachers in LOTUs would save about $500 a year and more should not be underestimated.

6. Recent teacher opinion polls indicate that 29 percent of NEA members and 21 percent of AFT members are dissatisfied with their national organizations. These are high percentages, especially in view of the lack of teacher information about NEA/AFT vulnerabilities, such as the excessive levels of union compensation.

7. The NEA/AFT have embarked upon an intensive campaign to organize all nonsupervisory, nonmanagerial school district employees. This constitutes a dras-

tic change in the NEA. Its governance structure, conventions, publications, programs—all must be changed to accommodate the shift to an industrial type union. Clearly, many teachers will prefer a teacher-only professional organization.

8. Many NEA members do not wish to be affiliated with the AFL-CIO. A sizable number of teachers who object to affiliation will be receptive to an alternative union.

9. Teachers opposed to unionization per se will support LOTUs as the lesser of two evils. Generally speaking, there is much less opposition to local unions than to regional, state, and/or national unions. When LOTUs and NEA/AFT affiliates go head to head in representation elections, teachers opposed to unions will vote for LOTUs.

The Strategic Implications of NEA/AFT Merger

Although LOTUs would be viable in the absence of an NEA/AFT merger, the merger would present a unique window of opportunity. In the absence of an alternative, most teachers will accept the merger. At the outset, they will pay dues to the merged organization, making it less likely that they will support an alternative organization. Furthermore, in the absence of an alternative, many non-members of the NEA or AFT will join the merged union; that has been the outcome under state and local mergers.

The media implications of the merger are also critical. The NEA and AFT are the alternatives to each other; the nonunion organizations receive virtually no attention from the media in the bargaining-law states. With a merger, this should change dramatically. Media and legislative committees looking for an "opposing point of view" will call a LOTU if there is one worth calling.

Needless to say, there are costs and problems associated with local only teacher unions. Such unions would not have the resources to persuade teachers elsewhere to join a local only union. On this issue, the NEA and AFT have an enormous advantage of scale. They can prepare materials to be used anywhere in the country; their cost is minimal when prorated over millions of members. Obviously, the costs for LOTU materials would be prohibitive if borne by teachers in a school district, or even a group of districts.

Furthermore, costs other than supportive materials would be unavoidable. It would be essential to identify potential activists and provide help with the decertification process. These are manageable problems, but their resolution would require a higher level of cooperation and sophistication about teacher unions than their critics have shown to date.

Of course, the NEA/AFT will try to counter any and all challenges to their revenues and power. Since the 1996 elections, the unions have adopted a softer rhetoric and a less adversarial stance. The changes thus far have been cosmetic, but they may not be if and when there is a real threat to union revenues. Just as the AFT triggered the unionization of the NEA, LOTUs may conservatize the merged organization. For this to happen, however, the LOTUs must be a credible membership threat.

State Legislators and School Boards

Most of the actions required to rein in teacher union power must be taken at the state and local level. Also, most can be addressed at either level. For example, school boards might decide individually to stop collecting union PAC funds at no cost to the union; state legislation might also prohibit the practice. Legislation has the advantage of avoiding a district-by-district confrontation over the issue; the district-by-district approach enables districts to act effectively in the absence of state legislation.

Because the underlying issues were discussed in previous chapters, I shall merely list the remedial actions that might be taken. Most are applicable to both the state and local levels. Obviously, the political dynamics will vary widely from state to state. For instance, consider the possibilities in a state that requires teachers to pay agency fees from the first day of employment.

1. Repeal the mandatory agency fee.
2. Repeal the mandatory agency fee, but allow local unions to bargain over it.
3. Legalize agency fees as a permissive but not a mandatory subject of bargaining.
4. Allow agency fees with new safeguards; for example, require unions and school boards to inform teachers of their right not to join the union each year.
5. Set a state limit on agency fees that protects payers from the illegitimate amounts now being collected.
6. Allow agency fees only for the local union.
7. Charge the union for payroll deduction.

At any given time, one or more of these options may be politically feasible while the others are not. I have not tried to show all the options on other issues, but awareness of them is critical, especially in situations in which a close vote is anticipated.

Generally speaking, the highest priorities should be: 1. Reducing the massive union revenues. 2. Ending taxpayer subsidies to the unions. 3. Enacting teacher "right to know" legislation, including full disclosure of union financial and political operations and union compensation. 4. Providing member bill of rights, including the right to be informed about union expenditures without any stonewalling by the union. 5. Treating teacher bargaining as political action, which it is. 6. Abolition of agency fees. 7. Abolition of school board col-

lection of PAC funds or allowing payroll deduction for teachers' choice of PAC.
8. Providing meaningful deterrents to union violation of member rights or the
rights of agency fee payers. 9. Requiring instead of prohibiting competition to
provide services to school boards.

Note that some of these actions are already incorporated in federal labor law
governing private sector unions. Some would remedy deficiencies in the federal
legislation. For example, when the federal legislation was enacted, fringe benefits
were not a major component of union compensation, hence the reporting requirements relating to them are not as informative as they should be. Also, I have
not included policies that would wipe out teacher unionization per se. Of course,
the NEA/AFT will argue that this would be the outcome, but their rhetoric on the
issue will be suspect. In 1947, Congress enacted the Taft-Hartley Act to remedy
various abuses by private sector unions. The AFL-CIO bitterly opposed the act,
even referred to it as "slave labor" legislation. Nonetheless, in the next ten years organized labor achieved unprecedented levels of membership and revenues.

Alternative Systems of Representation

The literature on private sector unions is replete with suggested changes in
labor legislation. Whatever their private sector viability, most of these suggestions are not applicable to public sector labor relations. Meanwhile, we lack
constructive alternatives to collective bargaining in public education, even at
the conceptual level. For instance, exclusive representation is the foundation of
unionization in the United States, but not everywhere else. Even in the United
States, exclusive representation is being challenged as the guiding principle of
employee representation. Although a comprehensive analysis of exclusive representation would take us too far afield, some of the basic objections to it should
be mentioned, since they may affect the teacher unions.[6]

As we have seen, some teachers are net losers under exclusive representation.
This is obvious in the case of teachers who are laid off but would not have been
except for union negotiated contracts. Teachers nearing retirement often want
the union to bargain for salary increases at the high end of the salary schedule.
Such increases would increase their retirement benefits, which are based on their
terminal salaries. To meet the demands of the younger teachers, however, the
union may negotiate a reduction of steps on the salary schedule, thereby leaving
the top salaries unchanged. Consequently, retiring teachers may receive lower
pensions the rest of their lives because the union emphasized different priorities.

Of course, these issues cannot always be resolved to everyone's satisfaction.
My point is that only some teachers are losers as a result of collective bargaining.
Who they are, and how much they lose has to be determined on a case-by-case

basis. Nevertheless, the examples suggest the inherent inefficiency as well as the unfairness of exclusive representation. To protect their interests, teachers must devote time and energy to persuading the union to accept their priorities. Otherwise, their priorities will be ignored in the bargaining process. In other words, union members are faced with substantial costs simply to protect their interests within the union. They must attend union meetings, proselytize supporters, criticize alternatives, distribute literature, and so forth. Most NEA/AFT members are not in a position to do these things. Furthermore, their efforts would often be futile regardless.

An actual private sector case illustrates the problem. In *Emporium Capwell* v. *Western Community Organization,* a group of black employees felt that the union had not adequately pursued a grievance alleging racial discrimination against black employees. The black employees picketed the employer without union permission and were fired as a result. The black employees sued the company, alleging that the firing was a violation of their right under the National Labor Relations Act to take concerted action. The firings were upheld by the U.S. Supreme Court on the grounds that the black employees were trying to negotiate with the employer, something only the union as exclusive representative is allowed to do.[7]

Regardless of the outcome, The *Emporium Capwell* case illustrates a critical point. Subgroups of employees frequently feel inadequately represented, and also that it would be futile to try to persuade the union to support their position. Five mathematics teachers may be unable to convince 500 other teachers to support a differential for mathematics teachers, no matter how justified it may be. Majority rule within the union is no guarantee that the just claims of subgroups within the union will be respected. Furthermore, in dealing with the union, the subgroups or individual employees are at a disadvantage; they lack the resources to fight the union, whereas the union has ample resources to defend its position against dissidents.

None of the foregoing assumes dishonesty or corruption within the union, although these things happen in unions as in most organizations. However, as with any organization whose members reflect diverse interests and views, the process of adopting a majoritarian position can be extremely time consuming as well as expensive. On the other hand, if each employee was represented by an organization of his or her own choice, employees would not be so concerned about adequate representation through the union. Employers might have to negotiate with more than one union, but the employees would not have to argue their position through a union that was opposed to it.

In the Netherlands, employees must join a union, but it is the employees choice of union. This was also permitted in the United Kingdom until 1976, when labor relations law was changed to allow employers and unions to specify which union the employees are required to join. All systems of employee representation have advantages and disadvantages, but there is need to consider alternative systems of employee representation as well as alternative organizations.

Alternative Organization or Alternative System of Representation?

Typically, a representation election or decertification petition among teachers involves a vote on the following options:

_____ NEA affiliate
_____ AFT affiliate
_____ No union

If none of the options receives a majority, a runoff is held among the two highest options on the first ballot. Suppose, however, that instead of voting only on their choice of union, if any, teachers could also vote for a different system of representation. The new option might be based on proportional representation, with a minimum number of teachers required to be entitled to formal representation. Or the option might provide various statutory benefits in lieu of union representation. For instance, if there were no union representation, tenured teachers might be entitled to state supported legal counsel in tenure hearings.

One can easily imagine several alternatives which might be offered as an option to exclusive representation or collective bargaining, and only experience can demonstrate their feasibility. Politically, options would be more attractive than repeal of the bargaining laws. If proposed legislation merely offered teachers additional options, the NEA/AFT would have to oppose options for their members. For instance, suppose teachers could vote for a different system of representation instead of being limited to voting for a different union or no union. Obviously, the NEA/AFT would be hard pressed to argue that their members are not capable of choosing among the options.

The Netherlands system minimizes union political activity to which members are opposed. The reason is that employees who object to the union's political program are free to join a different union. In the United States, choice of union would not completely eliminate union political activity. There would continue to be disagreements within the union on federal aid to education, multicultural education, special education, and so forth. Still, union resources would be less likely to be devoted to political activities opposed by union members. For instance, Catholic teachers in public schools may be concerned about NEA/AFT opposition to government assistance for denominational schooling. Quite possibly, a sizable number might prefer a teacher union not opposed to such assistance.

In my opinion, it may not be necessary to repeal the teacher bargaining laws. It will be necessary, however, to provide teachers with a choice between collective bargaining and a less expensive, less adversarial system of representation that is consistent with representative government. To survive in the 1960s and 1970s, the NEA transformed itself into a union. The abrupt change in organizational philosophy and structure was facilitated by the fact that unionization led to increased membership and revenues. Any movement away from exclusive representation, however, will probably require downsizing the NEA/AFT, a major obstacle to their acceptance of any alternative to the status quo.

Parents and the PTA

Regrettably, the prospects for parental empowerment vis-à-vis the teacher unions are extremely poor. On the one hand, teacher organizations have millions of members, billions in revenues, and thousands of staff members serving a clientele with a career stake in the status quo. On the other hand, parents are represented through an organization with high turnover, one-dollar-a-year dues, and a governance structure that ensures teacher union control. Even if nonparent teachers were expelled from the PTA or pulled out, it is doubtful whether the PTA could be an effective proponent of parental interests in school affairs.

School choice inclusive of private schools would empower parents, but most parents are not going to be activists on the issue. Parents want to help their children. Becoming an activist for policies that may never materialize, or may materialize too late to help their own children, does not appeal to most parents. Most support school choice as a concept but are not willing to devote personal time or resources to achieving it.

Although parent organizations without teacher membership might be helpful, formidable obstacles would remain. Teachers would still encourage parents to join the PTA and discourage them from joining any other parental organization. With both the teacher unions and the PTA determined to thwart the formation of an independent parent organization, the latter would be severely disadvantaged. School management might also prefer the PTA since it does not challenge board acquiescence to union demands.

When a social institution breaks down, it is often difficult to decide whether to fix or replace it. With respect to the PTA, an effort to replace it may be the most effective way to fix it. This is not a very optimistic message, but the realities should not be ignored for the sake of a feel good but futile message. Consumer organizations are seldom effective in eliminating monopolies or their negative effects. Typically, a competing producer is essential for this purpose. It is difficult to see how the PTA can overcome the various reasons why consumer organizations are unable to counter producer monopolies.

What We Can and Cannot Do

In the private sector, union decline may be attributed partly to union success. Organized labor was instrumental in enacting statutes on safety, the work environment, worker preferences in bankruptcy, leaves, and workmen's compensation, to cite some of the most prominent. To some extent, these legislative benefits weakened worker support for unions. New union objectives may not be as justified or appeal to workers as much as the objectives that have been achieved. The same phenomenon occurs in education. The state associations were responsible for enacting teacher tenure laws, but teachers sometimes feel less need for the union as a result. Organizations that achieve their objectives do not go out of business; they adopt new objectives. The latter, however, may not be as defensible or as appealing as the initial ones. Controversy over what unions have accomplished in the past may be irrelevant to their future; the fact, if it be a fact, that the teacher unions have accomplished a great deal in the past would not justify their existence in their present mode.

The most hopeful development relating to the NEA/AFT is that they have become a political issue. More precisely, their political role can no longer be obscured by cant about the "bipartisan" or "nonpartisan" nature of public education. According to my dictionary, "cant" is the "insincere use of pious phraseology"; the term is precisely applicable to NEA/AFT efforts to characterize their activities as "bipartisan" or "nonpartisan" or motivated by "pupil welfare."

For almost 150 years, the "nonpartisan" structure of public education has obscured the fact that politics is the process by which we establish our priorities. Labeling education "nonpartisan" and having schools managed by "nonpartisan" school boards and state departments of education has shielded public education and teacher unions from the kind of scrutiny accorded "partisan" or "political" issues. The fallacy inherent in a "nonpartisan" approach to public education is not a recent discovery, but public perception has lagged far behind the political realities. The controversies over state aid to education, school integration, and school choice illustrate the political nature of educational issues. Nevertheless, their political nature has been muted by the belief that we should take education out of politics. The genesis of this naive belief was the fear that a political party or interest group would indoctrinate young minds to its point of view. To forestall any such outcome, public education was established formally as a "nonpartisan" governmental agency.

In the past, the contradictions between the nonpartisan structure of public education and the political realities were brushed aside, as if the political realities were the exceptional case. School boards were labeled nonpartisan offices, as if eliminating political labels eliminated the political realities. Now that the Republican presidential nominee and the chairman of the Republican National Committee have explicitly criticized the teacher unions, there is no going back to the time when the unions could pose as bipartisan organizations interested primarily in the welfare of children.

As a result of the 1996 elections, every union issue discussed in this book will be in play afterward—not because the issue has been discussed here but because candidates for public office can no longer ignore them. Union PAC funds, financial disclosure, agency fees, and taxpayer subsidies, to cite just a few topics, will be subject to political and academic inquiry on an unprecedented scale. This scrutiny will lead to basic changes in the NEA and AFT and in our system of teacher representation. We will not see teacher unions more supportive of educational reform, but they will be less able to prevent it. Regrettably, this outcome is a necessary but not a sufficient condition for quantum improvement in American education. Those who believe that curtailing union power to block reform is sufficient are as misguided as those who believe the unions will subordinate union and teacher welfare to student achievement. The task ahead is to get to the point where we can choose among alternatives that are now foreclosed by the teacher unions.

Appendix A

NEA-PAC: A COMMENTARY

Initially, I planned to include the 1996 NEA-PAC Questionnaire and Adden-
dum as Appendix A. Answers to the questions on the questionnaire are the
basis for NEA political support. My purpose was to show that NEA-PAC endorsements are based upon several major noneducational issues, such as support for the Equal Rights Amendment and the Clinton administration's health
care plan. Instead of interpreting the criteria for NEA support, my intention
was to have the NEA-PAC's Questionnaire speak for itself. I also requested permission to publish the jurisdictional agreement between the NEA and AFT.

To my astonishment, the NEA declined my request to publish the NEA-PAC
Questionnaire and the jurisdictional agreement on the grounds that the documents are "intended for organizational use, and are not available for publication." NEA refusal to grant permission to publish the NEA-PAC Questionnaire
illustrates its determination to avoid scrutiny of its actions. Candidates for public office can hardly expect to avoid public disclosure of their answers to the
questionnaire. Surely, all citizens should be informed about candidate commitments to special interest groups, and would be concerned about candidates who
refuse to disclose the commitments they have made in political campaigns. In
this case, the NEA-PAC Questionnaire reveals the discrepancy between the
NEA's claim to endorse on the basis of educational issues, and the fact that its
endorsements are based on support for the NEA's left wing social agenda.

NEA refusal to permit publication of the jurisdictional agreement is additional evidence of NEA determination to avoid member and public awareness

of its policies. The jurisdictional agreement was not intended solely for the internal use of NEA members. The AFT is an equal partner to the agreement, and nothing in it precludes the AFT from showing it to whomever it wishes. The agreement was widely disseminated at the AFT convention, where it was formally approved by unanimous convention vote. AFT permission to publish the jurisdictional agreement was subject only to the requirement that the agreement be published in full. This had been my intention from the outset.

Appendix B

ESTIMATED AFT REVENUES

A FT revenues for 1996–97 in the text were set forth as follows:

$ 86,000,000	Estimated, National office
$105,000,000	Estimated, State federations
$159,922,000	Estimated, Local and regional federations
$350,922,000	Estimated, Total AFT revenues

The national office estimate is based on AFT reported revenues of $84.3 million for 1995–96, adjusted upward for anticipated increases in membership and dues. This estimate is undoubtedly close to the actual figure. The estimates for state and local revenues are much less certain and require explanation.

In sixteen states, no state federation filed IRS Form 990 for a recent year. Either they included too few locals or their revenues were less than the $25,000 filing threshold. An additional complication is that AFT fund transfers often follow a different path than in the NEA.

I first estimated an amount for combined state and local federations by multiplying the NEA budget by the percentage that AFT membership is of NEA membership. My assumption was that average dues in the two unions are substantially similar; certainly this is true for national dues. Because both unions are concerned that the other one will try to recruit teachers through lower dues, there is a tendency for their dues to be substantially similar, however, the AFT enrolls a higher percentage of members who pay little or no dues. Only about

500,000 of the AFT's 907,000 members are regular full-time teachers, a much lower proportion than in the NEA. On the other hand, a higher proportion of AFT teachers are in urban districts that charge relatively high dues. Thus, AFT membership includes higher proportions of both high and low dues paying members, whereas most NEA members fall in the middle of the dues range. My assumption that average dues in the two unions are substantially similar splits the difference. I could be wrong by plus or minus 20 percent.

My assumed allocation between state and local federations was based primarily on state federation returns on IRS Form 990 for 1993 and 1994, also from a few state federation returns since then. The local federations are conservative and may well be too low, but at least the national and state estimates should be very close to the actual revenues.

JURISDICTIONAL AGREEMENT BETWEEN THE NATIONAL EDUCATION ASSOCIATION AND THE AMERICAN FEDERATION OF TEACHERS (AFL-CIO)

Preamble

The National Education Association ("NEA") and the American Federation of Teachers, AFL-CIO ("AFT") believe that, as a single national organization, they more effectively could advance the interests of their members.

Towards this end, NEA and AFT are engaged in negotiations in an effort to create a merged national organization that reflects the core principles upon which NEA and AFT are based.

To facilitate this outcome, NEA and AFT desire to promote cooperative effort between themselves and their state and local affiliates and to avoid jurisdictional disputes and other organizational rivalry in the interim.

Accordingly, in consideration of the mutual promises contained herein, NEA and AFT agree as follows:

A. Representative Status

1. Except as otherwise provided in subsection A(2) below, NEA and AFT will respect the established representative status of the other party and its affiliates.* For purposes of this Section, the term "established representative status" means any situation in which NEA or AFT, or an NEA or AFT affiliate, is recognized as an exclusive representative of employees pursuant to a state or federal statute, city

*The term "affiliate" as used herein includes other nonaffiliated subordinate bodies, such as NEA UniServ Councils.

or county ordinance, executive order, administrative regulation or employing institution policy for the purpose of negotiating a collective bargaining agreement, or otherwise dealing with the employer regarding wages, hours, and/or other terms and conditions of employment. In those situations in which representative status, as a matter of law or policy, must be reestablished after a set period of time even in the absence of any changes in the composition or preferences of the group of employees involved, the established representative status will be deemed to continue. Under this Subsection A(1), NEA and AFT are prohibited from engaging in any activity, or assisting, participating in, or condoning any activity engaged in by an affiliate, that is designed, or that reasonably can be expected, to interfere with or terminate an established representative status, including, without limitation, seeking to represent employees by an affiliate of the other organization, seeking to decertify an affiliate of the other organization, or taking any action to secure a reorganization of a collective bargaining unit that would have the effect of ousting an affiliate of the other organization from its status as an exclusive representative. NEA and AFT will make good faith efforts to encourage and convince their affiliates to withdraw any pending representation petitions in which one organization is challenging the status of the other as defined herein.

2. In any situation in which exclusive recognition as provided herein has been achieved without a secret ballot election and such recognition does not carry with it the right to negotiate collective bargaining agreements, the prohibitions of this Section A shall not apply if NEA of AFT elects to treat the situation as one governed by Section C of this agreement.

B. Affiliation

1. Except as otherwise provided in Subsection B(2) below, NEA and AFT will not (a) engage in any campaign to cause an affiliate of the other organization to terminate said affiliation, and will not assist, participate in, or condone any such campaign engaged in by its affiliates; or (b) grant affiliation to any organization that is affiliated with the other party as of the effective date of this agreement.

2. The prohibition in Subsection B(1) above will not apply to a newly-created organization that results from the merger of an NEA affiliate and an AFT affiliate that is consistent with the applicable NEA and AFT guidelines for affiliate mergers.

C. Membership

1. In those situations where neither NEA or AFT has exclusive representative status as defined in Section A(1), NEA and AFT shall respect the relationship between the other party and its affiliates and their members in the manner and extent provided in this Section C.

2. NEA and AFT desire to stop jurisdictional disputes and membership competition between their affiliates through the establishment of Cooperation Agreements wherever possible. Therefore, NEA and AFT shall encourage the establishment of Cooperation Agreements between local affiliates of their respective organizations. They will encourage their respective state affiliates to promote and support such local Cooperation Agreements and will provide technical and other assistance to facilitate them.

Cooperation Agreements shall cover areas of mutual interest to the parties' respective members, including termination of organizing activity aimed at inducing or encouraging members of one organization to drop their membership in that organization and become members of the other organization. Cooperation Agreements may explore the potential for local merger. However, actual, formal, merger discussions may not take place unless and until they are approved by the appropriate state and national organizations, and only then if contemplated local merger would be consistent with applicable NEA and AFT policies or guidelines for local affiliate mergers.

In those situations in which membership is renewed annually, the membership relation will be deemed to continue from year-to-year, and for purposes of this Section C, membership will be considered terminated only if an individual fails to join, and is removed from the membership list, for the successor membership year.

3. a. Where a Cooperation Agreement exists which has been approved by NEA and AFT and their state affiliates, neither NEA nor AFT shall engage in any activity, or assist, participate in or condone any activity by an affiliate to induce or encourage members of one party and its affiliates to terminate their membership and/or become members of the other party and its affiliates, provided the local Cooperation Agreement is being observed by the local parties and the state affiliates.

b. Where a local Cooperation Agreement does not exist, but the local parties have commenced discussions leading to such an agreement, neither NEA nor AFT shall engage in any activity, or assist, participate in or condone any activity by an affiliate to induce or encourage members of one party and its affiliates, provided good faith discussions concerning a local Cooperation Agreement are continuing and there is no activity by either local or state affiliates to induce or encourage terminations or changes in membership while discussions are continuing.

4. Where either NEA or AFT believes that any of the conditions in Section C(3) are not being met with regard to observing and respecting Cooperation Agreements, continuing good faith discussions regarding such agreements and respecting membership relationships while discussions occur, it may refer the matter to the Implementation Committee established under Section G. The Implementation

Committee will oversee efforts to resolve the matter. If the Implementation Committee determines that a local or a state affiliate has failed to meet the conditions of Section C(3), it will refer the matter to the Presidents of NEA and AFT. If the Presidents of NEA and AFT concur in the determination of the Implementation Committee, NEA or AFT, as the case may be, will take such action as is necessary and sufficient to correct the situation and the local or state affiliate involved will not be entitled to the protections of this Agreement until the situation is corrected.

5. Where there is no local Cooperation Agreement and no discussion leading to such an agreement, and either NEA or AFT believes that such an agreement is necessary and appropriate, it may refer the matter to the Implementation Committee. If the Implementation Committee concurs that a local Cooperation Agreement is necessary and appropriate, it will oversee efforts of the locals and state affiliates to promote and establish such an agreement. After such efforts, if the Implementation Committee determines that a local has unreasonably failed to enter into a local Cooperation Agreement or a state affiliate has unreasonably failed to support efforts to establish a Cooperation Agreement, it will refer the matter to the Presidents of NEA and AFT. If the Presidents of NEA and AFT concur in the determination of the Implementation Committee, NEA or AFT, as the case may be, will take such action as is necessary and sufficient to cause the local or state affiliate cease its conduct, and the local or state affiliate involved will not be entitled to the protections of this Agreement until the situation is corrected.

6. Where changes occur in statute, ordinance, executive order, regulation or employing institution policy such that either NEA or AFT has the opportunity to achieve the status referred to in Section A in any employee group in which AFT or NEA has members but the other organization does not, the other organization shall not engage in organizing activity as defined in Section A above.

7. With or without Cooperation Agreements, NEA and AFT, as well as their affiliates, shall not offer reduced dues to members of the other organization as an inducement to join, and shall not provide any form or instructions for withdrawing membership from the other organization.

D. Adverse Publicity

NEA and AFT will not make any public statements or publicly distribute any documents that are designed to defame, or that reasonably can be expected to have the effect of defaming, the other party, its affiliates, or its officers and representatives. The prohibition in this Section D will not apply to statements or documents concerning policy differences with the other organization.

E. Actions by Affiliates

1. NEA and AFT will publicize this Agreement among their affiliates, and will send a copy of this Agreement to such affiliates as they deem appropriate, including at a minimum all of their state affiliates.

2. NEA and AFT will urge their state affiliates, where appropriate, to enter into counterpart state-level agreements, and will provide appropriate assistance to their state affiliates in this regard.

3. Unless otherwise provided in a counterpart state-level agreement, NEA and AFT will urge their affiliates not to take any action to undermine the express provisions of this Agreement. If NEA and AFT believes that an affiliate of the other party has taken, or proposes to take, an action to undermine the express provisions of this Agreement, it may submit the matter to the Implementation Committee that is established by Section G of this agreement. If the Implementation Committee determines that the action in question undermines the express provisions of this agreement, it will so report to the Presidents of NEA and AFT. The President of NEA or AFT, as then case may be, will attempt to persuade the affiliate not to take the action in question and/or to take whatever measures may be necessary to remedy the situation. If this attempt is unsuccessful:

   a. NEA or AFT, as the case may be, will publicize to the members of the non-complying affiliate and to its other affiliates that the affiliate is not in compliance with the purposes and objectives of this Agreement; and

   b. The non-complying affiliate will not be entitled to the protections provided by this Agreement until the non-compliance is terminated and/or remedied.

F. Waivers

If NEA or AFT claims that, because of special circumstances, it would be contrary to basic concepts of unionism, injurious to the interests of the employees involved, or in violation of core organizational principles to comply with a provision of this Agreement, it may submit the matter to the Implementation Committee. If the Implementation Committee determines that there is adequate justification for allowing a waiver of said provision, the Implementation Committee may grant a waiver on such terms as it deems appropriate. The party making the claim will comply with the provisions of this Agreement unless and until a waiver is granted.

G. Implementation Committee

Not later than ten (10) days after the effective date of this Agreement, an Implementation Committee, consisting of four (4) members appointed by NEA and four (4) members appointed by AFT, will be established. The Implementation Committee will be responsible for assuring the proper implementation of this Agreement. NEA and AFT will pay the expenses incurred by their respective members in connection with the work of the Implementation Committee, and any mutually incurred expenses will be paid equally by NEA and AFT.

H. Effect of Agreement

A failure by NEA or AFT to insist upon strict compliance with any provision of this Agreement will not constitute a modification or waiver of that provision, nor will it preclude NEA or AFT thereafter from insisting on such strict compliance. This Agreement may be modified only by a written document that is approved and executed as provided in Section J of this Agreement.

I. Enforcement of Agreement

1. Any dispute that may arise as to the interpretation or application of this Agreement may be referred by NEA or AFT to the Implementation Committee for resolution. If the Implementation Committee is unable to resolve the dispute within ten (10) days after such referral, the dispute may be submitted, by either NEA or AFT, to the Permanent Arbitrator, who will proceed in accordance with the Voluntary Expedited Labor Arbitration Rules of American Arbitration Association then in effect. The fees and expenses of the Permanent Arbitrator, and any other mutually-incurred expenses of the arbitration, will be paid equally by NEA and AFT. Separately incurred expenses will be paid by the party incurring them.

2. The Permanent Arbitrator will have no authority to add to, detract from, or modify the terms of this Agreement. The Permanent Arbitrator will have the authority to impose the remedy that he or she deems appropriate, including assessing damages or ordering specific performance of this Agreement, provided that the Permanent Arbitrator may not require NEA or AFT to disaffiliate or impose a trusteeship on any affiliate. The arbitration provided for in this Section will be the exclusive method for resolving any disputes that may arise as to the interpretation or application of this Agreement. The decision of the Permanent Arbitrator will be final and binding upon NEA and AFT, and his or her award

may be enforced in any court of competent jurisdiction. Unless otherwise agreed to by NEA and AFT, the arbitration will take place in Washington, D.C.

3. The Permanent Arbitrator will be [INSERT NAME]. If [INSERT NAME] is for any reason unable to serve as the Permanent Arbitrator in connection with any dispute, [INSERT SECOND NAME] will serve as Permanent Arbitrator for that dispute.

4. This Agreement will be governed by the laws of Washington, D.C.

J. Duration

This Agreement will become effective on January 1, 1997. This Agreement may be terminated at any time by NEA or AFT upon 60 days written notice to the other party In the absence of such notice, this Agreement will remain in effect until NEA and AFT merge to establish a single national organization or until midnight May 31, 1998, whichever is earlier.

_____

_____

Approved by the NEA Board of Directors, July 1, 1996
Approved by AFT Convention, August 5, 1996

Appendix D

RANKINGS BY EXPENDITURES, STATE TEACHER UNION PACS

	Rank	Largest State Teacher Union PAC
Alabama	1	Alabama Voice of Teachers for Education (A-VOTE)
Alaska	2	NEA Alaska PAC for Education
California	1	California Teachers Association PAC (CTA)
Idaho	1	PAC for Education
Illinois	1	Illinois PAC for Education
Kansas	1	Kansas Political Action Committee (Kansas PAC)–(KNEA)
Montana	1	
Nebraska	1	Nebraska State Education Association
New York	1	Voice of Teachers for Education/Committee on Political Education of the NYS United Teachers (AFT-affiliate)
Oklahoma	1	Oklahoma Education Association PAC
Wisconsin	1	Wisconsin Education Association Council (WEAC)
Missouri	2	Missouri National Education Association Political Action Committee

	Rank	Largest State Teacher Union PAC
North Carolina	2	North Carolina Association of Educators PAC for Education
Michigan	3	Michigan Education Association PAC
Colorado	4	Colorado Education Association
New Jersey	4	New Jersey Education Association Political Action Committee
Ohio	4	Ohio Education Association Educators PAC, Ohio Education Association (combined)

NOTES

Chapter 1. Introduction: Why This Book?

1. Myron Lieberman, *The Future of Public Education* (Chicago: University of Chicago Press, 1960), p. 179.
2. Marjorie Murphy, *Blackboard Unions* (Ithaca, N.Y.: Cornell University Press, 1990), pp. 180–181.
3. Leo Troy, "The Great Transformation: From Private to Public Unionism in Atlantic Community Nations," *Government Union Review* (Fall 1989).
4. Section 8 (d), National Labor Relations Act. 49 Stat. 449 (1935) as amended, 1947, 1951, 1958, 1959, 1974.

Chapter 2. The Takeoff

1. The most comprehensive account of this period, including the 1961 New York City election, is found in Myron Lieberman and Michael H. Moskow, *Collective Negotiations for Teachers* (Chicago: Rand McNally, 1966), pp. 35–40, 137–138, 619–674.
2. Greg Saltzman, *The Growth of Teacher Bargaining and the Enactment of Teacher Bargaining Laws,* unpublished doctoral dissertation, University of Wisconsin, 1981; Sterling D. Spero, *Government as Employer* (New York: Remsen Press, 1948); and Marjorie Murphy, *Blackboard Unions: The AFT & The NEA, 1900–1980* (Ithaca, NY: Cornell University Press, 1990) are the best accounts of the early AFT.
3. See Myron Lieberman, *Education as a Profession* (Englewood Cliffs, NJ: Prentice Hall, 1956), pp. 334–372, on compulsory membership before collective bargaining.
4. Thomas H. Eliot, Nicholas A. Masters, and Robert H. Salisbury, *State Politics and the Public Schools* (New York: Alfred A. Knopf, 1964).
5. David Selden, *The Teacher Rebellion* (Washington, D.C.: Howard University Press, 1985), pp. 56–58. The book was never mentioned in AFT publications although it was published while Shanker was AFT president.
6. For a summary of NEA/AFT differences on legislative issues, see Lieberman and Moskow, *Collective Negotiations for Teachers,* pp. 91–247.
7. Saltzman, *The Growth of Teacher Bargaining,* p. 58.

8. For a sympathetic insider's account of the NEA's transition to union status, see Allan M. West, *The National Education Association: The Power Base For Education* (New York: The Free Press, 1982).

Chapter 3. NEA/AFT Objectives

1. *NEA Handbook, 1996–97*, p. 177.
2. Ibid., p. 243.
3. John E. Berthoud, *The Fiscal Impact of the NEA's Legislative Agenda* (Arlington, VA: Alexis de Tocqueville Institution, March 4, 1996), p. 3.
4. *Health Care Reform: How Can NEA Members Impact the National Debate* (Washington: NEA, 1993), p. 4.
5. Berthoud, *The Fiscal Impact of the NEA's Legislative Agenda*, p. 3.
6. Progressive Caucus Platform, disseminated at 1996 AFT convention, Cincinnati, Ohio (not paginated).
7. Myron Lieberman, "Your RNC Contributions at Work," *Human Events*, April 29, 1994, p. 3.
8. Personal observations by the author at the 1994 NEA convention.
9. Ibid; also personal observations by the author at a meeting of the Republican Educators Caucus at the NEA building, December 8, 1993.
10. Haley Barbour, E.D., *Agenda for America* (Washington: Regnery Publishing Inc., 1996).
11. Dan McKillip, *A Merger in the Offing?* Paper prepared in December 1992 for NEA affiliates considering merger. Bruce Markens, *The Prospects of NEA-AFT Merger Based on the New York Experience*, paper presented at the 1995 AERA Convention, April 18–22, San Francisco. Markens was a leader of the Teacher Action Caucus in the UFT.

   Although I cannot confirm the accuracy of McKillip's figures, his analysis of the AFT caucus system is squarely on target.
12. Information provided by Bruce Markens, UFT Executive Board member from Manhattan in 1994.
13. Ibid.
14. Gary K. Clabaugh and Edward G. Rozycki, "Politics, Consensus, and Educational Reform," *Educational Horizons* (Fall/Winter 1989), pp. 7–12.
15. For an excellent discussion of how this comes about, see Timur Kuran, *Private Truths, Public Lies* (Cambridge: Harvard University Press, 1995).

Chapter 4. Bargaining with the NEA/AFT

1. See Harry T. Edwards, R. Theodore Clark, Jr., and Charles B. Cramer, *Labor Relations Law in the Public Sector*, 4th ed. (Charlottesville, VA: Michie Company, 1991); and Gene Geisert and Myron Lieberman, *Teacher Union Bargaining* (Chicago: Precept Press, 1994), pp. 87–89, 249–253.
2. *NEA Strategic Plan and Budget Fiscal Year 1996–97* (Washington: National Education Association, 1996), p. iii.
3. Provided confidentially to the author; however, the goals listed are cited because they are commonplace.

4. "What Gives You the Right to Do That? An Index to Chapter Chair Rights," published by *United Teacher,* United Teachers of Los Angeles, August 25, 1995, p. 7.

5. National Education Association, *Strategic Plan and Budget, Fiscal Year 1995–1996.* Presented to the Representative Assembly, Minneapolis, MN (July 1995), p. iv.

6. *Perry Education Association* v. *Perry Local Educators Association,* 460, U.S. 37 (1983).

7. Article D, Exclusive Rights to CATA/PSEA/NEA. *Agreement Between Coatesville Area Teachers Association and Coatesville Area School Board,* August 28, 1993–August 27, 1997.

8. *NEA Handbook, 1996–1997,* pp. 344–345.

9. See Richard Epstein, *Bargaining with the State* (Princeton, NJ: Princeton University Press, 1993).

10. *City of Madison, School District No. 8* v. *Wisconsin Employment Relations Commission,* 429 U.S. 167 (1976).

11. See Robert S. Summers, "Public Sector Bargaining Substantially Diminishes Democracy," *Government Union Review* (Winter 1980), pp. 1–33.

Chapter 5. Union Political Operations

1. Press releases, Federal Election Commission, June 7, 1996 and July 11, 1996.

2. Political Affairs Division, *How to Raise Money for NEA-PAC: Education's Defense Fund* (Washington: National Education Association, n.d).

3. *Federal Election Commission* v. *National Education Association* 457 F. Supp. 1102 (District of the District of Columbia 1978).

4. "Washington Education Association Attacks EFF," *EFF's Washington Journal* (Olympia, Wash.: Evergreen Freedom Foundation, March, 1996).

5. Denise L. Baer and Martha Bailey, "The Nationalization of Education Politics: National Education Association PAC (NEA-PAC) and the 1992 Elections," in Robert Biersack, et al., eds., *Risky Business* (Armonk, NY: M.E. Sharpe, 1994), pp. 65–78.

6. NEA-PAC, *Operating Procedures* (Washington: National Education Association), 1995. The procedures were subject to revision at the June 1997 NEA-PAC Council meeting.

7. Government Relations, *How to Participate in Party Politics* (Washington: National Education Association, 1986), p. 15.

8. William Form, *Segmented Labor, Fractured Politics* (New York: Plenum Press, 1995), p. 263.

9. Ibid.

10. Myron Lieberman and Charlene K. Haar, "Teachers' Pet Party," *The Weekly Standard,* June 24, 1996, pp. 12–13.

11. National Education Association Government Relations *How to Participate in Party Politics* (Washington: National Education Association, 1986).

12. Joshua Goldstein "PACs in Profile" (Washington: Center for Responsive Politics, 1995).

13. For a much higher estimate see James T. Bennett, "Private Sector Unions: The Myth of Decline," *Journal of Labor Research,* Vol. XII, (Winter 1991), pp. 1–12.

14. *The People's Case* (Washington: National Education Association, n.d.), p. 26.

15. Haley Barbour, ed., *Agenda for America, A Republican Direction for the Future* (Washington: Regnery Publishing, Inc., 1996).

16. Robert Dole, *Acceptance Speech at the Republican National Convention,* San Diego, California, August 15, 1996.

17. *Program Accomplishment Report* 1992–93 (Washington: National Education Association, 1993), pp. 39–40.

18. National Education Association, *Strategic Plan and Budget, Fiscal Year: 1995–96* (Washington: National Education Association, 1995), p. iv.

19. Office of Government Relations, *How to Conduct the NEA Congressional Contact Team Program* (Washington: National Educational Association, n.d.)

20. William Form, *Segmented Labor, Fractured Politics* (New York: Plenum Press, 1995), pp. 293–336.

21. Ibid., pp. 317–318.

22. *Regents of the University of California* v. *Bakke,* 438 U.S. 265 (1978).

Chapter 6. State Teacher Unions

1. National Center for Education Statistics, *Digest of Education Statistics* 1994 (Washington: U.S. Department of Education, 1994); and Research Division, 1994–95 *Estimates of School Statistics* (Washington: National Education Association, 1995), p. 22.

2. Mario M. Cuomo *The Diaries of Mario Cuomo* (New York: Random House, 1983).

3. Unpublished survey of local teacher union PACS by Education Policy Institute, 1996.

4. Marilyn Perkins, member, Board of Directors, California Teachers Association, "The California Public Schools: We Work Wonders," *Commentary on CTA's 1993 Advertising Campaign.*

5. *VEA-PAC Candidate Questionnaire,* Virginia Education Association, 1994.

6. Letter from Bill Press, chairman, California Democratic Party to CTA President Del Weber, November 29, 1993.

7. Indiana, Utah, and Washington were states in which legislation was introduced in 1995. The efforts were successful in Indiana and Washington.

8. Rephrased from *Organization Handbook* (Burlingame, CA: California Teachers Association, n.d.), p. 329.

9. Ibid., pp. 330–331.

10. Statement by Ken Khachigian, Principal Strategist, *Yes on 174, A Better Choice,* October 21, 1993.

11. Stephen Glass, "A Pension Deficit Disorder," *Policy Review* (Winter 1995), pp. 71–74.

12. Sample program for UniServ unit directors published by California Teachers Association, May 1989.

13. *CTA Handbook,* May 1989 Revision, p. F–7.

14. Government Relations, *Guide to Congressional Contact Teams* (Washington: National Education Association, 1987) pp. 35, 44–45; *How to Raise Money for NEA-PAC; Education's Defense Fund* (Washington: National Education Association, n.d.), p. 7.

15. For a summary of the factors bearing on state teacher union influence, see Ronald J. Hrebenor and Clive S. Thomas, eds., *Interest Group Politics in the Midwestern States* (Ames: Iowa State University Press, 1993), pp. 11–12.

16. Alan Ehrenhalt, *The United States of Ambition* (New York: Times Books, 1991), pp. 164–189.

17. Hrebenor and Thomas, *Interest Group Politics in the Midwestern States,* pp. 346, 354, 361.
18. Stephen Glass, "A Pension Deficit Disorder, Teacher Unions Betray Their Members," *Policy Review* (Winter 1995), pp. 71–74.
19. NEA and NCSEA, Assessment of the 1992 Political Action Program Executive Summary, November 15, 1993, 9 pp.

Chapter 7. The War Against Competition and Contracting Out

1. See NEA Resolution F–27, "Subcontracting/Contracting Out," *NEA Handbook, 1995–1996* (Washington: National Education Association, 1995), pp. 310–311. See also *AFT Demands Accountability for Private Managers of Public Schools,* New Release (Washington: American Federation of Teachers, July 17, 1994).
2. Affiliate Services Division, National Education Association, *The People's Cause: Mobilizing for Public Education* (Washington: National Education Association, 1994); Center for the Preservation of Public Education, *Contracting Out: Strategies for Fighting Back* (Washington: National Education Association, n.d.).
3. Center for the Preservation of Public Education, *The People's Cause: Mobilizing for Public Education* (Washington: National Education Association, n.d.)
4. Statement of Goals—The Paraprofessional and School Related Personnel Division of the American Federation of Teachers, n.d.
5. AFT-on-line, n.d.
6. Edward M. Gramlich and Patricia P. Koshel, *Educational Performance Contracting* (Washington: Brookings Institution, 1975), pp. 29–30.
7. U.S. Office of Economic Opportunity Office of Planning, Research and Evaluation, *A Demonstration of Incentives in Education* (Washington: Government Printing Office, 1972).
8. Battelle Columbus Laboratories, *Final Report on the Office of Economic Opportunity Experiment in Educational Performance Contracting* (Columbus, Ohio: Battelle Memorial Institute, 1972), p. 142.
9. Hartford data based on interviews with Hartford Board of Education members and items in the *Hartford Courant,* October/November, 1995.
10. Public Employee Department, AFL-CIO, *The Human Costs of Contracting Out, A Survival Guide for Public Employees* (Washington: Public Employee Department, AFL-CIO, 1993).
11. On January 19, 1994, the Mackinac Center for Public Policy praised the Michigan Education Association for contracting out cafeteria service, custodial work, security, and mailing services, sometimes to nonunion firms. *Mackinac Center Praises MEA for Management Excellence, Questions Double Standard* (Midland, MI: Mackinac Center for Public Policy, January 19, 1994).

    The author has attended meetings in the MEA building, sponsored by MEA, in which the food service was catered by outside companies.
12. This is a conservative estimate based on perusal of NEA's *Strategic Plan and Budget, Fiscal Year* 1995–1996 (Washington: National Education Association, 1995).
13. Ibid., *The People's Cause: Mobilizing for Public Education*
14. AFT-on-line, 1995.

15. *AFT Demands Accountability For Private Manager of Public Schools,* AFT news release, July 17, 1994.

16. *Annual Reports of the National Endowment for Democracy,* 1983 to 1995 (Washington: National Endowment for Democracy).

17. *NEA Calls For Teacher Retirement Plans to Sell Investments in Companies Supporting Privatization Efforts,* NEA news release, annual convention in New Orleans, LA, July 4, 1994.

18. Robert J. Shiller, Maxim Boycko, and Vladimir Korobov, "Popular Attitudes towards Free Markets: The Soviet Union and the United States Compared," *American Economic Review,* 81, June 1991, pp. 385–400.

Chapter 8. Education's Gravy Train

1. National Staff Organization, *NEA/AFT Merger/Successor, A Declaration,* unpaginated and undated memorandum disseminated at 1996 NEA convention.

2. *NEA Handbook, 1995–1996,* p. 44.

3. NEA Secretary-Treasurer, *Financial Reports* (Washington: National Education Association, 1995).

4. For an example, see "NEA tangles with union staffers over payroll cutbacks, benefits," *Great Falls (MT) Tribune,* September 4, 1994.

5. Contract between the Indiana State Teachers Association (ISTA) and the Professional Staff Organization (PSO), September 1, 1993 to August 31, 1996. My analysis is from Bill Styring, "Inside the ISTA Payroll," *Indiana Policy Review* (December 1993), pp. 23–31. To my knowledge, ISTA has never challenged Styring's data or analysis.

6. Agreement between the California Teachers Association (CTA) and the California Staff Organization (CSO), September 1, 1995 to August 31, 1998.

7. Mike Antonucci, "Teachers Can't Match Union Staff's Benefits," *Inside California* (November, 1996, p. 5).

8. "In-house union on NJEasy Street," *The Trentonian,* May 5, 1994, p. 3.

9. Ibid.

10. McElroy is a plaintiff in Rhode Island litigation seeking to avoid his eviction from the state's teacher retirement system. In 1987, McElroy was one of several teacher union officials who were allowed to buy credit in the system for their years of service as union officials. McElroy paid $34,386 for an annual pension of $64,344, with projected lifetime benefits of $618,806. The state of Rhode Island sought to evict McElroy and other NEA/AFT officials from the retirement system, and the litigation had not been resolved when this manuscript went to press. For a more detailed account of this shocking pension grab by NEA/AFT officers, including indictments of some, see Myron Lieberman and Charlene K. Haar, "The Great Rhode Island Ripoff: A Commentary" : *Government Union Review* (Spring 1995), pp. 27–41.

11. AFT Return, FY 1995, IRS Form 990, Return of Organization Exempt from Income Tax.

12. NYSUT Return, FY 1995, IRS Form 990 Return of Organization Exempt from Income Tax.

13. Article IX, Section 5, *Agreement between the American Federation of Teachers Staff Union and the American Federation of Teachers, January 1, 1995 to December 31, 1997.*

14. Ibid, Article IV, Section 7.

Chapter 9. Paying the Bills: NEA/AFT Revenues

1. Mackinac Center for Public Policy, *Michigan Education Special Services Association: The MEA's Money Machine* (Midland, MI: Mackinac Center for Public Policy, November 1993).
2. Ibid.
3. All data on the WEA Insurance Group is from WEA Insurance Group, *1995 the Year in Review* (Madison, WI, WEA Insurance Group, 1996). Some AFT affiliates also have arrangements with commercial vendors that raise conflict-of-interest issues.
4. "Chicago Teachers Union to Create Graduate School," *Education Week,* October 18, 1995, p. 16.
5. "Your Benefits: State Public Pension Funds and Amounts," *NEA-Retired Magazine,* NEA Publishing, May 1996, p. 4.
6. Stephen Glass, "A Pension Deficit Disorder," *Policy Review* (Winter 1995), pp. 71–74.
7. *NEA Now,* vol. 20, no. 4 (June 1981).
8. New Business Item 2, adopted at the 1996 NEA Annual Convention, Washington, July 1–5, 1996.
9. "WEA Challenger Network News," care of Barb Amidon, Olympia, WA (no date, post-marked February 12, 1996).
10. Resolution H–10, *NEA Handbook,* 1996–97, pp. 325–326.

Chapter 10. Free Economic Riders or Forced Political Passengers?

1. *Ellis* v. *Brotherhood of Railway, Airline and Steamship Clerks, et al* 466 U.S. 435 (1984).
2. *Abood* v. *Detroit Board of Education* 431 U.S. 209 (1977).
3. *Chicago Teacher Union* v. *Hudson* 475 U.S. 292 (1986).
4. *Lehnert* v. *Ferris Faculty Association* 111 S. Ct. 1950 (1991).
5. *NEA Strategic Focus Plan and Budget, Fiscal Year* 1996–97 (Washington: National Education Association, 1996), p. iii.
6. *CTA Membership/Agency Fee Report,* as of September 30, 1995 (Burlingame, CA: California Teachers Association, 1996).
7. *How To Raise Money for NEA-PAC: Education's Defense Fund* (Washington: National Education Association. n.d.), p. 7.
8. "The AFT helps generate mandate for change," *American Teacher,* December 1992–January 1993, p. 7.
9. See "Report of AFT President David Selden," *AFT Officers' Reports to American Federation of Teachers Convention* (Washington: American Federation of Teachers, 1972), p. 70.
10. Statement of Raymond J. LaJeunesse, Jr., Staff attorney, National Right to Work Legal Defense Foundation, Concerning The National Education Association, National Press Club, July 1, 1996. In response to an inquiry from the author, NEA General Counsel Robert H. Chanin asserted that there have been only "a relative handful of court cases involving the collection and expenditure of agency fees by NEA and its affiliates" and that the unions have been "wholly or largely successful" in these cases. *Letter,* Robert H. Chanin to Myron Lieberman, April 7, 1997. The differences between the NRTWLDF and Chanin statements may be due to differences over the inclusion of cases before ad-

ministrative agencies, cases that are not reported, cases in which the unions were the plaintiffs, and multiple cases that were consolidated. It should be noted, however, that in his petition for certiorari in the Bromley case, Chanin stated that:

> As the instant lawsuit illustrates, although most nonmembers are content to pay a service fee that is either equal to the full amount of union dues or a reduced fee calculated by the union, nonetheless the law of large numbers assures that there is a ready pool of would-be plaintiffs to challenge service fees (for whom the Right to Work Foundation provides legal representation at no cost, and without regard to the small financial stakes involved). As a result, service fee litigation has become a staple of the federal courts' diet.

Bromley v. Michigan Educational Association, 82 F. 3d 686 (6th Cir. 1996), *cert. denied,* 117 S. Ct. 682 (1997). Petition for certiorari filed with the Supreme Court, p. 17.

Inasmuch as my interest is in any evidence from challenges to agency fees, the NRTWLDF data provides a much more comprehensive basis for evaluating the extent of excessive agency fees.

11. Information provided by National Right-to-Work Legal Defense Foundation, March 5, 1996.
12. "Teacher Unions, Long Far Apart, Discuss a Merger," *New York Times,* June 23, 1993, p. 18.
13. Ibid.
14. *Steele* v. *Louisville & N.R.* 323 U.S. 192 (1944).
15. Article 11, Charter Draft of November 1989. Some members of the European Community allow union security provisions that violate Article 11. Cited in Sheldon Leader, *Freedom of Association* (New Haven, CT: Yale University Press), p. 290.
16. *Abood* v. *Detroit Board of Education* 431 U.S. 209 (1977), pp. 258–59.
17. Office of Government Relations, *You and Politics: A Workbook Introduction* (Washington: National Education Association, 1977), p. 3.

Chapter 11. AFT President Albert Shanker: Visionary or Union Apologist?

1. Article V and VI, AFT Constitution, Correct as of July 1994, pp. 6–7.
2. Peter Schrag, "The World of Teaching," *Sacramento Bee,* August 14, 1994, p. 9. According to the *Washington Post* of January 28, 1993, Shanker was "Known as the father of collective bargaining for teachers for his efforts in the 60s and 70s."
3. Myron Lieberman and Michael H. Moskow, *Collective Negotiations for Teachers* (Chicago: Rand McNally & Company, 1966), pp. 47–54. This is the most detailed study of the emergence of teacher bargaining in the 1960s; Shanker is not mentioned once in the entire book.
4. Chester E. Finn, Jr. *We Must Take Charge* (New York: The Free Press, 1991), p. 90.
5. Chester E. Finn, Jr. "Towards Excellence in Education," *The Public Interest,* No. 120 (Summer 1995), pp. 41–45. A 1996 article recognizes union opposition to school choice but urges less union emphasis on it without any recommendation on how to deal with union opposition. See Chester E. Finn, Jr., "How the Republicans Lost the Education Issue," *Weekly Standard,* November 15, 1996, pp. 29–31.
6. David Kearns and Denis P. Doyle, *Winning the Brain Race* (San Francisco: Institute for Contemporary Studies Press, 1989), p. 18.

7. Kearns and Doyle, *Winning the Brain Race*, p. 44.
8. On the twenty-fifth anniversary of Shanker's "advertorials" in the *New York Times*, Diane Ravitch, former assistant secretary of education in the Bush administration, asserted a wish that it were possible to clone Shanker. Note also that the daughters of Ben Wattenberg, a prominent analysts for the American Enterprise Institute, and Michael Usdan, president of the Institute for Educational Leadership (the nation's largest educational policy organization), hold important staff positions in the AFT's national office.
9. *Proceedings of the 1983 AFT Convention* (Washington: American Federation of Teachers, 1983), p. 87.
10. Albert Shanker, "Where We Stand," Advertisement, *New York Times*, August 15, 1993, p. E7.
11. From Henry Light Nunn, *The Whole Man Goes to Work* (New York; Harper & Row, 1953), p. 32, in Carl Golden, *Organized Labor Source Materials for the Study of Labor in America*, 2d ed. (New York: United Federation of Teachers, 1991), p. 77.
12. *Catalog*, 1994–95 George Meany Center for Labor Studies (Silver Spring, MD: George Meany Center for Labor Studies, n.d.).
13. Advertisement in *United Teacher*, published by United Teachers of Los Angeles, February 2, 1996, p. 12.
14. I have Shanker's word for it. AFT Press Conference September 9, 1995, Washington, D.C.
15. *In the Matter of the Dispute Between American Federation of Teachers and Service Employees International Union*.
16. Max Green, *Epitaph for American Labor* (Washington: AEI Press, 1996), p. 2.
17. Albert Shanker, "Where We Stand," *New York Times*, July 22, 1990, p. E7.
18. Green, *Epitaph for American Labor*, pp. 39–43.

Chapter 12. Takeoff Promises, Landing Realities

1. David McCord Wright, ed., *The Impact of the Union* (New York: Harcourt, Brace and Co., 1951).
2. *The Effect of Collective Bargaining on Teacher Salaries* (Reston, VA: Public Service Research Council, 1981).
3. Richard B. Freeman and Casey Ichnioski, eds., *When Public Sector Workers Unionize* (Chicago: University of Chicago Press, 1988. The quotations are by different authors.)
4. Milton Friedman, "Some Comments on the Significance of Labor Unions for Economic Policy," in *The Impact of the Union*, pp. 204–259.
5. New Business Item, "Preservation of Public Education," and NEA News Release, July 4, 1994; *NEA Handbook*, 1994–95, p. 379.
6. Roberta Romano, *Politics and Public Pension Funds* (New York: Manhattan Institute, 1994).
7. Stephen Glass, "A Pension Deficit Disorder," Teacher Unions Betray Their Members," *Policy Review* (Winter 1995), pp. 71–74.
8. Barry T. Hirsch, *Labor Unions and the Economic Performance of Firms* (Kalamazoo, MI: W.E. Upjohn Institute, 1991), pp. 113–125.
9. Albert Shanker, "A Reply to Myron Lieberman," *Phi Delta Kappan* (May 1979), pp. 652–654.
10. Ronald G. Ehrenberg and Robert S. Sith, *Modern Labor Economics*, 5th ed. (New York:

HarperCollins, 1994). pp. 512–516. Ehrenberg and Smith state that the state and local public sector unions "appear to have had a smaller effect on the relative wages of their members than unions in the private sector" but they do not say by how much.

11. See Dale Ballou and Michael Podgursky, *Teacher Pay and Teacher Quality* (Kalamazoo, MI: W.E. Upjohn Institute, 1996). My analysis of the topic relies heavily on this publication, which I find persuasive.

12. For a case study, see Myron Lieberman, "The Costs of Collective bargaining in the Modesto School Districts: A Case Study," *Government Union Review* (Winter 1981), pp. 3–33.

13. Lawrence Mishel and Paula B. Voos, eds., *Unions and Economic Competitiveness* (Armonk, NY: M.E. Sharpe, Inc., 1992), pp. 33, 70–72. Of course, many authors of publications critical of the union role are employed or subsidized by organizations that would benefit from the criticisms.

14. Sam Peltzman, "The Political Economy of the Decline of American Public Education," *Journal of Law and Economics* (April 1993), p. 12 in the text.

15. Caroline Minter Hoxby, "How Teachers' Unions Affect Education Production," *Quarterly Journal of Economics* (August 1996), p. 707. For a union response and a rebuttal by Hoxby see Albert Shanker, "Strong Teacher Unions, Better Teachers," *Wall Street Journal*, October 17, 1996, p. A23 and Caroline Hoxby, "Unions' Effect on Schools," *Wall Street Journal*, October 31, 1996, p. A23.

16. Eric A. Hanushek, *The Productivity Collapse in Schools*, Working Paper No. 8 (Rochester, NY: W. Allen Wallis Institute of Political Economy, University of Rochester, December 1996). See also Eric A. Hanushek and Stephen G. Rivkin, "Understanding the Twentieth-Century Growth in U.S. School Spending," *Journal of Human Resources*, Vol. XXXII, No. 1 (Winter 1997), pp. 35–68.

17. Richard Vedder, *School Daze: Productivity Decline and Lackluster Performance in U.S. Education, Policy Brief 171* (St. Louis, MO: Center for the study of American Business, Washington University, August 1996).

18. Paul W. Grimes and Charles A. Register, "Teacher Unions and Black Students' Scores on College Entrance Exams," *Industrial Relations*, Vol. 30 (Fall 1991), pp. 492–500.

19. Randall W. Eberts and Joe A. Stone, "Teacher Unions and the Productivity of Public Schools," *Industrial and Labor Relations Review*, Vol. 40 (April 1987), pp. 354–363.

20. F. Howard Nelson, Michael Rosen, and Brian Powell, *Are Teachers Unions Hurting American Education?* (Milwaukee, WI: Institute for Wisconsin's Future, 1997), p. 18.

21. Carole Baldwin McWilliams, *The Impact of Collective Bargaining on Teacher Absenteeism* (doctoral dissertation, University of Utah, 1981, available from University Microfilms, Ann Arbor, Michigan).

22. Myron Lieberman, *Public Education: An Autopsy* (Cambridge: Harvard University Press, 1993), p. 105.

23. Attendance by the author and/or Charlene K. Haar at National PTA Conventions, 1994–96, and state conventions in Connecticut (1995), Maryland (1994), Virginia (1994), California (1994) and the District of Columbia (1995, 1996), also informal reports from PTA members in other states.

24. National PTA Position Statement, Reaffirmed 1987 (Chicago: National PTA 1987).

25. John E. Berthoud, *A Fiscal Analysis of NEA and AFL-CIO Contributions to 1996 Congressional Races*, Executive Summary (Arlington, VA: Alexis de Tocqueville Institution, 1996), p. 3.

Chapter 13. NEA/AFT Merger: Teachers in the AFL-CIO

1. Myron Lieberman, *The Future of Public Education* (Chicago: University of Chicago Press, 1959).
2. David Selden, *The Teacher Rebellion* (Washington: Howard University Press, 1985).
3. Leo Troy, *The New Unionism in the New Society* (Fairfax, VA: George Mason University Press, 1994).
4. Paul E. Peterson, *The Politics of School Reform* 1870–1940 (Chicago: University of Chicago Press, 1985), p. 15.
5. Marjorie Murphy, *Black Board Unions* (Ithaca, NY: Cornell University Press, 1990), pp. 180–181.
6. "AFT-NEA Joint Council," *NEA Today* (April 1997), p. 9.
7. Allan M. West, *The National Education Association: The Power Base for Education* (New York: The Free Press, 1980), pp. 157–161.
8. *NEA Handbook,* 1996–97, pp. 177–214.
9. "Teacher Unions, Long Far Apart, Discuss a Merger," *New York Times,* June 23, 1993, p. 18.
10. Article XX, AFL-CIO Constitution.
11. Louis Harris and Associates, "A Study on the Outlook for Trade Union Organizing" (New York: Louis Harris and Associates, Inc., November 1984). See also Leo Troy "Will A More Interventionist NLRA Revive Organized Labor?" *Harvard Journal of Law and Public Policy* (Spring 1990), pp. 583–633.

Chapter 14. What Is to Be Done?

1. The Kamber Group, *An Institution at Risk, an External Communications Review of the National Education Association* (January 1997).
2. Chase's contention that the NEA is in the process of reinventing itself to emphasize student achievement was set forth in his address to the National Press Club on February 5, 1997, and in several NEA advertorials in national media in the spring of 1997.
3. See a UFT advertorial, "We Are Changing the Rules to Fix the Schools," *New York Times,* March 14, 1997, p. A15.
4. Myron Lieberman, *Privatization and Educational Choice* (New York: St. Martin's Press, 1989). Available only from Education Policy Institute, Washington, D.C.
5. *NLRB* v. *Catholic Bishop of Chicago,* 440 U.S. 490 (1979).
6. For excellent discussion of exclusive representation issues, see Sheldon Leader, *Freedom of Association* (New Haven, CT: Yale University Press, 1992) and Edwin Vierira, Jr., "Exclusive Representation versus Freedom of Petition for Nonunion Public Employees—A Study in Irreconcilable Constitutional Conflict," 1977 *Detroit College Law Review,* pp. 499–611; "Are Public Sector Unions Special Interest Political Parties?" *DePaul Law Review,* Vol. 27, No. 2 (Winter 1978), pp. 293–382.
7. *Emporium Capwell* v. *Western Addition Community Organization,* 420 U.S. 50 (1075).

INDEX

Narragansett Public Library
35 Kingstown Rd
Narragansett, RI 02882